Introduction

Watching ocean animals, and learning about them, creates a sense of delight and awe. Look at how they move, how they hunt and how they hide!

Wouldn't it be great to catch some of that excitement in your own drawings?

This book shows you how, with step by step instructions. You'll be surprised how easy it is to draw, without tracing, a wide range of ocean animals.

Think of drawing in three steps. The first is getting all the shapes and pieces in the right place. Always draw lightly at first! The second is finishing the drawing–adding details, textures and shading. The final step is 'cleaning up' by erasing the lines you don't need.

In these pages, I will take you through all the steps. The first step will be shown in several drawings, as we draw lightly, putting the pieces together. The final drawing of each set shows a finished drawing, with details and shading added and the 'cleaning up' completed. You can find out more about finishing techniques by looking at the *Drawing Tips* section.

I think you'll be surprised by your own great drawings of ocean animals. Putting the pieces together, one step at a time, is much more rewarding than tracing! Have fun looking and learning!

Supplies

- **pencil** (any kind)
- **fine marker** (optional)
- **pencil sharpener**
- **eraser** (I like the kneadable type)
- **paper** (drawing paper erases best)
- **blending stump** if you want to do smooth shading (you can use your finger, too, but it's a bit messy)
- **place to draw**
- **POSITIVE ATTITUDE!**

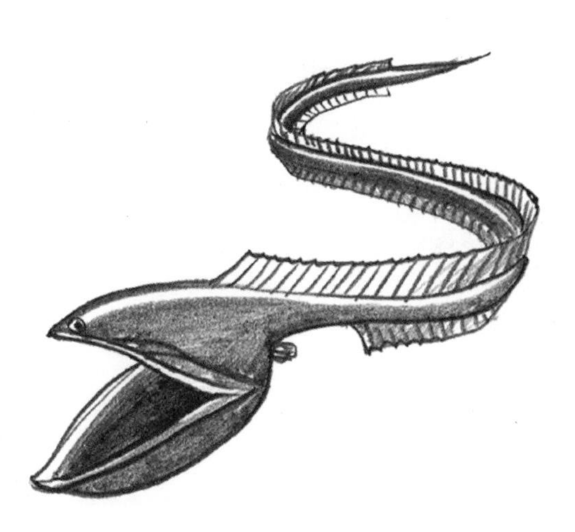

Drawing Tips

Always draw lightly at first!

Scales and fins

1 Start with your basic outline.

2 Add lines in the fins.

3 Make a 'checkerboard' with diagonal lines.

4 Round edges of diamond shapes to make scales.

Always draw lightly at first!

Drawing Tips

Contour scales

It's not easy drawing scales evenly, but with a little practice, this technique might work well for you.

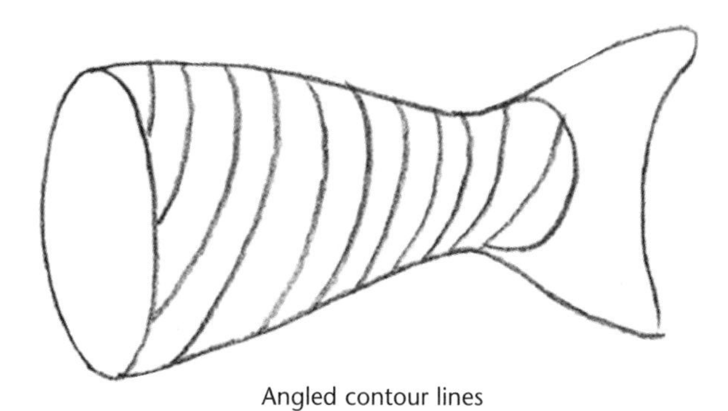
Angled contour lines

1. *Draw angled contour lines around the fish (not vertical contour lines).*

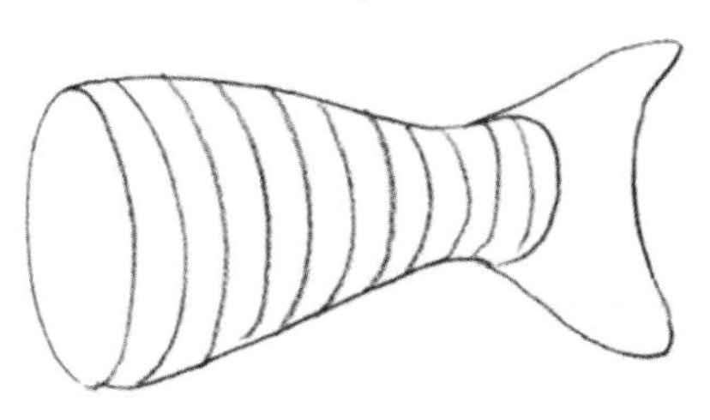
Vertical contour lines–not what you want

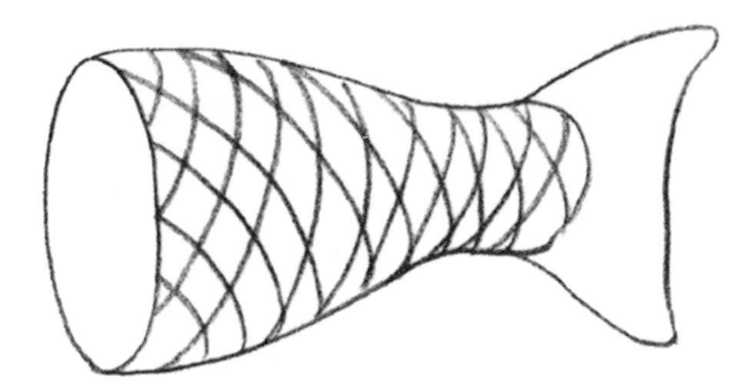
Angled contour lines going the other way

2. *Draw angled contour lines in the other direction, as evenly spaced as possible.*

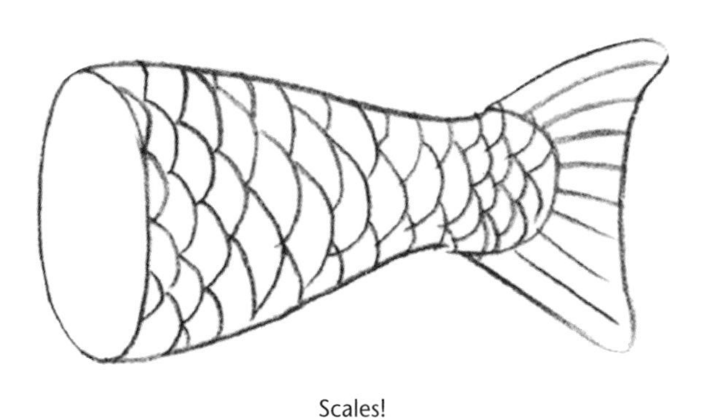
Scales!

3. *Carefully turn each small diamond shape into a scale shape. This will take some practice, but the results can be very impressive!*

Drawing Tips

Always draw lightly at first!

Contours

1. *Here's the outline of the moray eel. Because of the way it's drawn, the eel appears to be swimming toward you.*

   Now let's shade it.

2. *Just 'coloring' it with a pencil works, but you can do better. Here I've shaded the lazy way, using just back-and-forth lines.*

3. *A more effective approach: imagine the contours of the form–how the sides curve–and try to draw your shading lines so they follow the contours.*

4. *One step better is to think about light as you follow the contours. Make the top of the form a little lighter than the bottom. Can you see the difference, with the light and dark areas?*

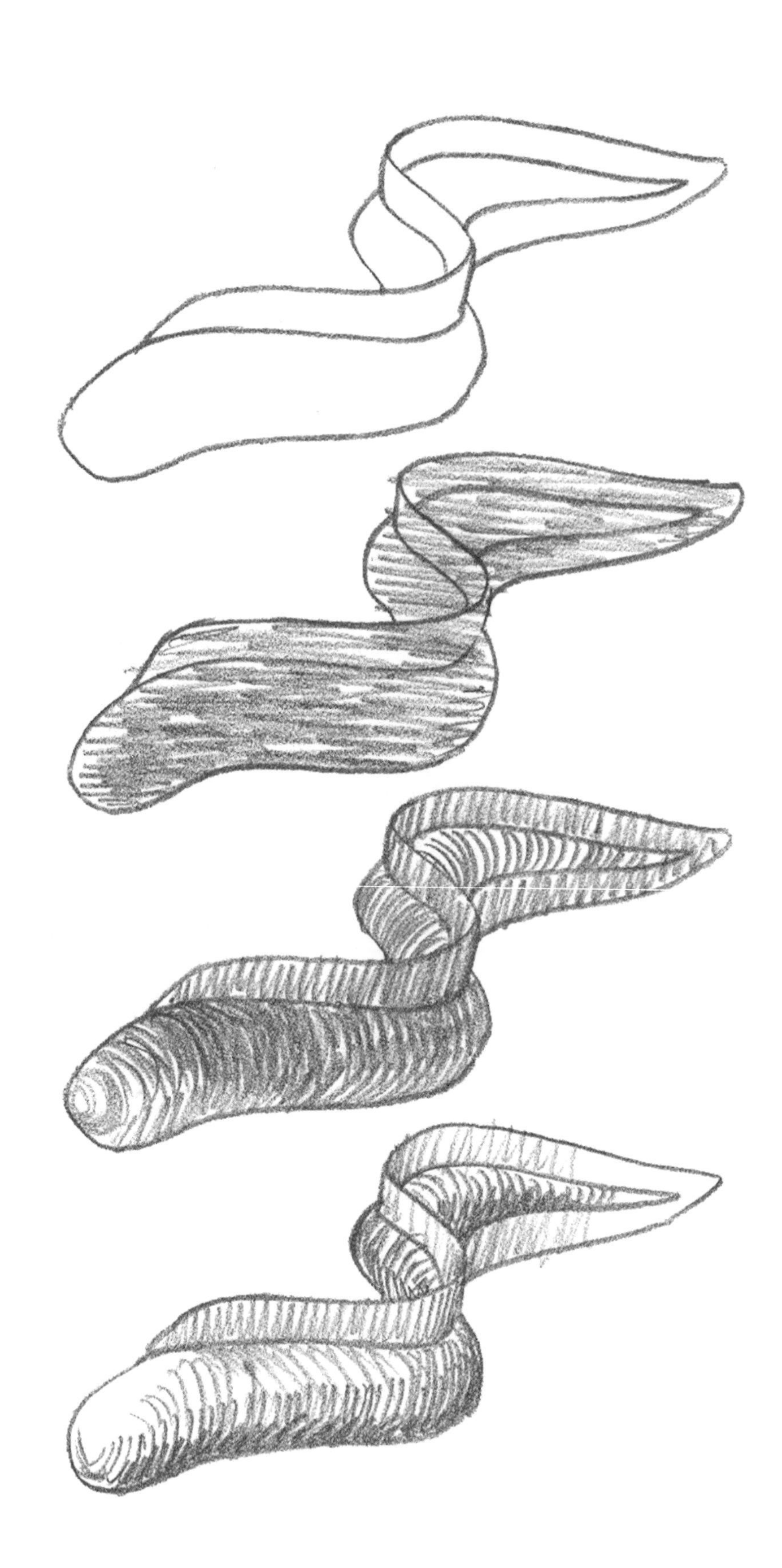

Always draw **lightly** at first!

Drawing Tips

Shading

Sometimes the effect you want is a very smooth surface, with no contour lines showing on it. When that's the case, try using a blending stump.

First, carefully shade, trying not to make any obvious lines.

Next, blend the pencil marks with a blending stump (or a piece of paper or paper towel, or even your finger–that's kind of messy, though...).

Finally, use your eraser to add highlights and clean up any smudges. This technique may take some practice, but it's worth it!

Blending stump–use to smooth out shading lines

Eraser (kneadable type)–use to add highlights and clean up smudges, edges

Contour patterns

Look at these two cylinders with spots on them. Which looks rounder? Why?

Notice that I've carefully drawn the pattern so that it appears to wrap around the right cylinder. When you add patterns to your drawings of ocean animals, look for ways to make the patterns 'bend' around the animal to show its form.

It takes practice, but it can make a big difference in your drawing!

Drawing Tips

Always draw lightly at first!

Basic Approach

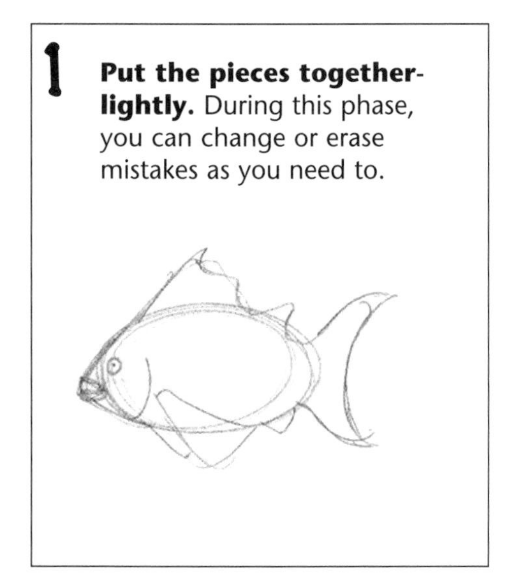

1 **Put the pieces together-lightly.** During this phase, you can change or erase mistakes as you need to.

2 **Finish the drawing.** Darken important lines, junctions, and details. Add shading and textures.

3 **Clean up.** Last step in your drawing: carefully erase any smudges.

Save your work!

Whenever you do a drawing–or even a sketch–put your initials (or autograph!) and date on it. And save it. You don't have to save it until it turns yellow and crumbles to dust, but do keep your drawings, at least for several months. Sometimes, hiding in your portfolio, they will mysteriously improve! I've seen it happen often with my own drawings, especially the ones I knew were no good at all, but kept anyway....

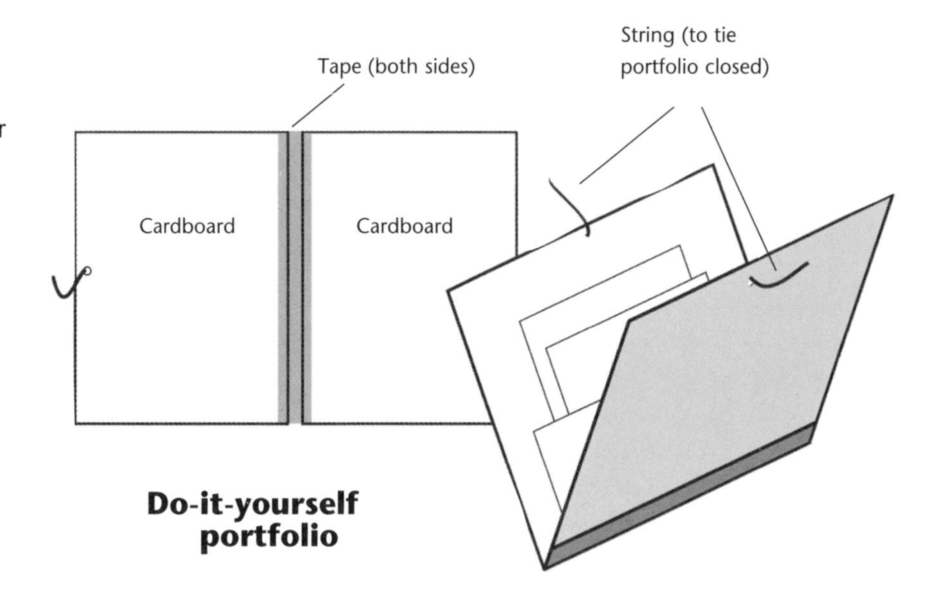

Do-it-yourself portfolio

Always draw lightly at first!

Great White Shark

Carcharodon carcharias.
Size: 6 m (19.5 ft). Diet: fish, seals, dolphins, unlucky humans. Large and aggressive! The great white shark has protective eyelids that cover the eyes during attacks.

1. *Draw a long, flat oval. Add a box at one end for the head, and two lines tapering at the other end for the tail.*

Nostril

Eye

Gill openings

2. *Add mouth, teeth, eye, nostril and gill openings.*

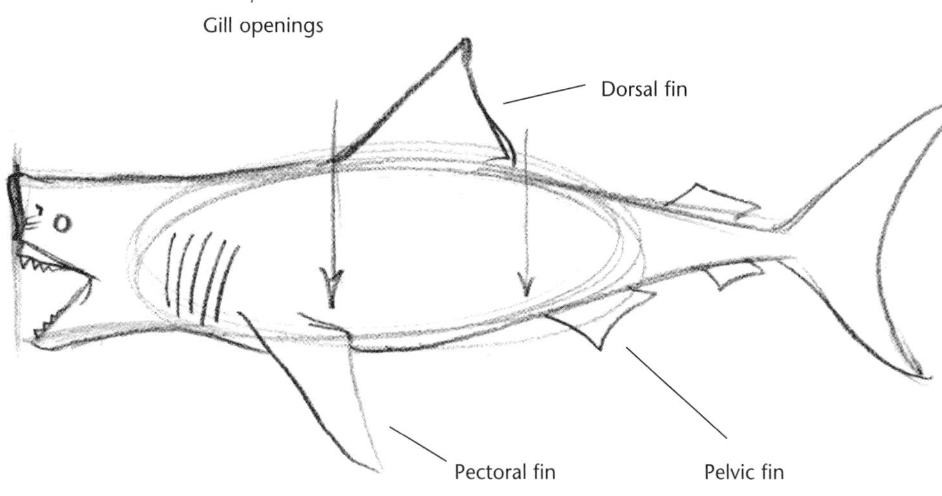

3. *Next draw the triangle-shaped dorsal fin on top, behind the center of your oval. Draw the pectoral fin behind the gill openings.*

   Draw the pelvic fin. It lies below the back of the dorsal fin. Add the two other small fins. Now draw the tail.

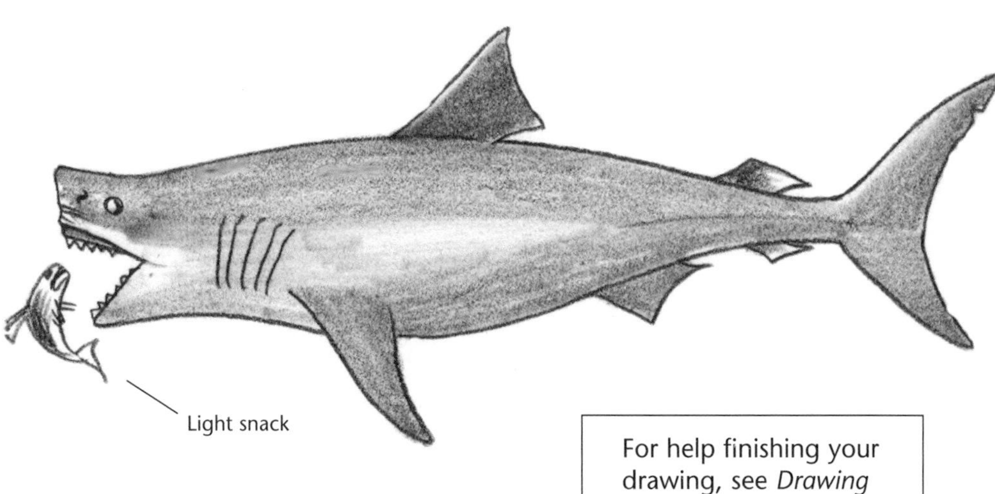

4. *Add shading. Make the outlines and details bolder. Erase the lines you don't need.*

For help finishing your drawing, see *Drawing Tips* on pages 2-6.

Shortfin Mako Shark

Always draw lightly at first!

Isurus oxyrhincus.
Size: 3-4 m (10-13 ft). Diet: tuna, mackerel, herring, sardines, squid.

1. *Start with a pointed oval. Notice the difference between the top and bottom. Draw two triangles for the tail. Which is bigger?*

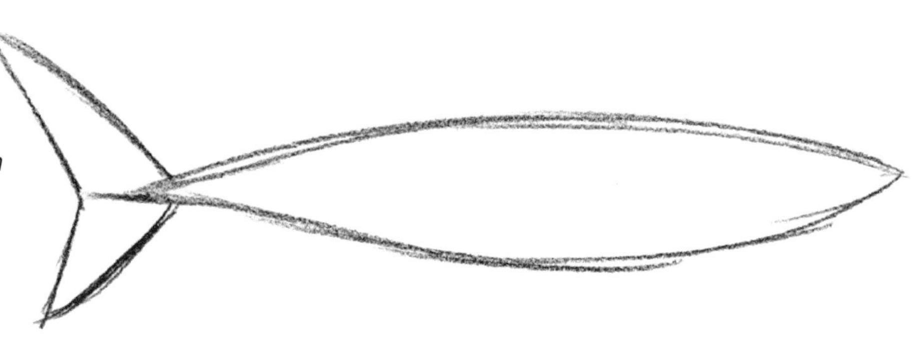

2. *Next, draw the dorsal fin, above the middle of the oval.*

   The back of the pectoral fin lines up with the front of the dorsal fin. Draw it.

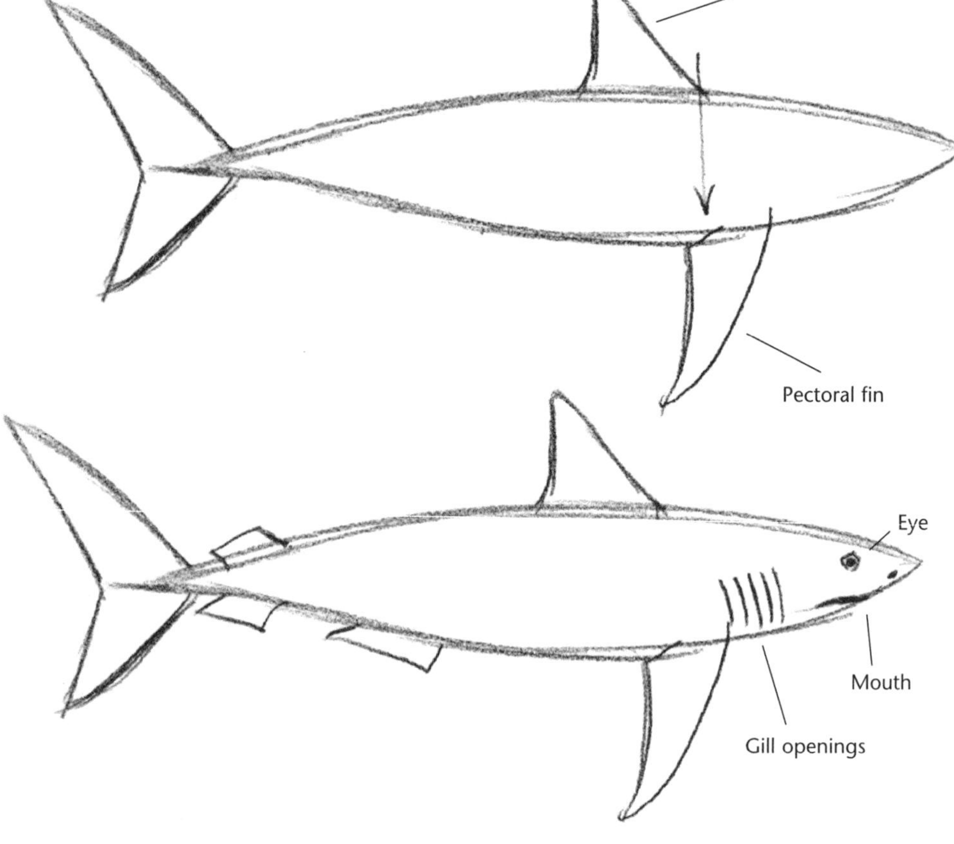

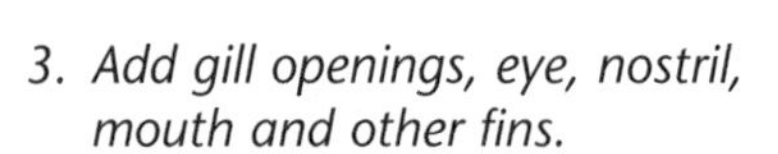

3. *Add gill openings, eye, nostril, mouth and other fins.*

4. *Add shading. Sharpen details (did you catch the notch in the tail?). Clean up with your eraser.*

Always draw lightly at first!

Hammerhead Shark

Sphyrna mokarran (Great hammerhead). Size: 6m (19.5 ft) Diet: fish, especially rays. With eyes facing out to the side, hammerheads have to turn from side to side as they swim.

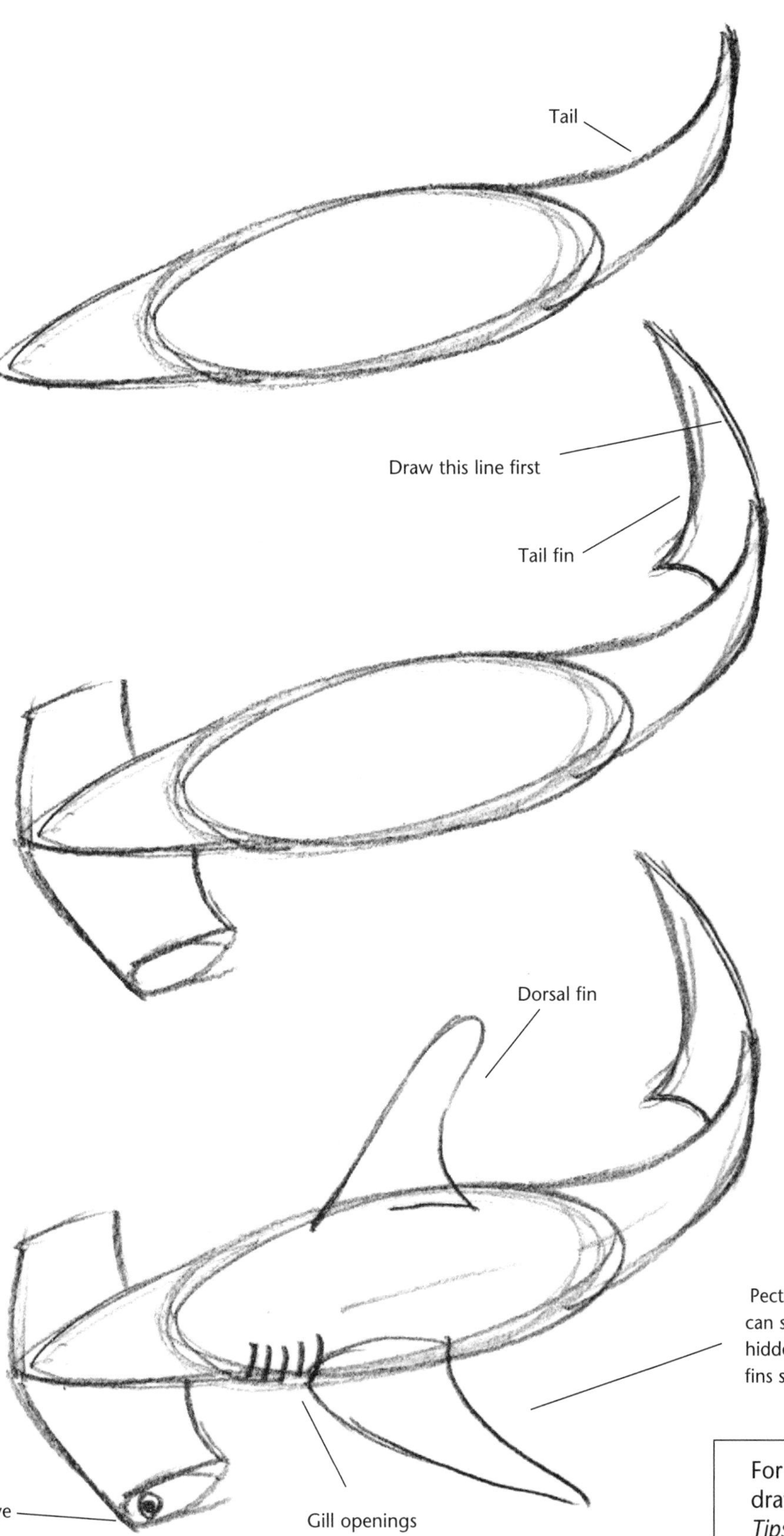

1. *Start with a tilted oval. Add a curving triangle for the tail, and a pointed end for the head.*

2. *Look at the curved tail fin. Draw it. Now look at the angle of the head. Draw it carefully, paying attention to angles.*

3. *Add the one eye you can see from this angle. Draw gill openings. Next add the pectoral and dorsal fins.*

Pectoral fin. At this angle, you can see one of two (the other is hidden by the body). Pectoral fins stick out to the side.

For help finishing your drawing, see *Drawing Tips* on pages 2-6.

Always draw lightly at first!

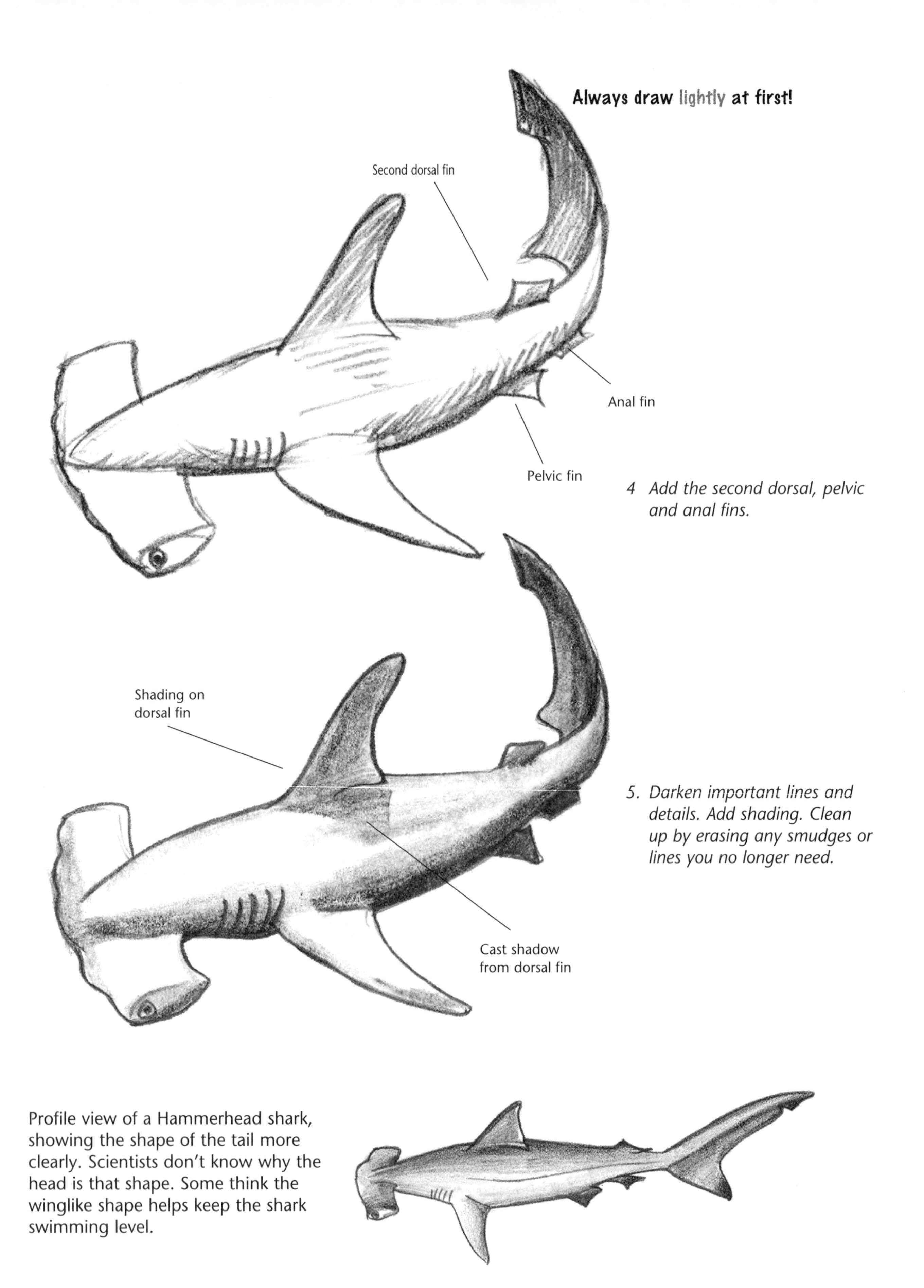

4 Add the second dorsal, pelvic and anal fins.

5. Darken important lines and details. Add shading. Clean up by erasing any smudges or lines you no longer need.

Profile view of a Hammerhead shark, showing the shape of the tail more clearly. Scientists don't know why the head is that shape. Some think the winglike shape helps keep the shark swimming level.

Always draw lightly at first!

Port Jackson Shark

Heterodontus portusjacksoni.
Size: up to 1.5 m (5 ft). Diet: probably mollusks, sea urchins and mollusks; feeds at night. Has stout spines in front of each dorsal fin.

Tail
Head

1. *Draw a long, flat oval with a rat-like tail. Add a slanting box shape for the head.*

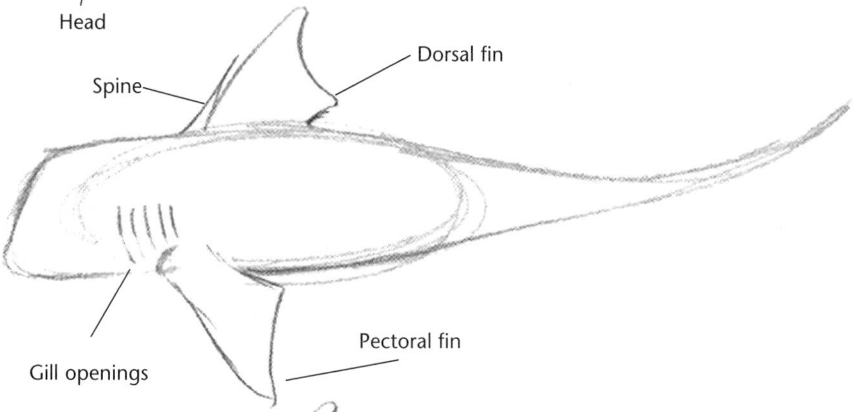

Dorsal fin
Spine
Gill openings
Pectoral fin

2. *At the front of the oval, draw gill openings and the pectoral fin. Add the dorsal fin, with its pointed spine in the front.*

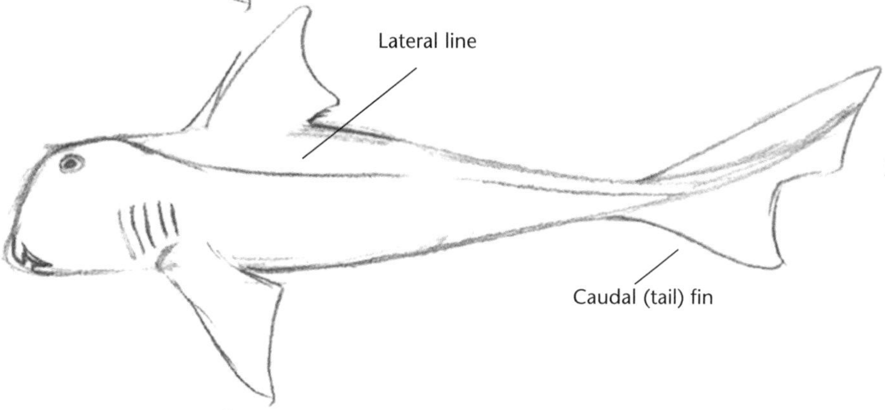

Lateral line
Caudal (tail) fin

3. *Draw the eye high in the head. Draw the mouth, quite unlike other sharks'. Carefully add the caudal (tail) fin, and the lateral line.*

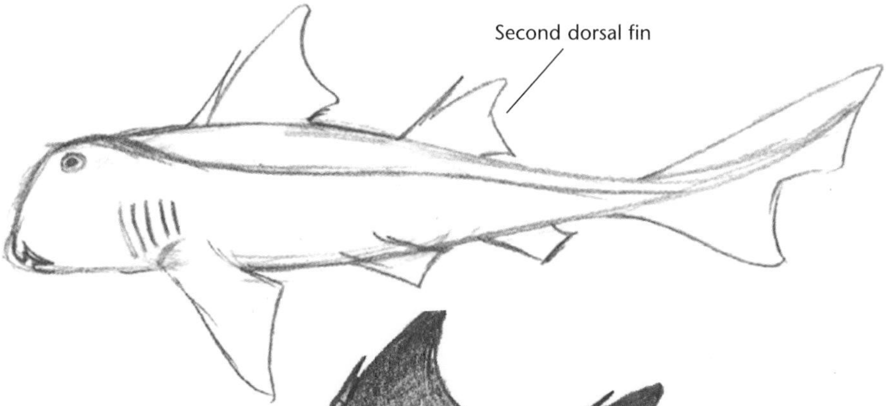

Second dorsal fin

4. *Draw the second dorsal fin, and the fins on the bottom.*

5. *Add shading. Sharpen outlines and details. Clean up with your eraser.*

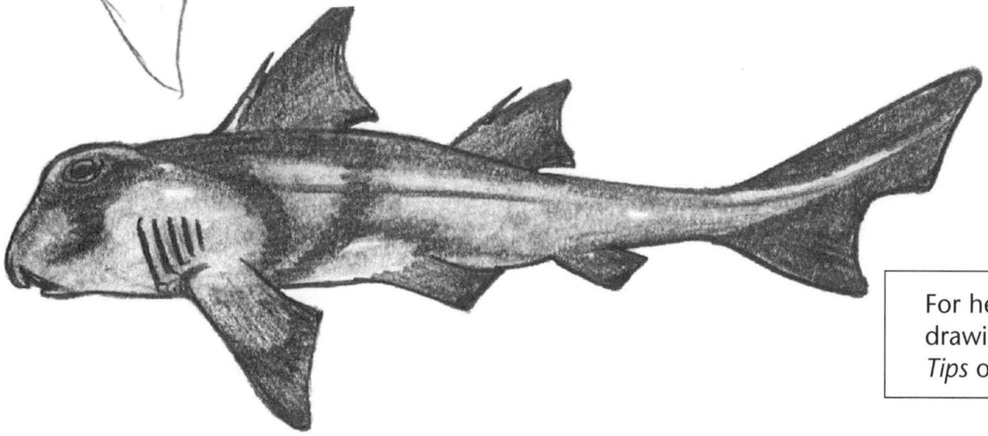

For help finishing your drawing, see *Drawing Tips* on pages 2-6.

Sting Ray

Always draw **lightly** at first!

Family *dasayatidae.* Size: 1.5 m (5 ft). Diet: Mollusks and crustaceans on the seabed. Graceful swimmers who live on sandy and muddy bottoms. The sharp spine can be used as a weapon. There are about a hundred species.

1. *Start with a box shape. Add the pointed tail with its spine. This is where the 'sting' in stingray comes from.*

2. *Make the outline wiggly. Add eyes, gills and spiracles, which are where the ray breathes in (its mouth is on the bottom; it breathes out through its gills). Carefully erase your straight lines.*

3 *Sharpen outlines and details. Add the little lines around the outside. Add shading. Clean up any smudges with your eraser.*

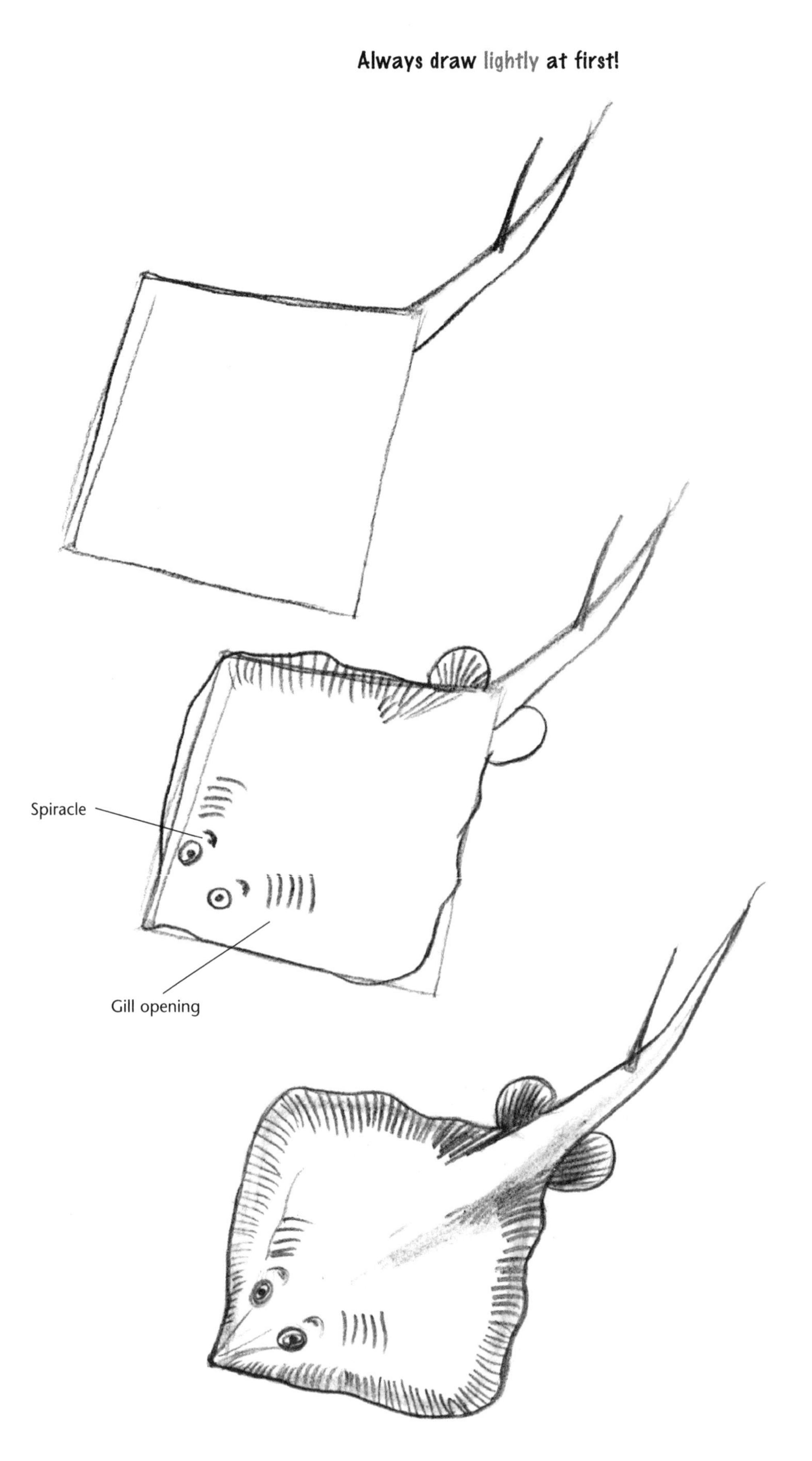

Always draw lightly at first!

Atlantic Manta

Manta birostris.
Size: up to 6.7 m (27 ft) wide. Diet: plankton, fish and crustaceans. The 'hands' on either side of the mouth can be extended, or used as scoops to direct food into the mouth.

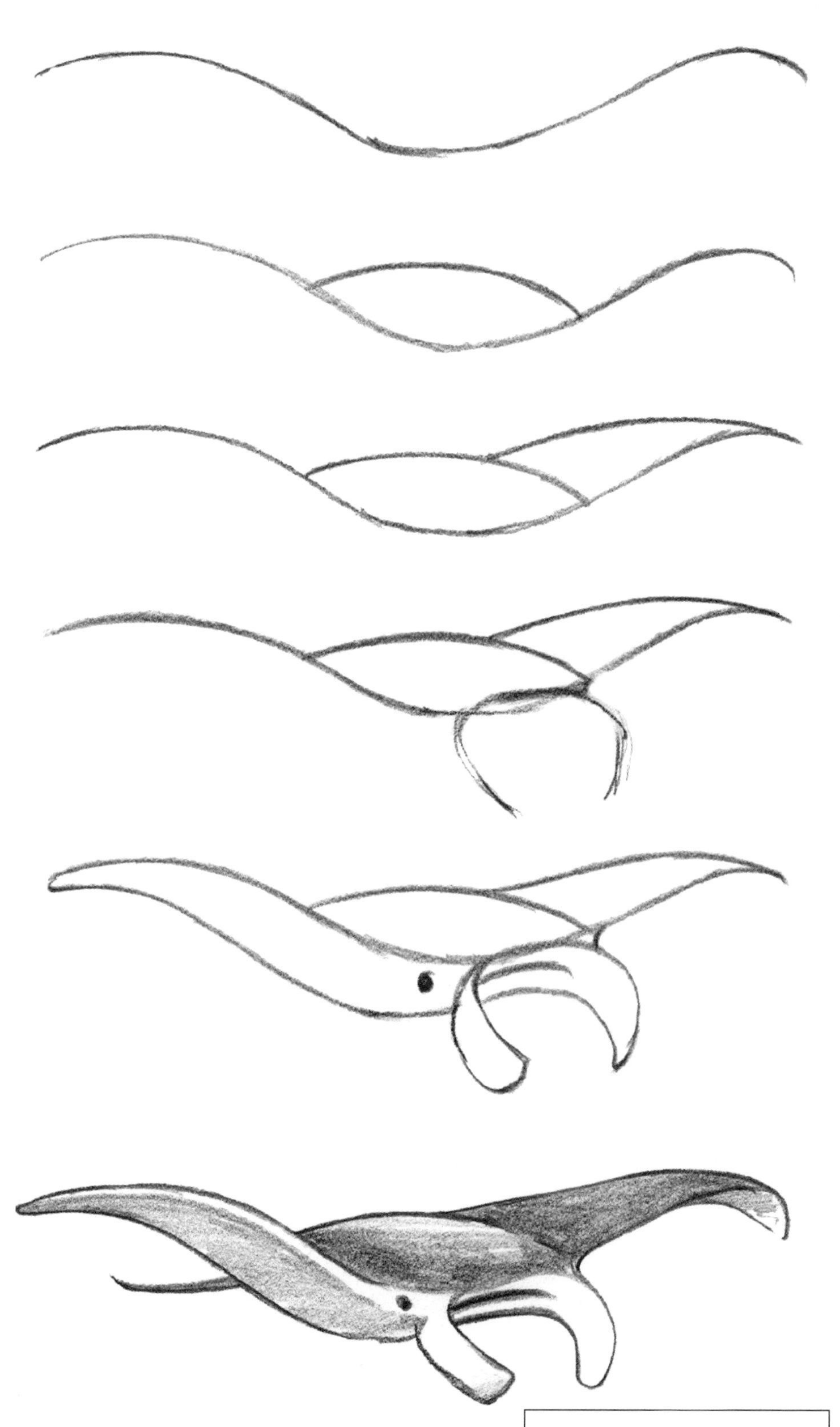

1. *Draw a big, swooping curve.*
2. *Add a bump in the middle.*
3. *Next draw an arching curve to make one 'wing.'*
4. *Lightly draw in a 'C' shape for the projections at either side of the mouth.*
5. *Add a line for the bottom of the closer wing. Draw the eye. Look carefully at my example to see how to finish the mouth.*
6. *Add the tail. Sharpen outlines, add shading, and clean up any smudges with your eraser.*

For help finishing your drawing, see *Drawing Tips* on pages 2-6.

White (Beluga) Whale

Always draw lightly at first!

Delphinapterus leucas.
Size: 4-6 m (13-20 ft). Diet: fish and crustaceans from the sea bottom. White whales sing a variety of songs. Nineteenth-century whalers called them sea canaries.

1. *Draw a large, flat oval with another oval overlapping it. Add a triangular projection at the other end for the tail.*

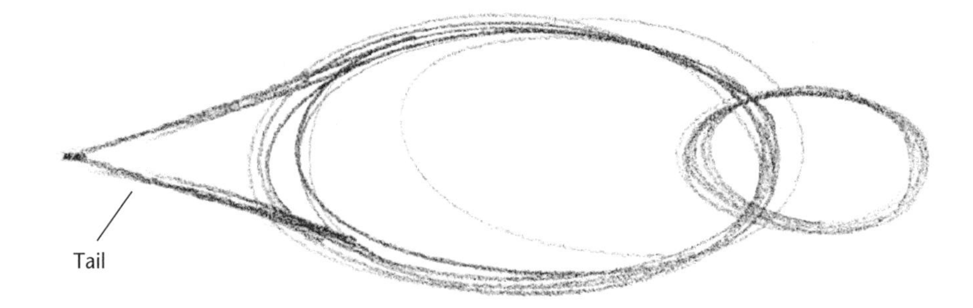

2. *Add two small triangles for the tail flukes. Draw the flipper on the lower front of the big oval. Draw the mouth upward like a smile. Add the eye.*

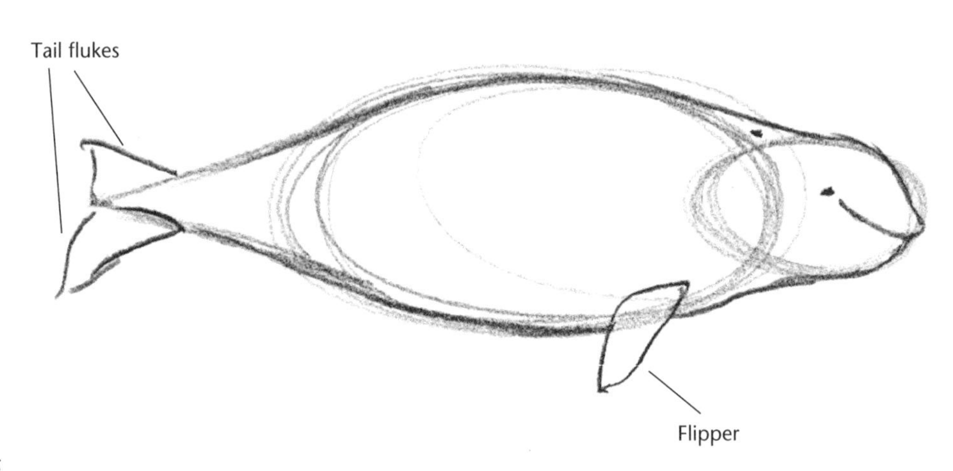

3. *Erase what's left of the ovals. Go over outlines. This whale is very light in color, so there's not much shading to do. Clean up any smudges with your eraser.*

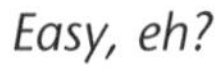
Easy, eh?

For help finishing your drawing, see *Drawing Tips* on pages 2-6.

Always draw lightly at first!

Blue Whale

Balaenoptera musculus.
Size: 25-32 m (82-105 ft). Diet: plankton. Strains food through the baleen plates attached to upper jaw. The largest mammal that has ever existed. Feeds in polar waters during summer months, eating four tons of tiny shrimp each day. Migrates to warmer waters to breed. Endangered.

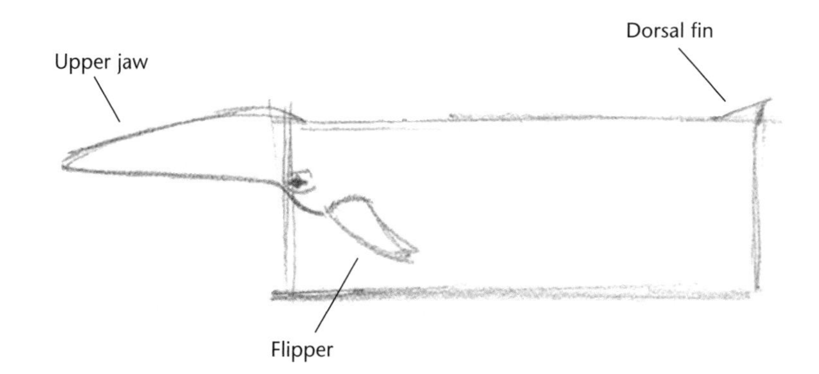

1. *Draw a long rectangle. Add the little dorsal fin. Add the eye. Draw the flipper. Add the upper jaw.*

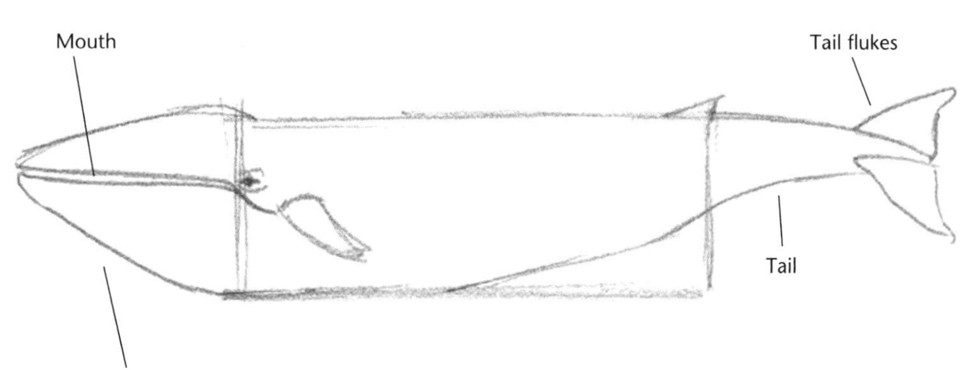

2. *Taper the bottom of the whale's body upward, and extend it to form the tail. Extend the top line of the rectangle to meet it. Add the tail flukes. Draw the lower jaw, leaving space to show the baleen plates in the mouth.*

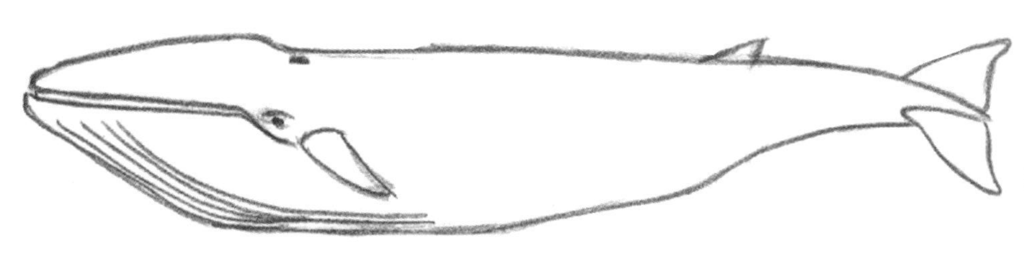

3. *Erase parts of the rectangle you no longer need, and go over the outline. Add the grooves on the lower jaw.*

4. *Add shading. Sharpen outlines and details (notice the baleen plates visible in the mouth). Clean up with your eraser.*

Humpback Whale

Always draw lightly at first!

Megaptera novaeangliae.
Size: 14.6-19 m (48-62 ft). Diet: plankton and fish. Strains food through the baleen plates attached to upper jaw. Many knobs and barnacles on body and very long flippers. Feeds in polar waters in the summer, and migrates to tropical waters for the winter. Endangered.

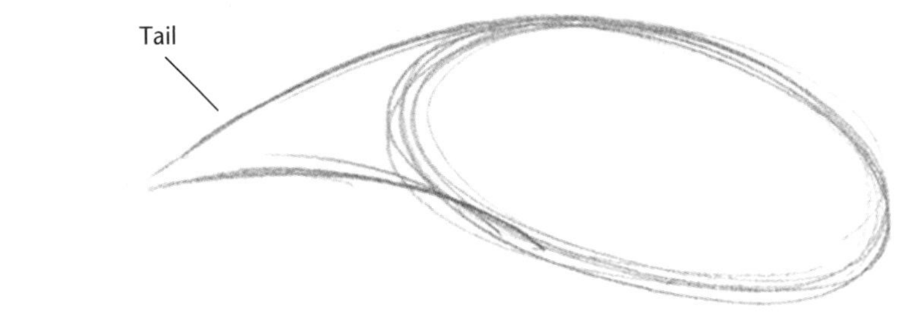

1. *Draw a tilted oval. At the high end, make a curving-down triangle for the tail.*

Top of head

2. *Draw the top of the head.*

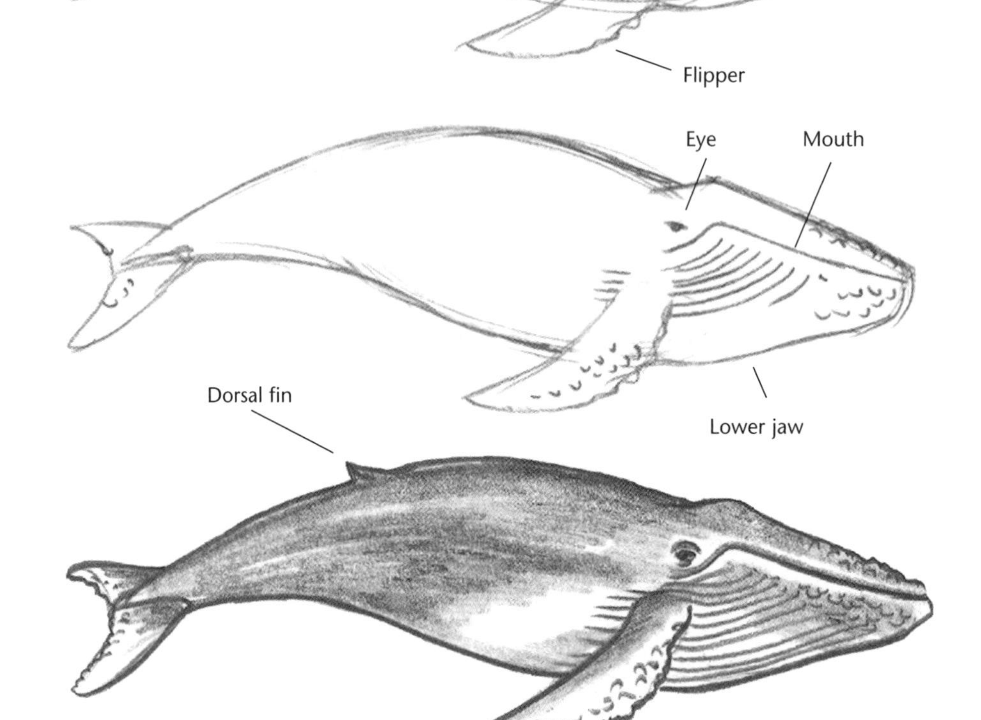

3. *Add the bottom of the head. Add a long, slightly curving flipper with one bumpy side. Draw two triangle shapes for the tail flukes.*

4. *Add a line for the mouth. Draw the eye. Add curved lines on the lower jaw. Add bumps and barnacles on the head and flipper.*

5. *Draw the dorsal fin. Add shading. Sharpen outlines and details. Clean up any smudges with your eraser.*

Great whale!

Listen to a recording of humpback whales singing sometime....

For help finishing your drawing, see *Drawing Tips* on pages 2-6.

Always draw lightly at first!

Bowhead Whale

Balaena mysticetus.
Size: 15-20 m (49-66 ft). Diet: plankton. The large vertical lines in the mouth are baleen, with which the whale strains plankton out of the water as it swims. Endangered.

Tail

Tail fluke

1. *Draw a box. Add three curving triangle shapes for the tail and tail flukes.*

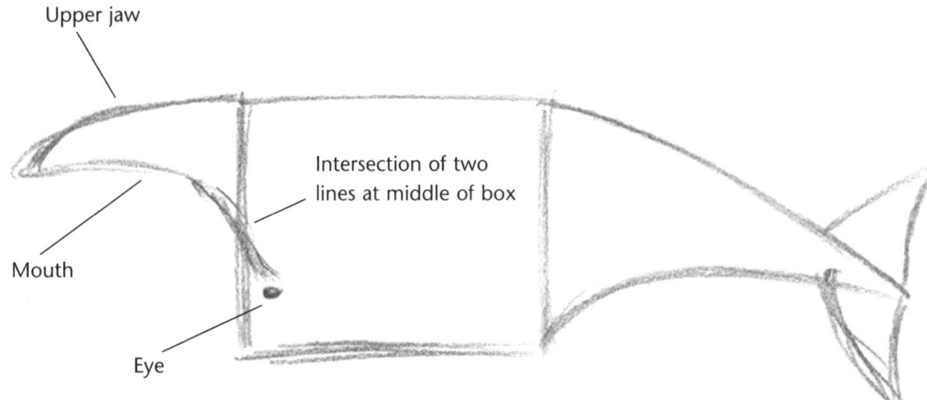

2. *Draw the upper jaw. Notice where the line for the mouth and the box intersect. Add the eye.*

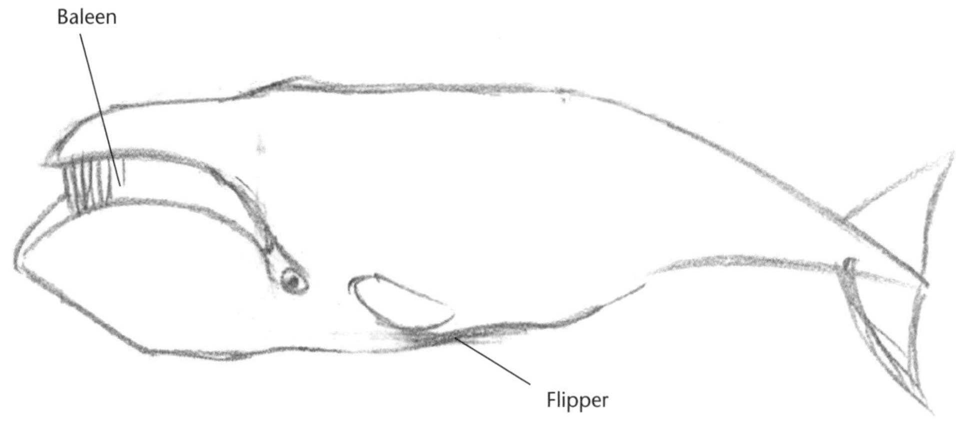

3. *Draw the flipper, then the bottom of the mouth, lower jaw, and baleen plates. Draw lightly and take your time! Add the flipper. Add the bump on top.*

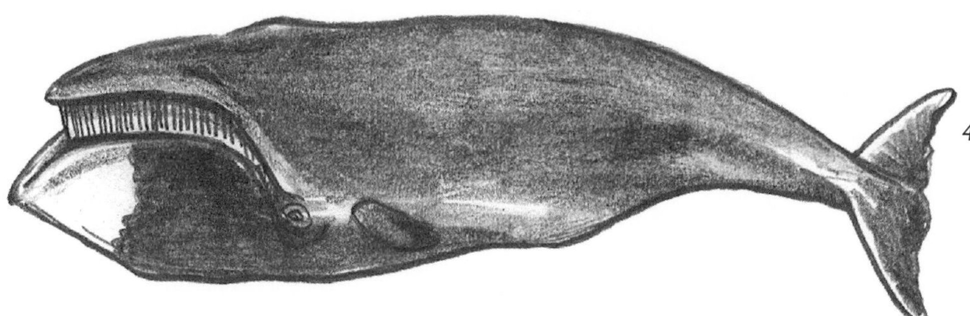

4. *Add shading. Sharpen outlines and details. Clean up any smudges with your eraser.*

Killer Whale (male)

Always draw lightly at first!

Orcinus orca.
Size: 7-9.7 m (23-32 ft). Diet: fish, squid, sea lions, birds. Males have the distinctive dorsal fin (smaller and curved on females and juveniles). Killer whales are black on top, and white on the bottom. Each has a unique pattern.

1. *Draw a long, flat oval. Add a triangle for the tail. Draw the head, with a bump on top.*

2. *Draw a very tall dorsal fin on top. Add flippers and tail flukes.*

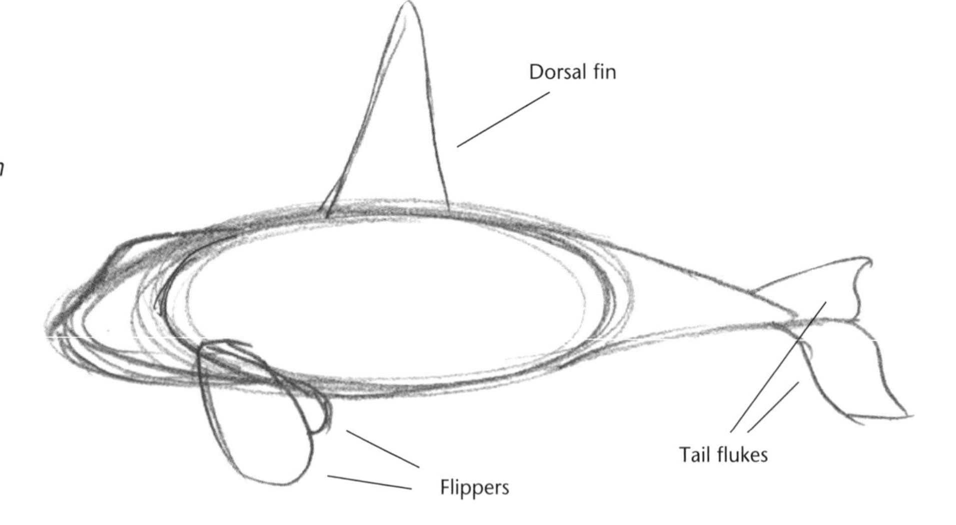

3. *Because of their strong black and white coloring, you may want to finish your drawing in ink or marker. Then you can carefully erase pencil lines.*

For help finishing your drawing, see *Drawing Tips* on pages 2-6.

Always draw **lightly** at first!

Atlantic Bottlenose Dolphin

Tursiops truncatus.
Size: 4 m (12 ft). Diet: fish. Highly intelligent animals who live in groups. These are the dolphins you usually see in movies or on TV.

1. *Draw a crescent shape.*

2. *Add a pointed nose, and two triangles for the tail flukes. Add the curved line on the side, and the eye.*

3. *Draw the flippers (you only see part of the far one, which I've shaded) and the dorsal fin.*

4. *Make your dolphin jumping out of the water if you like. Add shading. Sharpen outlines and details. Clean up any smudges with your eraser.*

California Sea Lion

Always draw lightly at first!

Zalophus californianus.
Size: 6 ft (1.8 m). Diet: fish, octopus, and squid. Unlike seals, sea lions can turn their rear flippers forward, which helps them move on land. Sea lions have ear flaps; seals don't.

1. *Draw three tilted ovals. Look carefully at how, and where, they connect. Also look at how they tilt.*

2. *Draw the forward-facing rear flippers and the front flipper. Connect the two largest ovals.*

3. *Draw the head, and lines to connect it to the middle oval. Add the ear, nostril, eye and whiskers.*

4. *Now add shading. Notice how I use short strokes of the pencil to suggest fur. Sharpen outlines and details. Clean up any smudges with your eraser.*

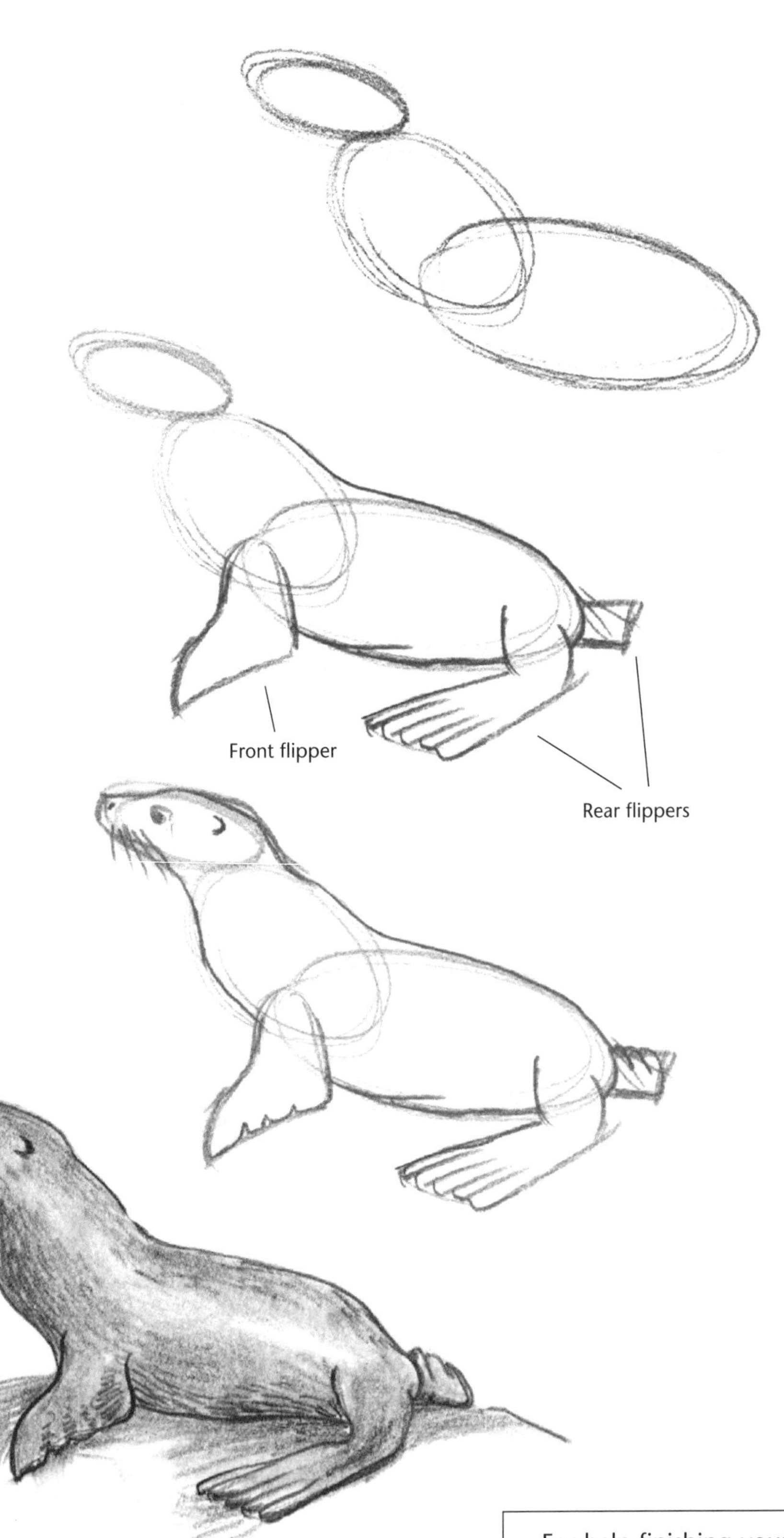

For help finishing your drawing, see *Drawing Tips* on pages 2-6.

Always draw lightly at first!

Walrus

Odobenus rosmarus.
Size: males 2.7-3.5 m (9-11.5 ft); females a bit smaller. Diet: mollusks, crustaceans, starfish, fish. They dive to feed, and use their tusks to help pick up food from the sea bottom.

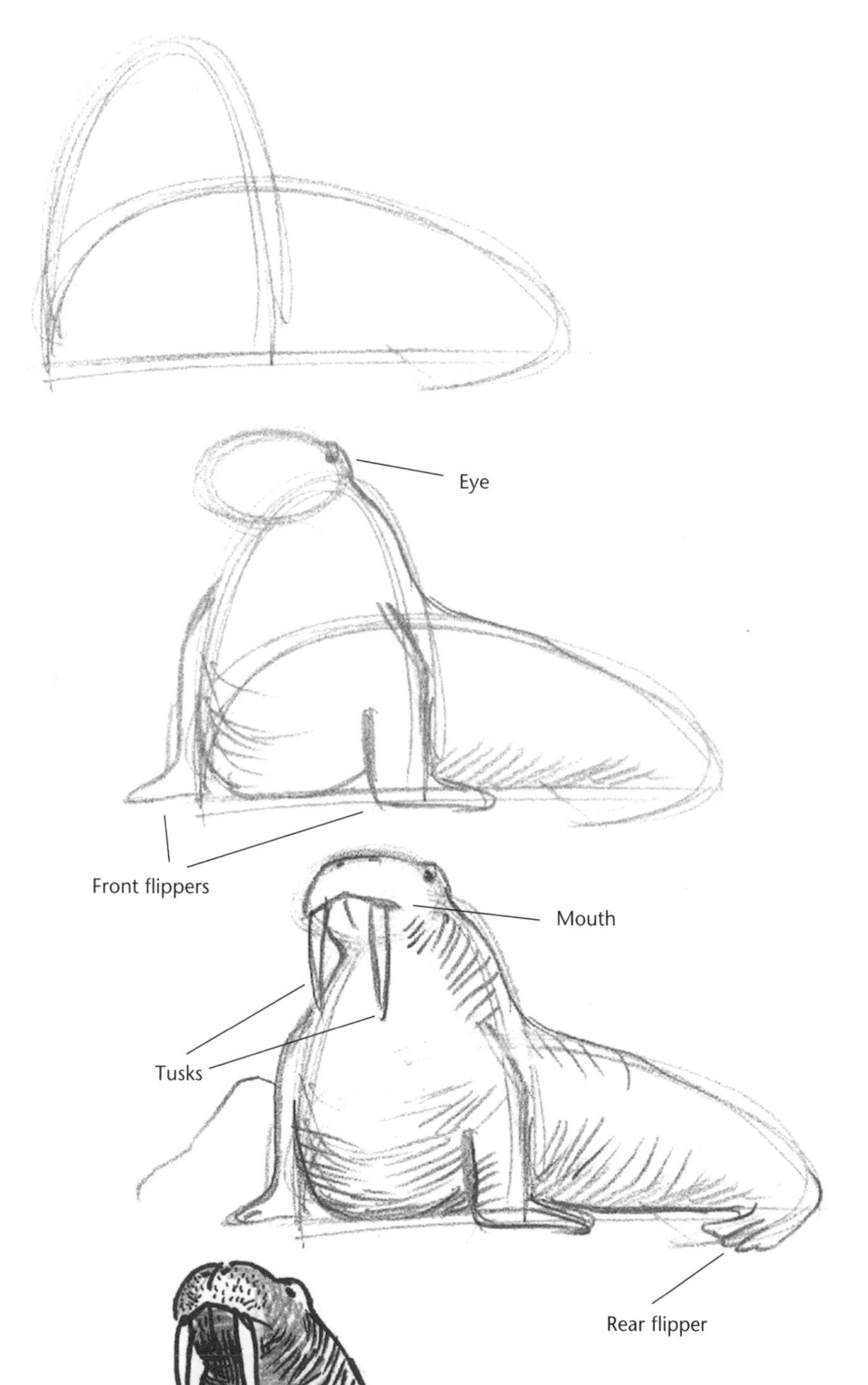

1. *Start with two simple shapes.*

2. *Add an oval for the head. Connect the back of the head in a smooth curve to the back. Draw the eye. Add the front flippers.*

3. *Draw mouth and tusks. Add wrinkles. Since the walrus has many wrinkles, you can use them to make the animal look more round (see* Drawing Tips *at the end of the book for ideas about drawing with contour lines).*

4. *Add shading. Sharpen outlines and details. Clean up any smudges with your eraser. I finished this drawing by going over key lines with a fine tip marker.*

Manatee

Always draw lightly at first!

Trichecus manatus (American manatee). Size: up to 3 m (10 ft). Diet: mainly vegetation, found at night by touch and smell. Manatees sleep in shallow waters, coming to the surface every few minutes to breathe–without even waking up!

1. Draw two overlapping ovals.

2. Add lines for wrinkles at the neck, and lines for the tail.

3. Draw the mouth and face. Add the rest of the tail and flipper.

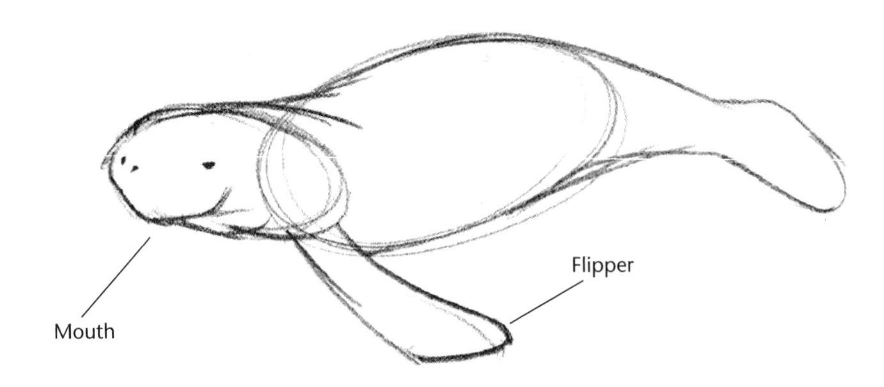

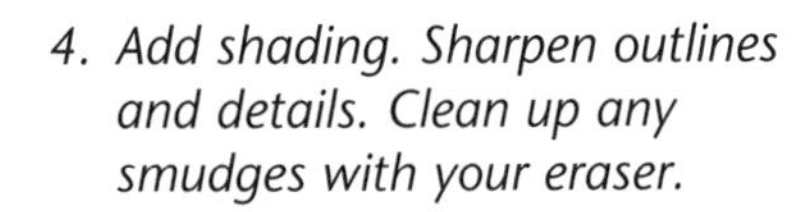

4. Add shading. Sharpen outlines and details. Clean up any smudges with your eraser.

For help finishing your drawing, see *Drawing Tips* on pages 2-6.

Always draw lightly at first!

Parrotfish

Scarus guacamaia (Rainbow Parrotfish). Size: 1.2 m (4 ft). Diet: Algae and coral, which it scrapes off reefs with a parrot-like beak. Like some other parrotfish species, this one can create a mucus 'sleeping bag' around itself at night to protect it from predators.

1. *Start with a long oval. Add a point at one end and a rounded shape for a tail at the other.*

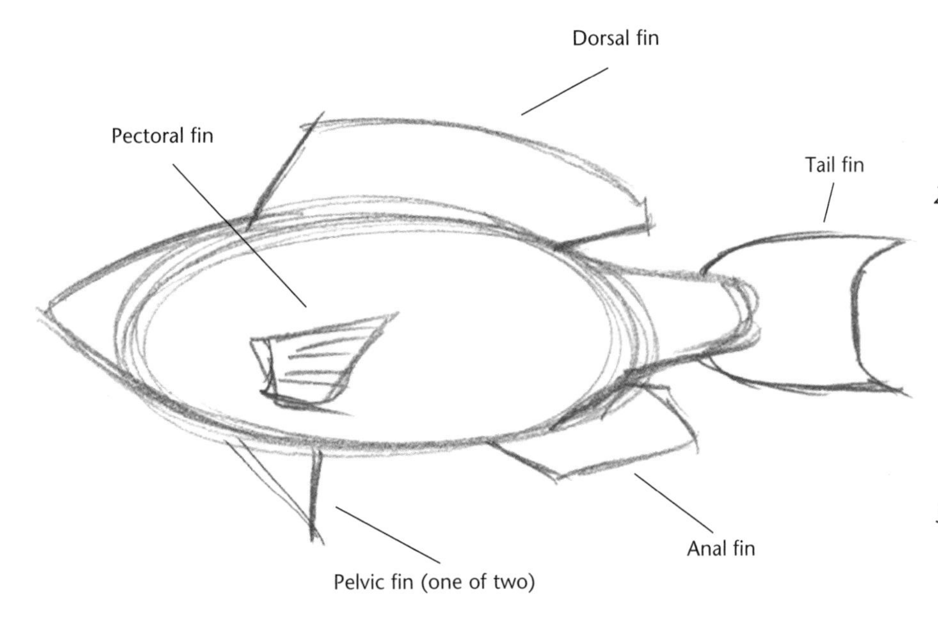

2. *Add the dorsal fin. Next draw the pectoral fin. Add the pelvic, anal and tail fins.*

3. *Draw the mouth, eye, and gill openings. Add scales, spines in the fins, and shading. Sharpen outlines and details. Clean up any smudges with your eraser.*

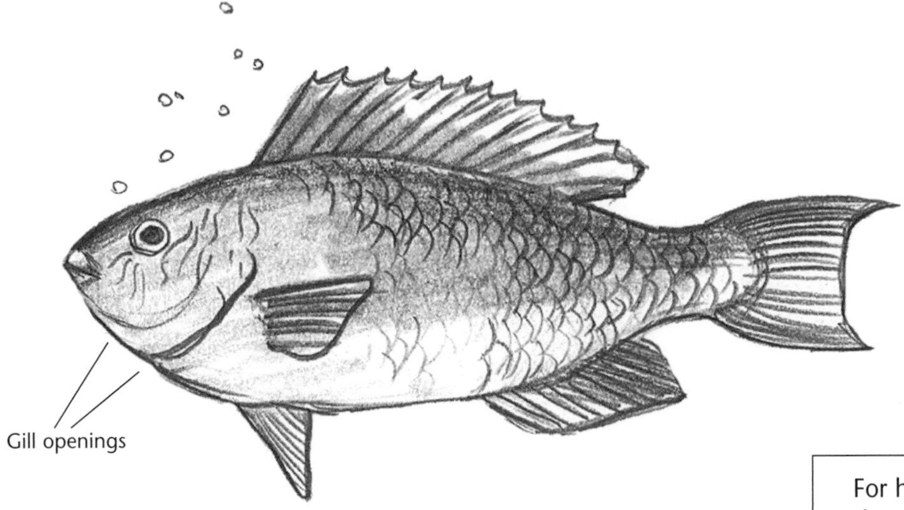

For help finishing your drawing, see *Drawing Tips* on pages 2-6.

Butterflyfish

Chelmon rostratus (copperband or beaked butterflyfish).
Size: 20 cm (7.5 in). Diet: small plants and animals that it pulls out of crevices in coral. The big spot on the tail is probably to fool predators into thinking it's the eye. The eye itself is partially camouflaged by the stripe running through it.

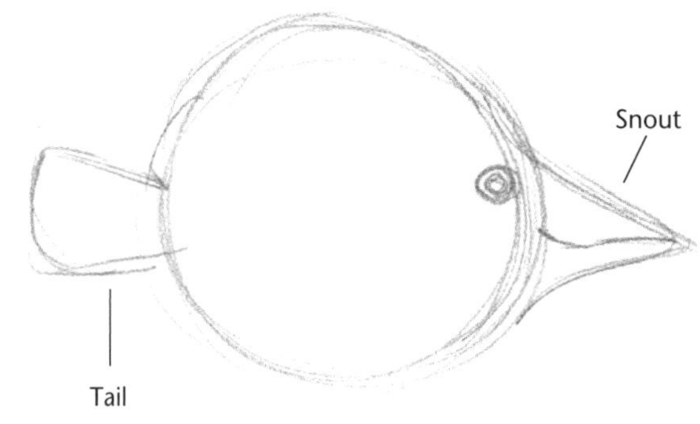

1. *Start with a light circle. At one end, in the middle, add the tail. At the other end, draw the long beaklike snout. Add a line for the mouth. Draw the eye.*

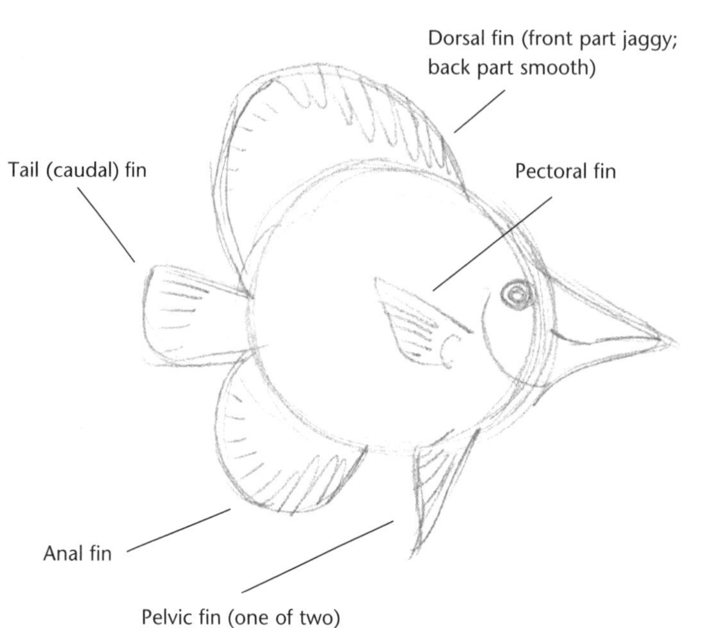

2. *Your next challenge is to draw all the fins with spines. Five fins are visible in this drawing. Draw them all!*

3. *Next, add the camouflage pattern, including the second 'eye' to fool attackers.*

4. *Darken the patterns. The eye and band on the tail are black. The stripes are copper-colored. Sharpen outlines and details. Clean up with your eraser.*

Lionfish

Pterois volitans.
Size: 38 cm (15 in). Lives in the Pacific and Indian Oceans. This is a "look but don't touch!" fish. Colorful fins conceal poisonous spines that will kill other fish and even people. Bright orange and reddish colors make this a very pretty fish. Just don't touch!

Always draw lightly at first!

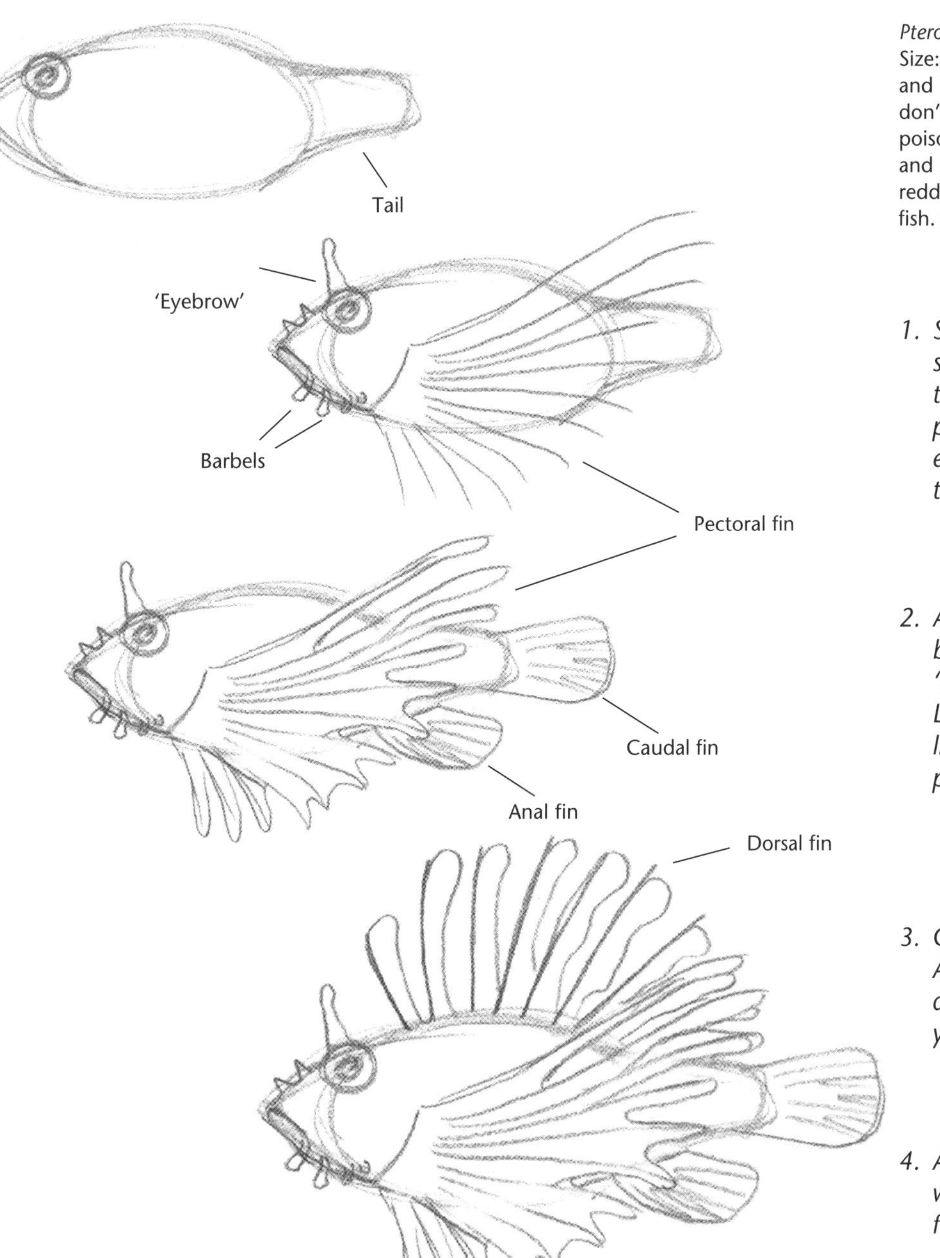

1. *Start with a simple oval shape. Add a rounded part for the tail at one end, and a point at the other. Draw the eye. Notice where it lies on the oval.*

2. *Add a line for the mouth, barbels on the chin, and the 'eyebrow' above the eye. Lightly draw radiating curved lines for the spines of the pectoral fin.*

3. *Complete the pectoral fin. Add the caudal (tail) fin and anal fin. Erase any body lines you no longer need.*

4. *Add the large dorsal fin, which is in many parts. At the front of each is a spine.*

5. *To sharpen the lines, you can go over outlines and important details with a fine marker. Clean up with your eraser.*

For help finishing your drawing, see *Drawing Tips* on pages 2-6.

Clown Anenome Fish

Always draw lightly at first!

Amphiprion percula.
Size: 6 cm (2.25 in). Diet: tiny crustaceans and other organisms. Lives in safety amidst the tentacles of sea anenomes, which kill other fish.

1. *Start with an oval. Add a rounded part at one end for the head. Draw a large eye and the mouth. Notice that the eye touches the outside of the oval. Add the tail.*

2. *Draw top and bottom fins in line with each other.*

3. *Add tentacles of the sea anenome, with some in front of the fish. Lightly erase lines that cross at the bottom of the fish.*

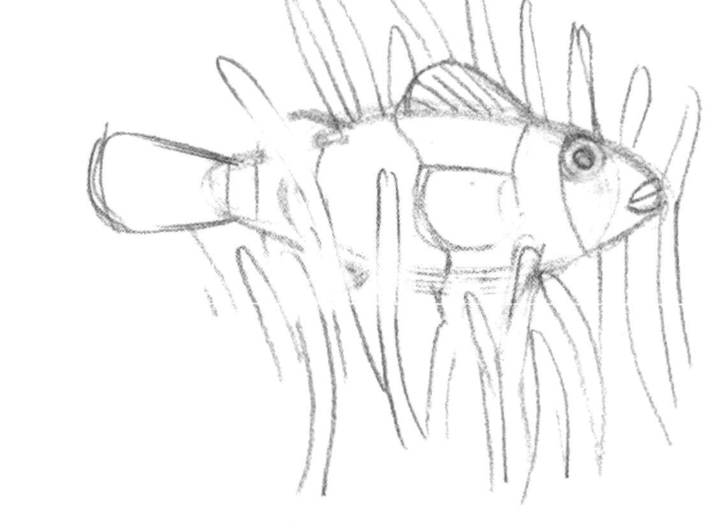

4. *Draw the bold pattern (orange, black and white if you're drawing in color). Add shading. Sharpen outlines and details. Clean up any smudges with your eraser.*

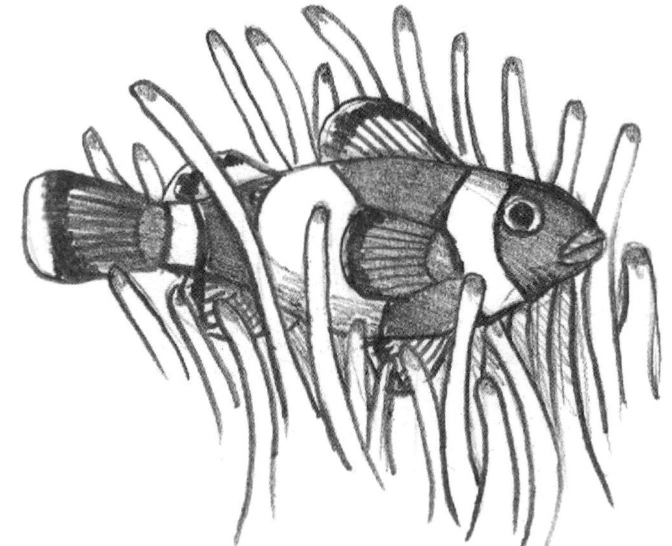

Always draw lightly at first!

Moray Eel

Mureana helena.
Size: 90 cm (35.5 in). Diet: fish, squid, cuttlefish. Hides in rock or coral crevices, waiting to lunge at prey swimming by.

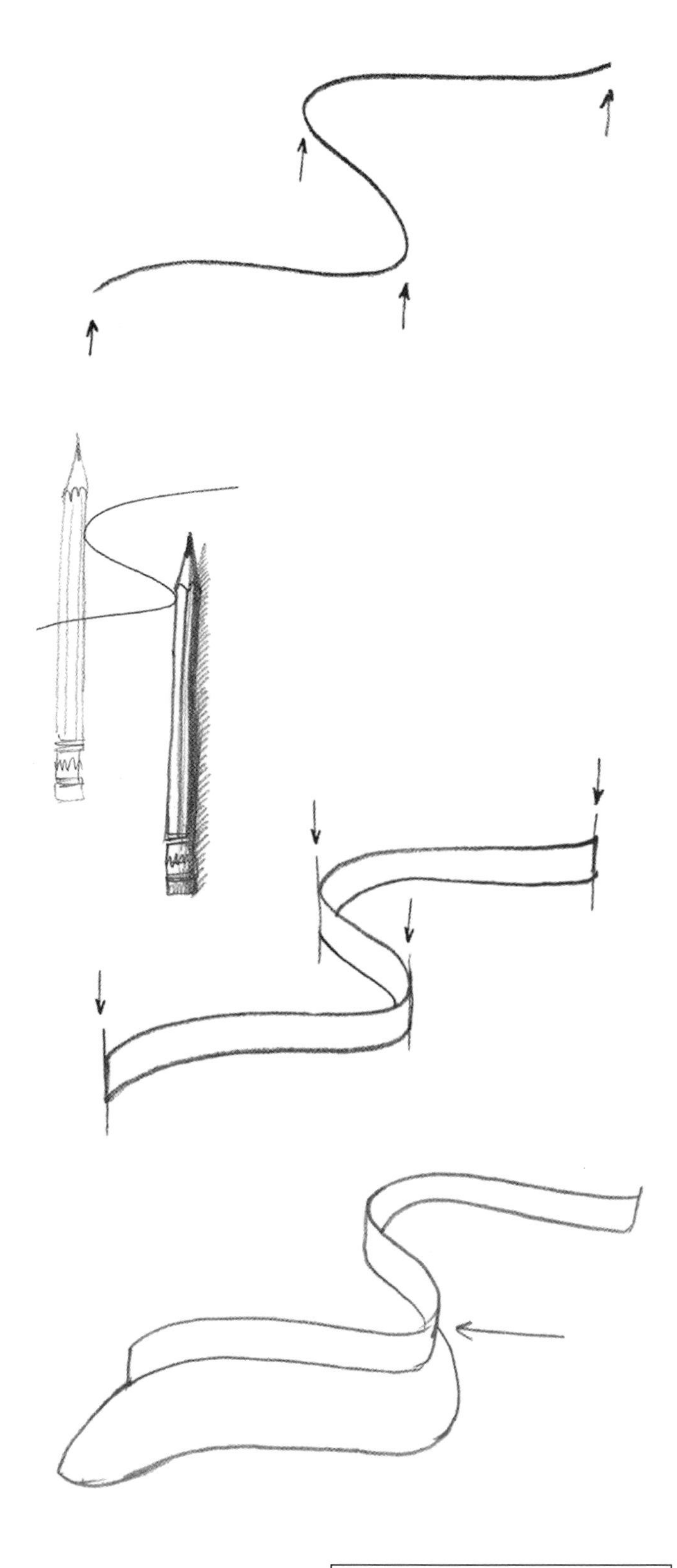

This drawing involves depth, and it's a bit more complicated. For that reason, I've broken it down to one line at a time.

1. *Start with a curvy line.*

2. *Add straight vertical lines at the ends and the curves. Hold your pencil flat on the paper if you have trouble seeing how to draw the vertical lines. Add more curved lines beneath the first ones, connecting to the vertical lines. See how you can turn it into a ribbon?*

3. *You may need a couple of tries to figure out the next few steps, so draw lightly at first! Pay special attention to the arrows.*

   From the left side of the ribbon, draw a sausage shape, with your line ending at the arrow.

For help finishing your drawing, see *Drawing Tips* on pages 2-6.

4. *Draw a small line to make the second part of the body…*

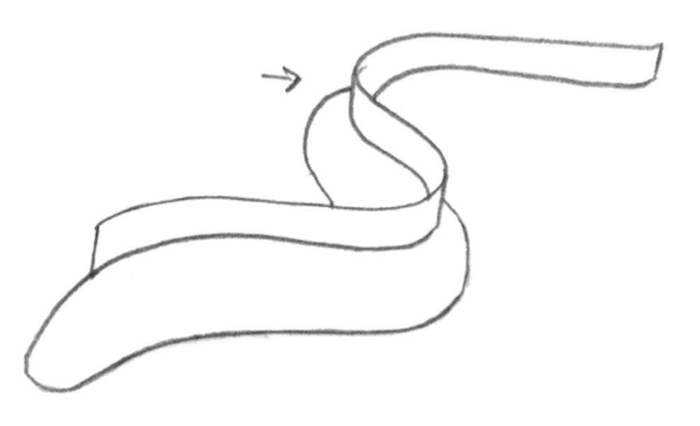

5. *Add a third line. Now you've drawn the entire body of the eel. Take a moment to look at your drawing. Does it look like it's swimming toward you?*

   Cool!

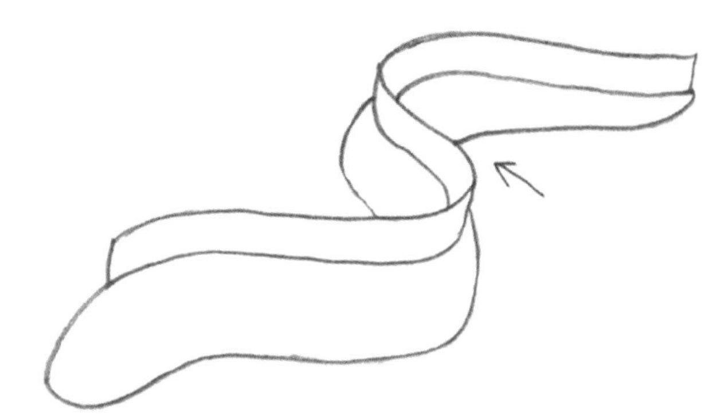

6. *Next add the ribbon-like fin along the bottom of the eel. Draw the mouth and eye. Add an angle to the front of the dorsal fin.*

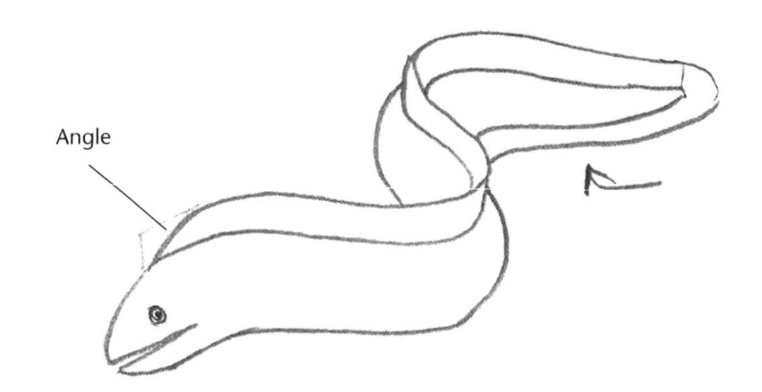

7. *Add shading and spots. See* Drawing Tips *at the end of the book for help with the pattern. Clean up any smudges with your eraser.*

Always draw lightly at first!

Octopus

Class *Cephalopoda,* genus *Octopus.* Mollusk with eight tentacles, or arms, with suction cups. Related to squid, cuttlefish, and nautilus, an octopus has no bones. It moves by squirting water out of the siphon, an opening under its head. Has three hearts, can change colors, and shoots clouds of black 'ink' in self defense. Size: varies among 50 varieties, from 8 cm (3 in) to 8.5 m (28 ft). Diet: clams, crabs, lobsters, mussels and other shellfish. Octopuses live along coasts; not just in coral reefs.

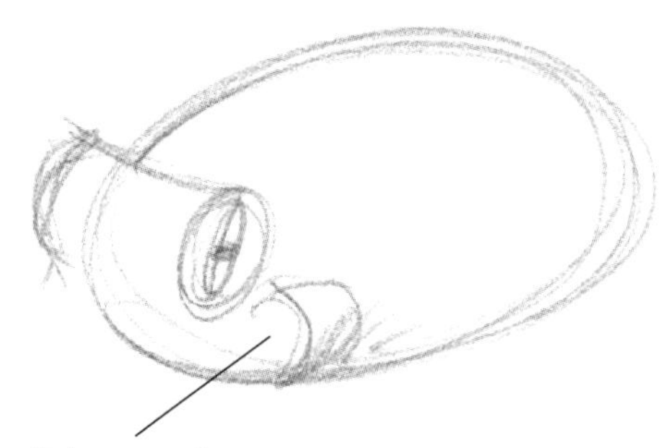

1. *Draw an oval for the body. Next draw a cylinder shape for the head, with an eye at the end. Add the opening for the siphon.*

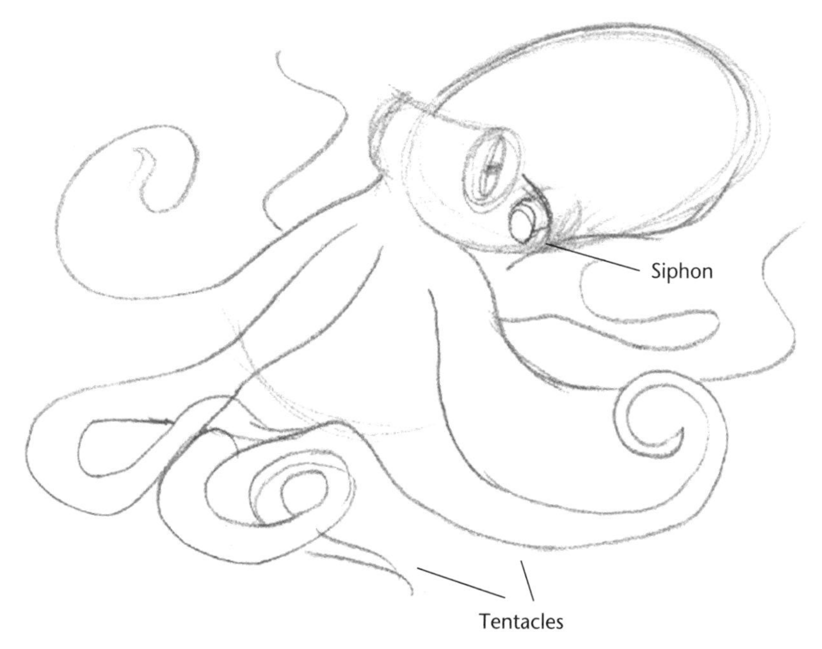

2. *Because the octopus has no bones, the tentacles can go just about any direction, often they're curled. Draw the siphon.*

   Suggestion: put tentacles curling every which way. Make a fun design!

3. *Draw suction cups on the bottom of each tentacle. When you like the design, you can go over your final lines with a fine-tip marker. Erase the pencil lines, add shading, and clean up with an eraser.*

For help finishing your drawing, see *Drawing Tips* on pages 2-6.

Green Turtle

Always draw lightly at first!

Chelonia mydas. Size: 1-1.5 m (3-4 ft). Diet: sea grasses and seaweed, some jellyfish and crustaceans. Endangered.

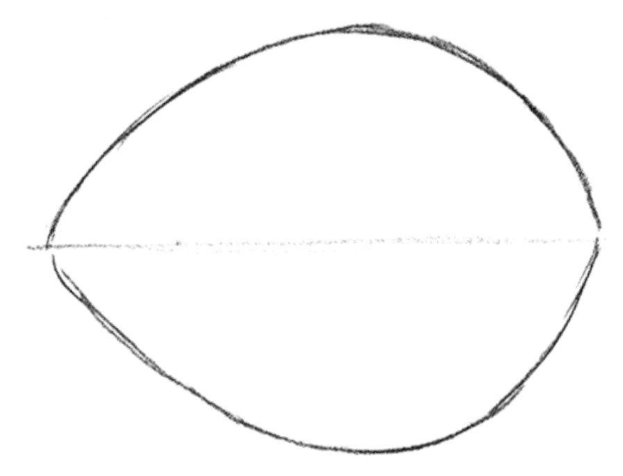

1. *Draw the outside of the shell, with center line.*

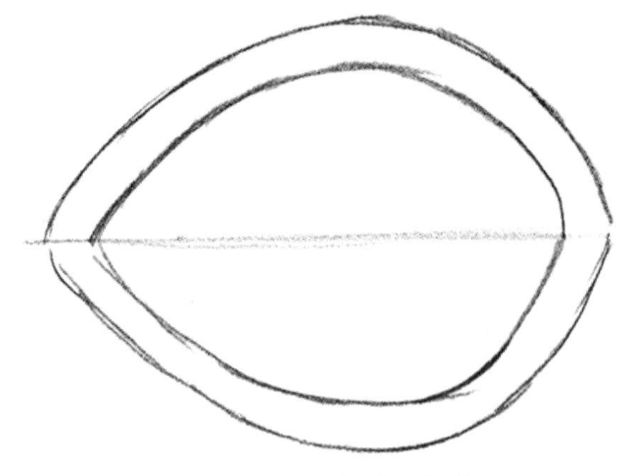

2. *Draw the same shape inside the shell.*

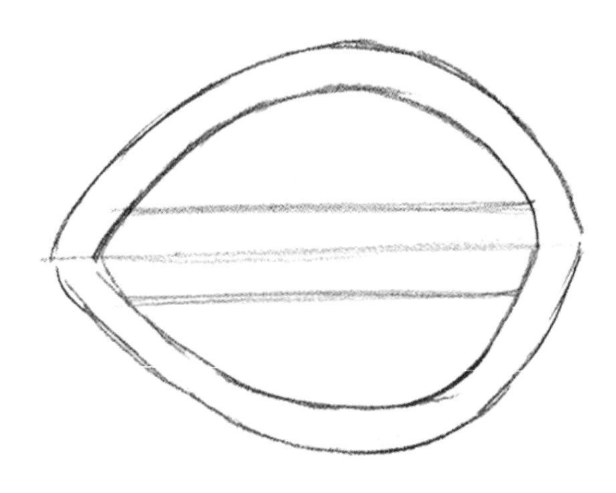

3. *Draw a line either side of the center line.*

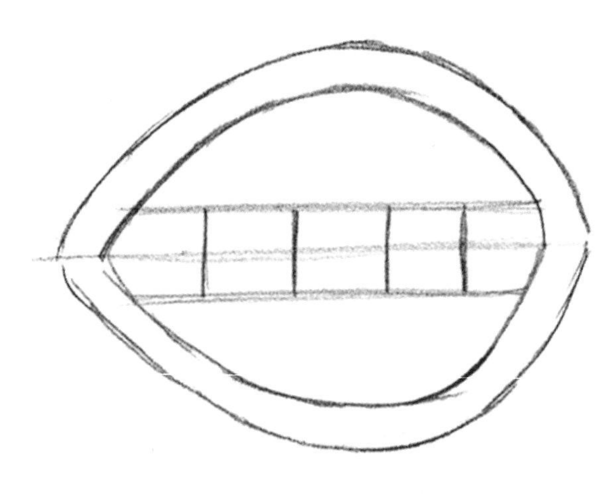

4. *Divide the center into five spaces.*

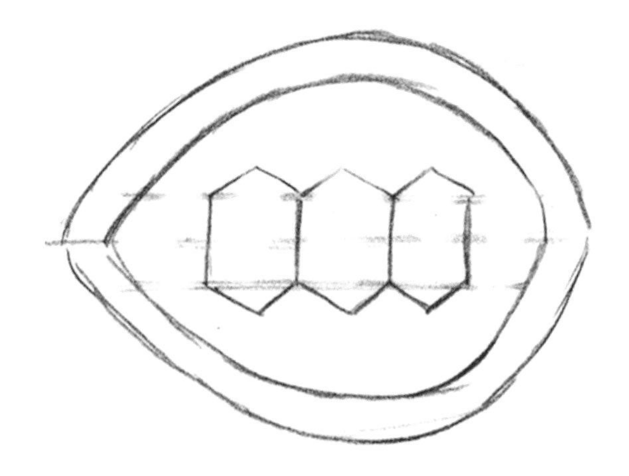

5. *Turn the middle three spaces into hexagons.*

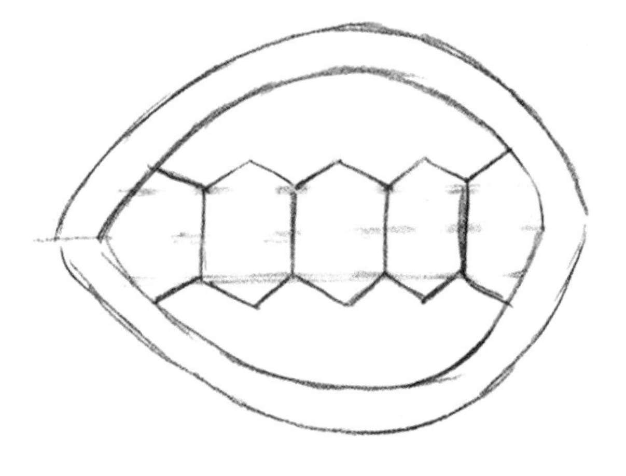

6. *Draw lines for the front and back segments.*

Always draw lightly at first!

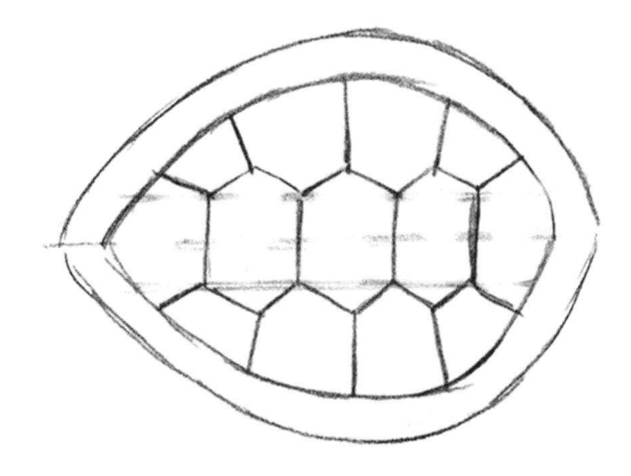

7. *Draw radiating lines from the hexagon points.*

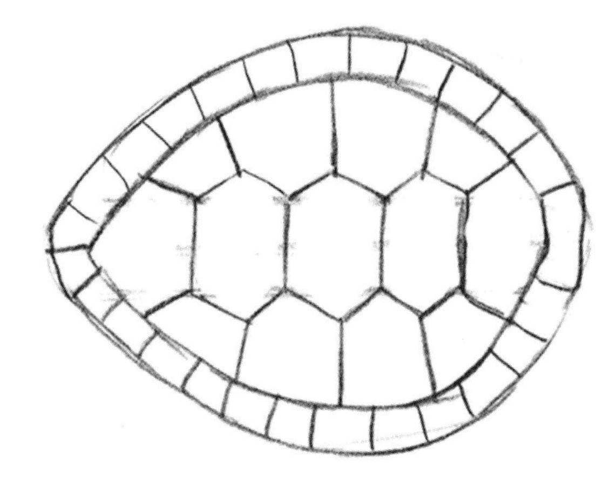

8. *Make lots of little segments on the outside rim. Now the hard part is done!*

9. *Add flippers and head. The front flippers have two parts. Notice which direction each part goes.*

10. *Draw the tail. Add shading and patterns of scales on the flippers and head. Sharpen outlines and details. Clean up any smudges with your eraser.*

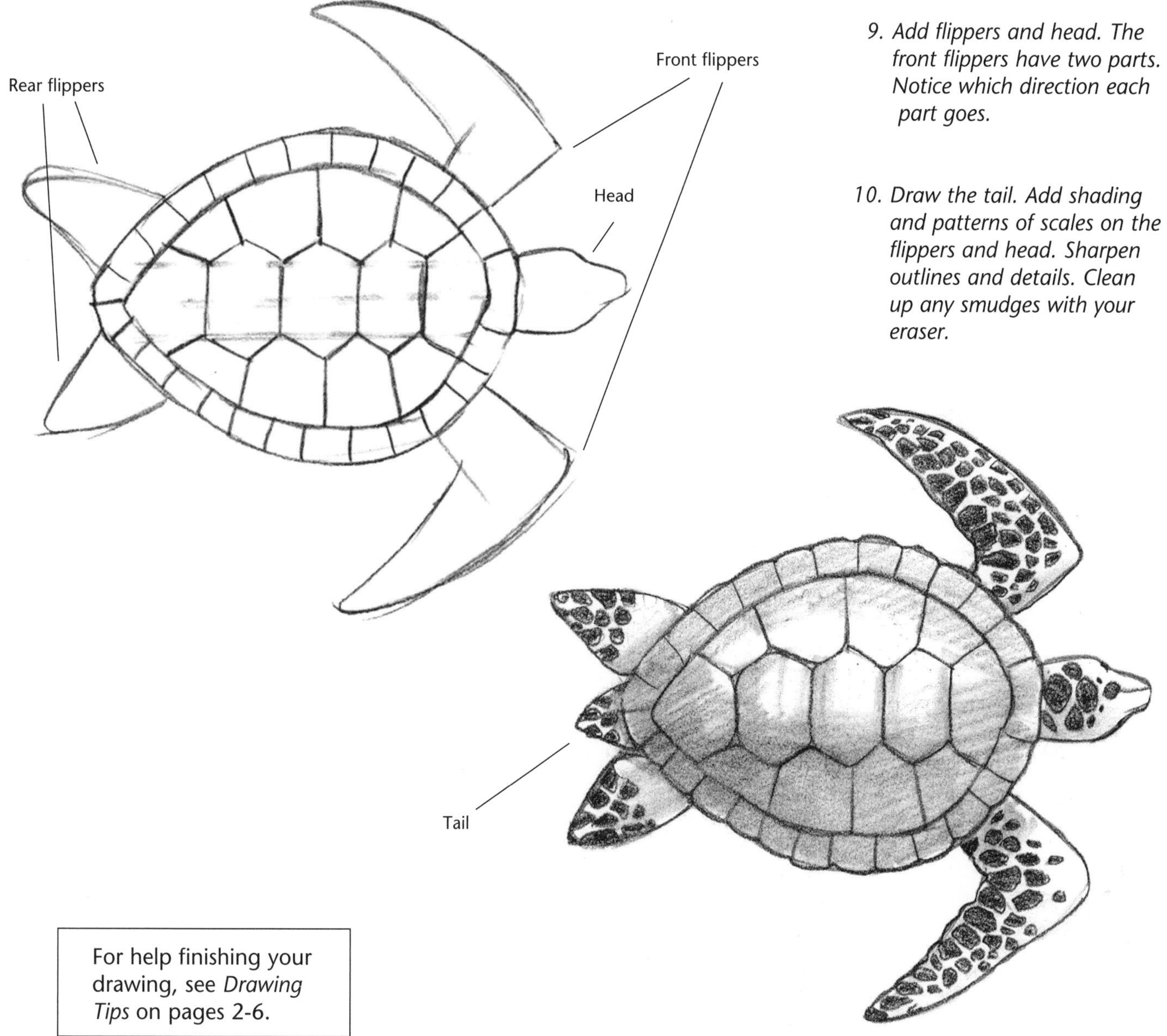

For help finishing your drawing, see *Drawing Tips* on pages 2-6.

17
KENT

Introduction

Find a **comfortable place to draw** – with decent light, so you can see what you're doing.

As you start to learn about car designs, shapes and proportions, don't worry too much about materials.

Use a **pencil that's longer than your finger.**

Sharpen your pencil when it gets dull!

Get a **separate eraser.** My favorite is a *kneaded* type, available in art supply and craft stores (the eraser on your pencil will disappear quickly).

For smooth shading with a soft pencil, consider a **tortillon, or blending tool**.

For practice drawings, use **recycled paper** – for example, draw on the back of old photocopies or computer printouts.

Always **draw lightly at first**, so you can erase problems as you need to.

Save your drawings and learn from them.

Enjoy drawing ***great*** cars!

Supplies

- **pencil** (any kind)
- **fine marker** (optional)
- **pencil sharpener**
- **eraser** (I like the kneadable type)
- **paper** (drawing paper erases best)
- **blending stump** if you want to do smooth shading (you can use your finger, too, but it's a bit messy)
- **place to draw**
- **POSITIVE ATTITUDE!**

Tips and Tricks: Some Basics

Use reference material: find pictures in magazines or books when you can't look at actual cars. Look at details, light and dark areas, and the effects of perspective from the camera angle.

Turn your paper as you draw to take advantage of the point of your pencil, and the natural way your hand draws curves.

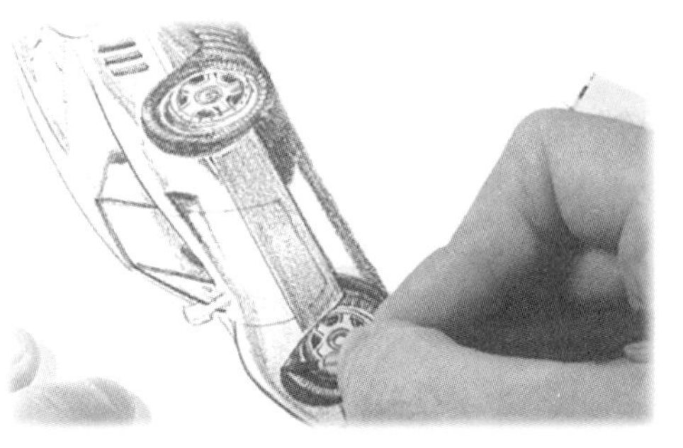

Put scrap paper under your hand to keep from smearing parts of the drawing you've already finished.

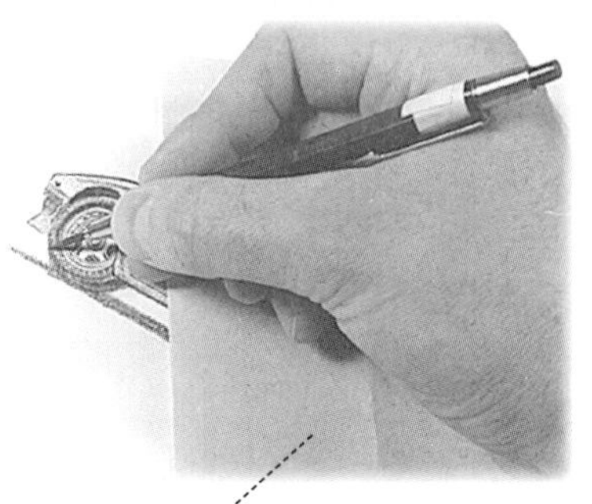

Protective paper keeps drawing clean

Use your eraser to create highlights and to clean up any smudged areas.

Kneadable eraser can be pinched into a point for close work

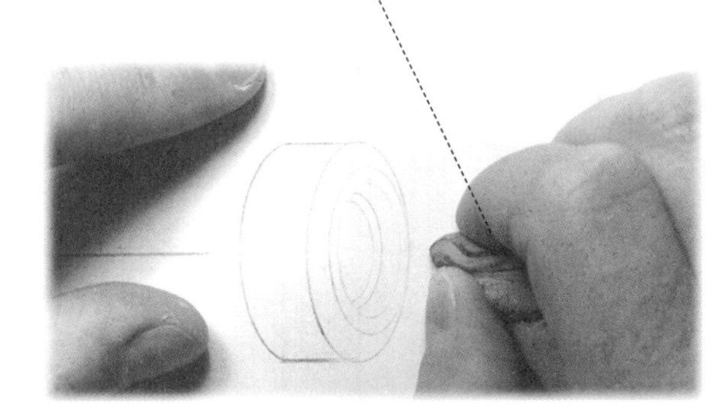

Use different pencils. Pencils range from 6B (softest and darkest) to 9H (hardest). A normal 2B pencil works well for sketching and shading, but a harder HB makes crisper lines – I even use a 5H, which is very hard, for very fine details.

For very smooth shading, use a soft pencil and a *tortillon*, a wound-up paper stick made for blending pastels.

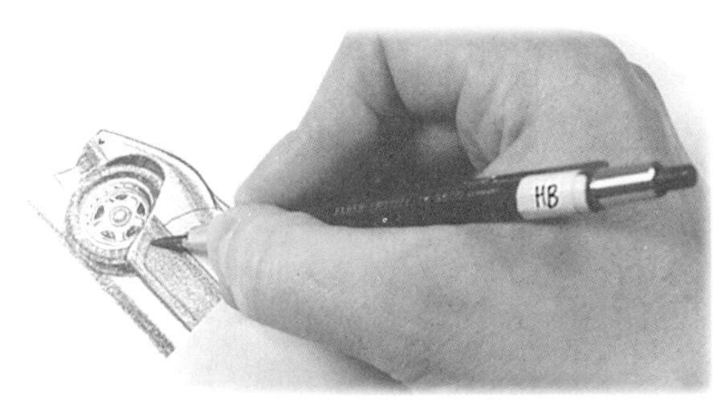

Tips and Tricks: Making Wheels Round

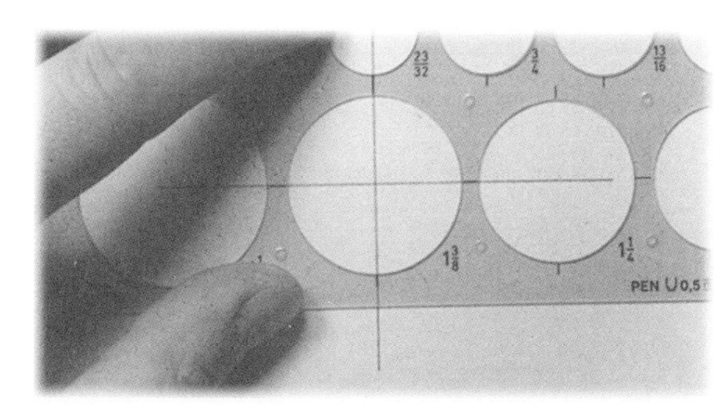

"Aren't wheels always round?" you ask. No, in fact, they're only round when you look at them in exactly the right way. Otherwise they're elliptical (see next page). Round wheels can be both fun and frustrating to draw.

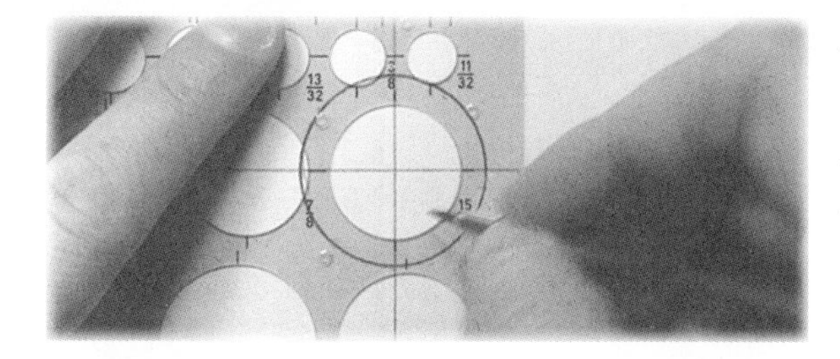

If you want perfect circles, you might want to try a transparent circle template. Make a horizontal and vertical line, then align them with the marks on the template. Then draw circle after circle, using different size holes in the template.

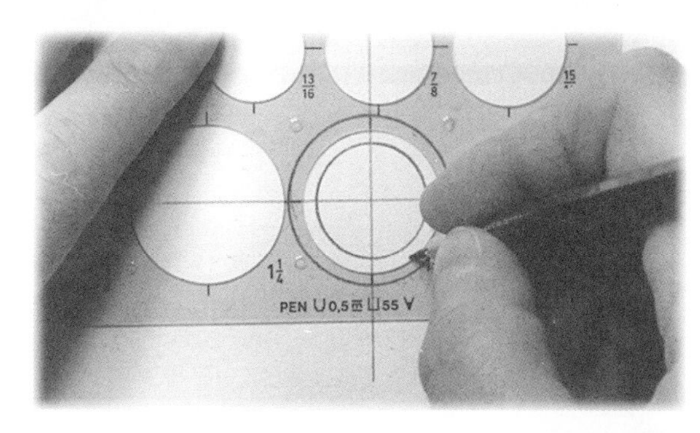

When you start looking at wheel (or hub cap) designs, you'll find a bewildering variety. Most are divided into five spokes or holes. But some have four, some have six, some have none, some have seven, or nine, or eleven, or...well, *count them for yourself!*

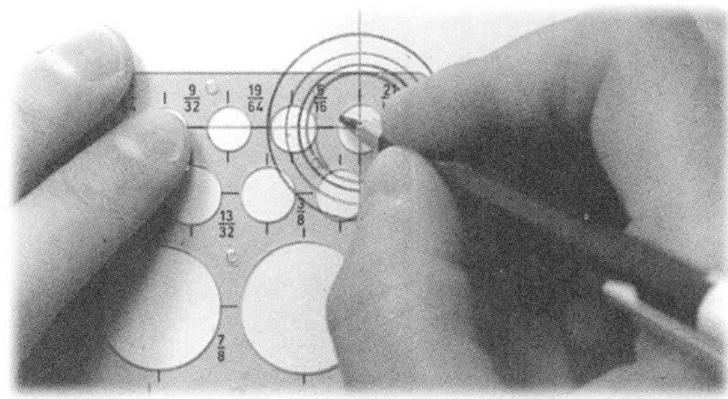

The more you look, the more you'll see. Have fun hunting for and drawing cool wheels!

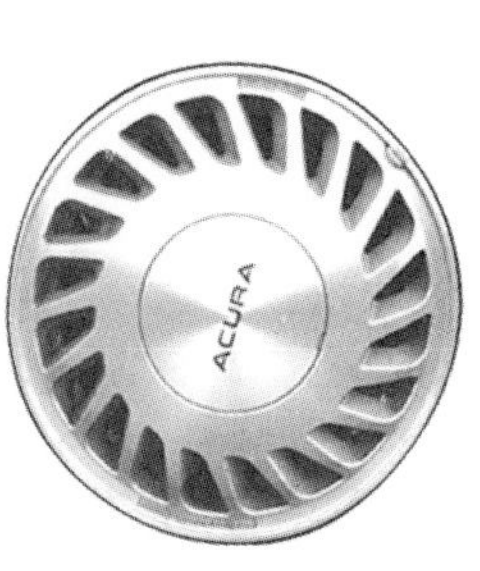

Tips and Tricks: Wheels from an Angle

Although I have a template for ellipses, I don't use it. I prefer to draw freehand.

These photos show how the ellipses go together to make a wheel from an angle.

Starting with a horizontal and vertical line, draw one ellipse. Next, slide the template along the horizontal line, and draw part of a second ellipse, the same size as the first.

Use a ruler to connect them to make the top and bottom of the tire. Now slide the template to the right, slightly beyond the first vertical line, and make a smaller ellipse.

Though you don't have to, you can add another, still smaller ellipse on the same vertical axis. Then slide the template left to the first vertical line for the rim of the wheel.

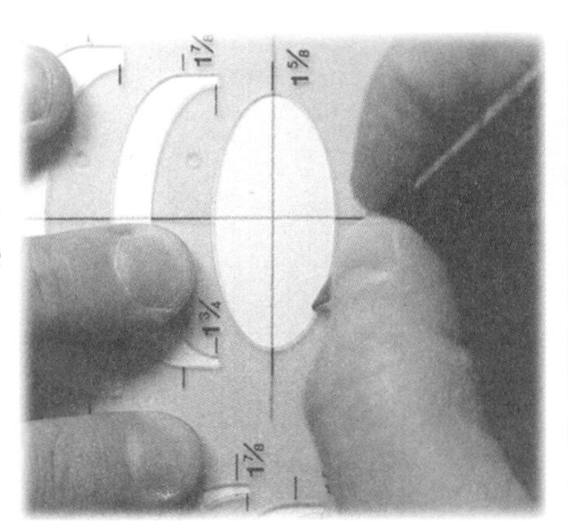

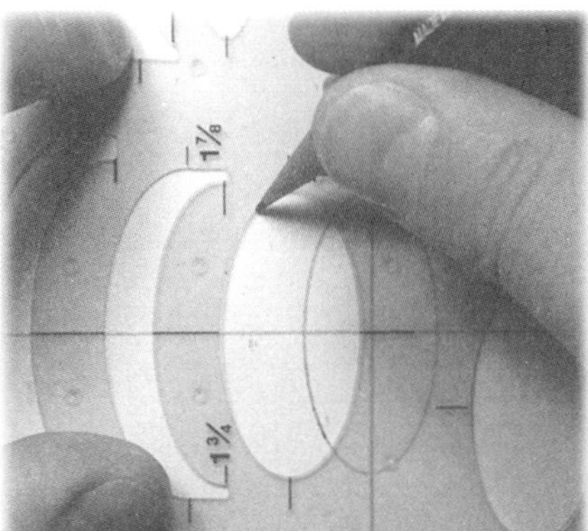

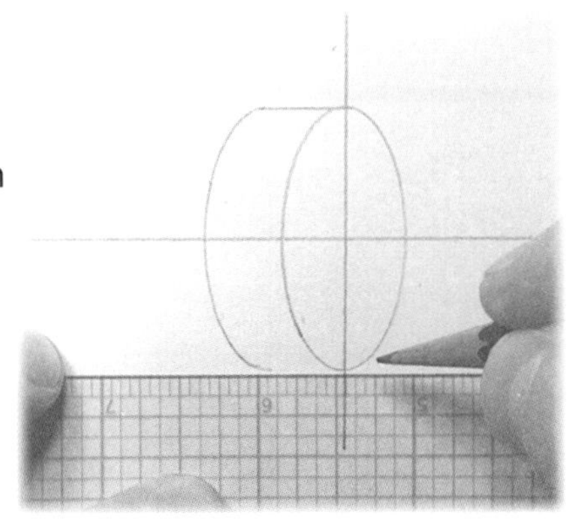

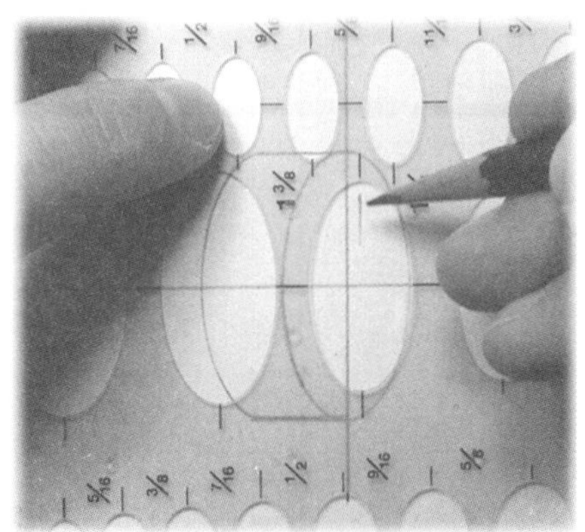

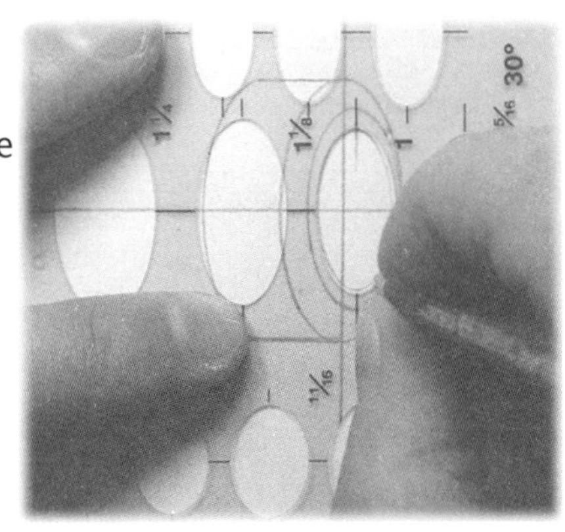

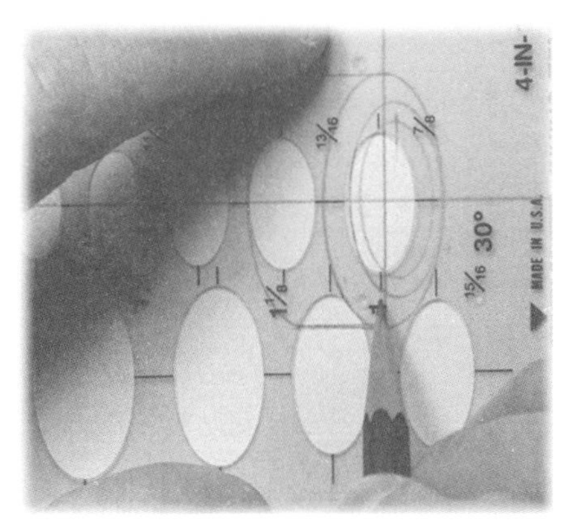

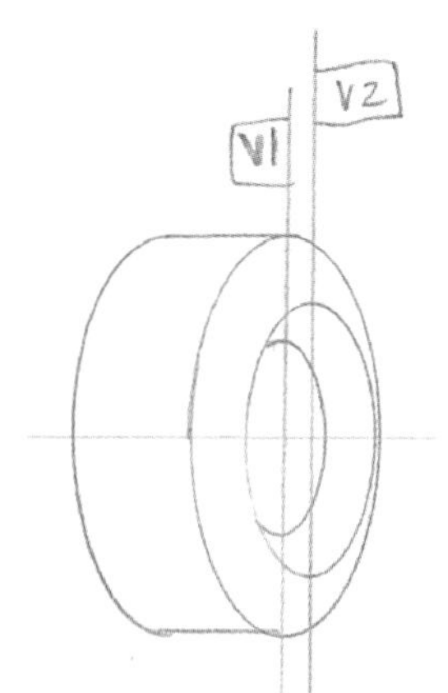

V1=vertical axis used for largest and smallest ellipse

V2=vertical axis used for smallest ellipse

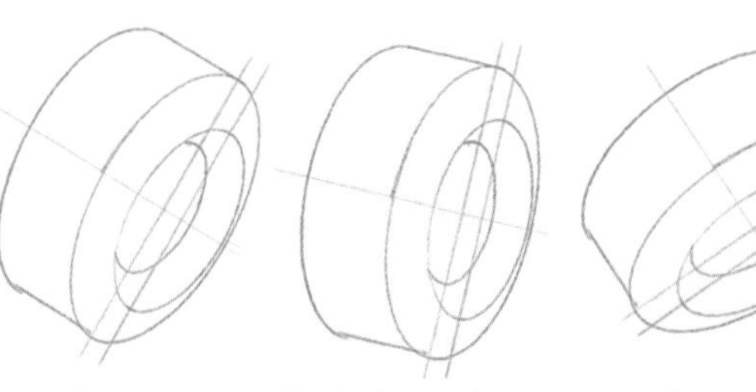

When viewing wheels from above, rotate the axes. Note that they remain perpendicular *to each other.*

Tips and Tricks: Imagination!

Here's my favorite drawing tip: use your imagination!

A 30-year-old Ford parked behind a warehouse (may not even run) suddenly takes to the air as it crashes over rugged terrain!

A pathetic-looking 1955 Fiat becomes a Lamborghini-stomping terror!

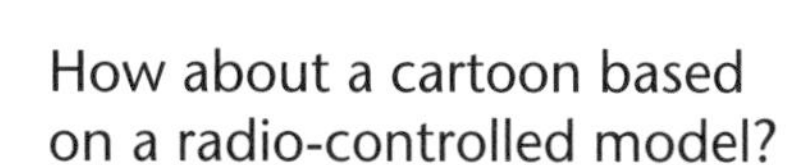

How about a cartoon based on a radio-controlled model?

Imagination: you've got it. Use it!

Dodge Stratus

*Before you start, look carefully at your **reference material**.*

For this drawing, your reference material will be this finished drawing (my reference material for this drawing was a magazine advertisement.)

Start with a light horizontal line for the ground.

The Ground.

Carefully draw a circle for the wheel.

A Wheel. Don't worry if it isn't perfectly round at first.

Always ask yourself: how many wheels (or wheel diameters) would fit between the front and back wheel?

You won't see many cars where the answer is two.

Nor will you see many cars where the answer is seven!

On the Stratus, the front and rear wheel are separated by about 3½ diameters, which is typical of many cars.

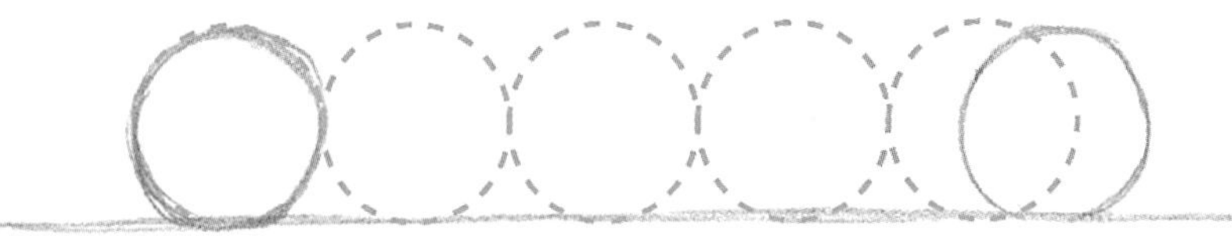

Always start out ***lightly***!

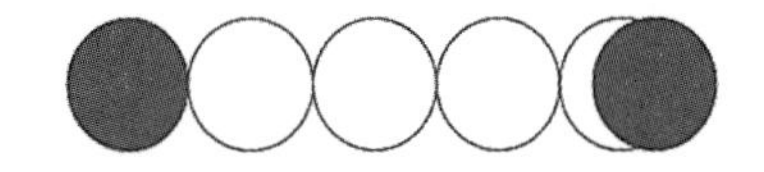

Carefully measure the distance between the wheels, then draw a light circle for the second wheel.

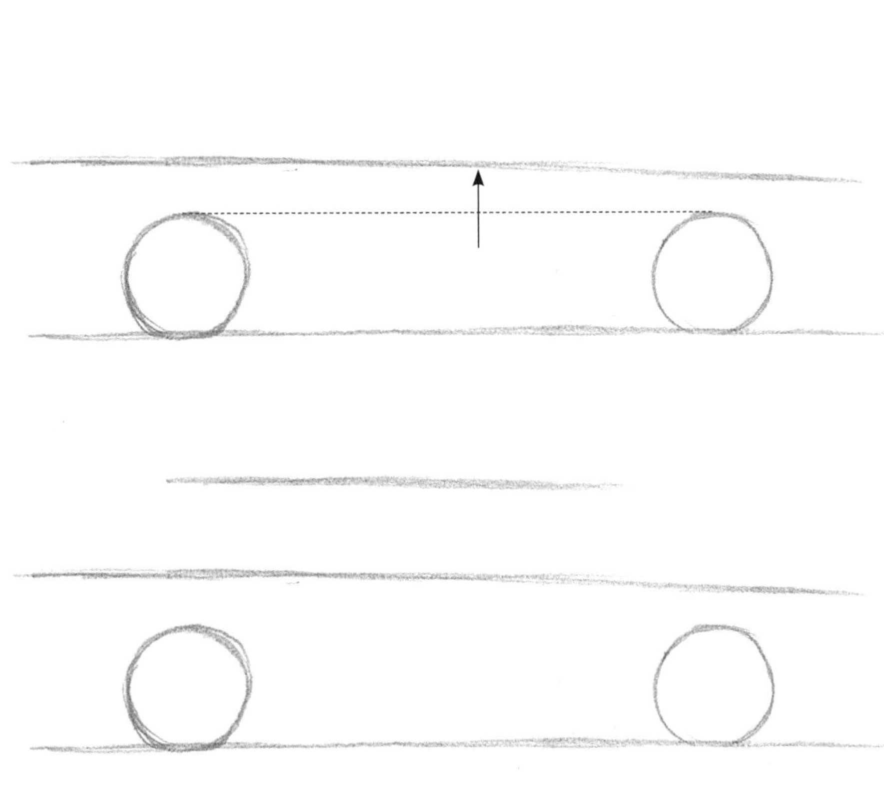

Look again at your *reference material.* Lightly draw the line at the bottom of the windows. Observe its height above the wheels, and notice how it slopes slightly down to the front.

Look again at your *reference material.* Find the top of the roof. Lightly draw this line.

*These three lines—the ground, bottom of window, and roof—are **basic lines** you'll need to draw **any** car.*

The details can be a little complicated at the front and rear end of the car. For now, just make a light vertical line to mark the front of the car, with another line cutting back to the wheel.

Look again at your *reference material* to see where to end the car. Make a light vertical line there, then another cutting forward to the wheel.

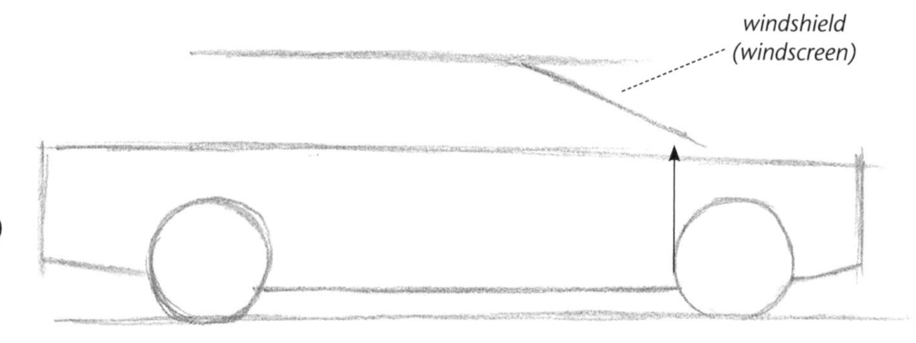

Look at the windshield. How far forward does it extend, compared to the back of the front wheel? *(This varies from car to car.)* Lightly sketch the windshield line.

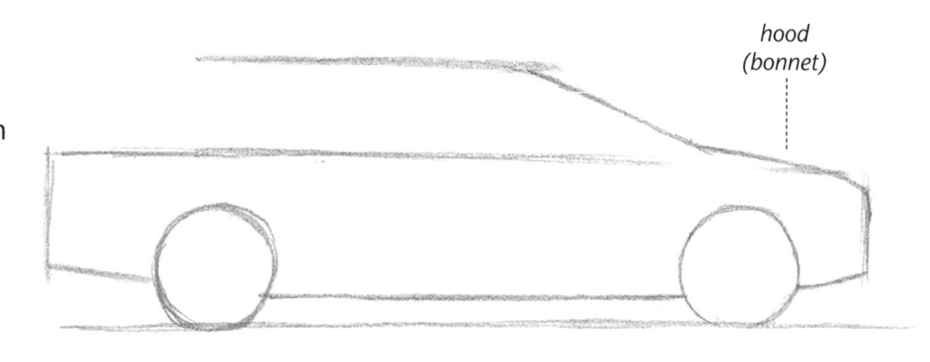

Add the line, joining the bottom of the windshield and carrying forward, with a slight curve.

Notice how the rear window and trunk are higher than the hood. Draw them. Now take another look at your *reference material*, and add the curves of the bumper and tail light.

Always start out ***lightly***!

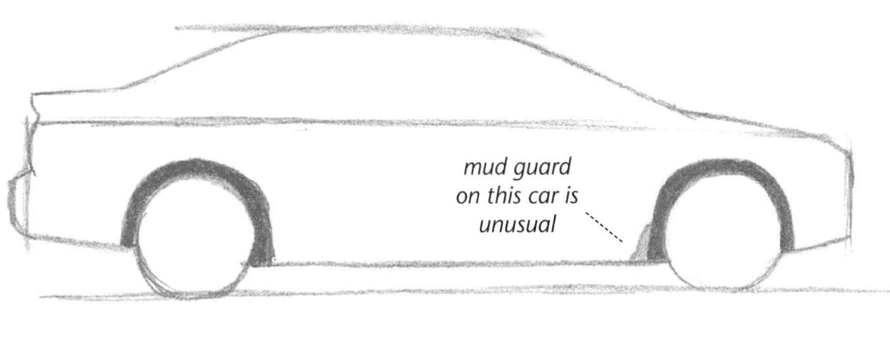

Extremely important... draw the dark cut-out portion of the body that surrounds the wheels. These dark *wheel wells* are key to making your car drawing look real!

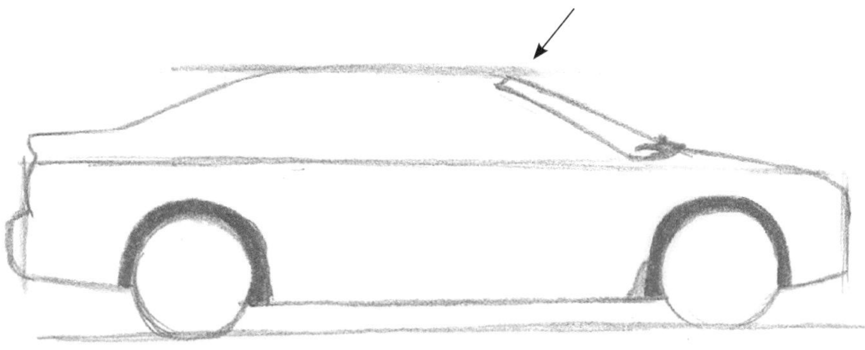

Add the side and top windshield lines (notice the angle at the top of the windshield). Draw windshield wipers.

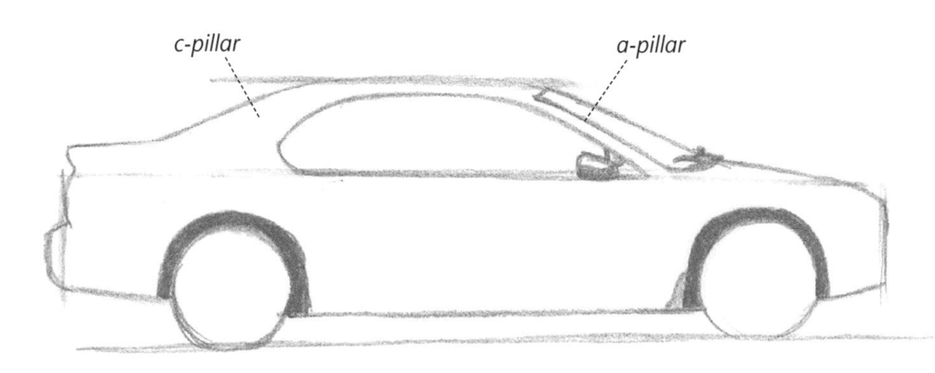

The outline of the side windows contributes much to the car's style. Draw the outline of the side windows. By drawing this shape, you've also drawn the A- and C-pillars. Add the mirror.

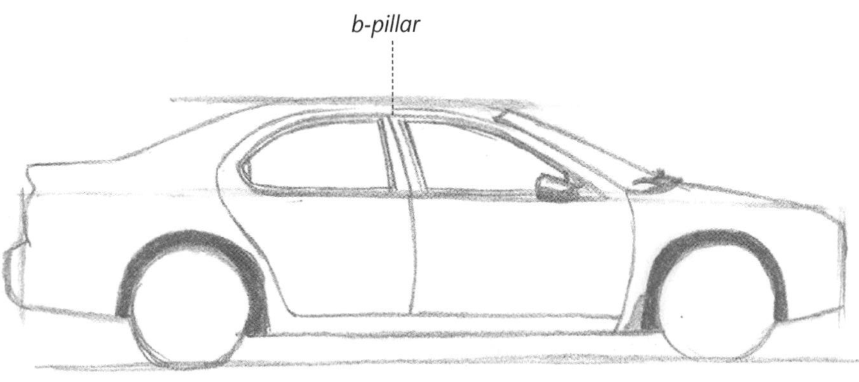

Look carefully at the size of the doors. Typically, on a four-door *sedan,* the front doors are bigger (a *coupe* has two doors). Outline the doors, windows and b-pillar (draw the door seam through the middle of it).

Why do chicken coops have two doors?

(Because if they had four doors, they'd be chicken sedans.)

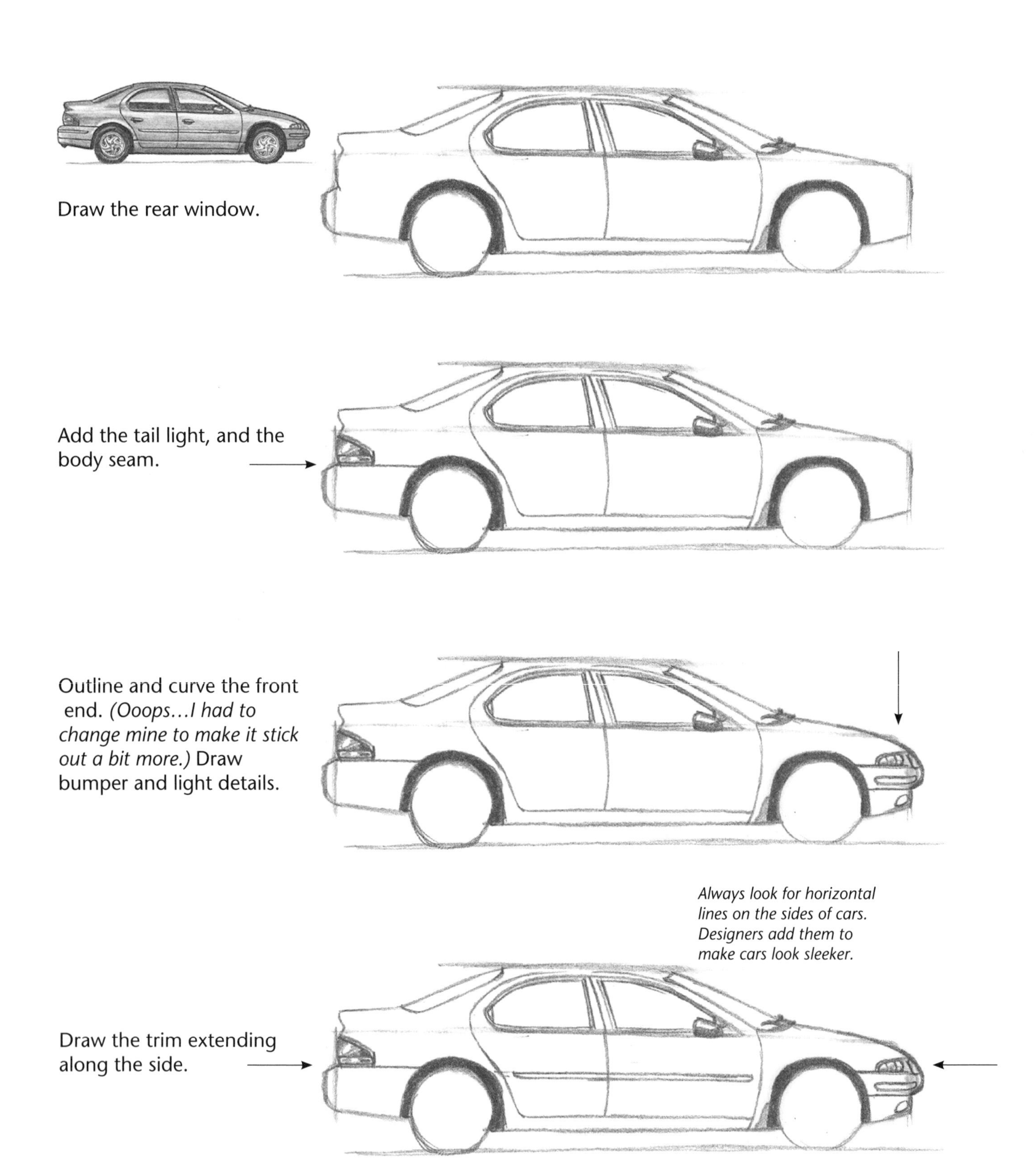

Draw the rear window.

Add the tail light, and the body seam.

Outline and curve the front end. *(Ooops...I had to change mine to make it stick out a bit more.)* Draw bumper and light details.

Always look for horizontal lines on the sides of cars. Designers add them to make cars look sleeker.

Draw the trim extending along the side.

Always start out ***lightly***!

Add another horizontal line, above the bottom of the doors, and extending to the rear end of the car.

Draw door handles. Erase guidelines you no longer need.

Look carefully at the *reference material,* and add shading to your drawing. You might smooth it, as I did, with a *tortillon* or blending tool. Then you can use your eraser to add highlights. Spend as much time as you need at this stage.

Turn your drawing as you draw to avoid smudging it with your hand.

Now sharpen your pencil and go over details and lines, making them as crisp as you can.

All done!

...just kidding!

Notice those *round things* the car sits on. They have two parts: the *wheel* and the *tire.* Draw a smaller circle in each tire for the real wheel.

Having trouble drawing circles?

Darken the tires. For best effect, leave a little highlight at the top of the top, and the top of the bottom.

Draw the pattern of the wheels.

Add details to the wheels, and shading.

All done!

(Really!)

Always start out ***lightly***!

Audi Avus

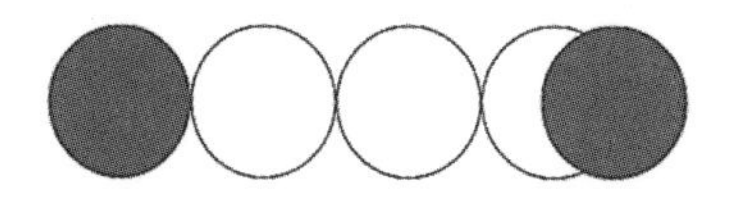

*Before you start, look carefully at your **reference material** (for now, my finished drawing).*

Draw the ground line. Using the wheel diagram above, draw the wheels the correct distance apart. Draw the basic body lines.

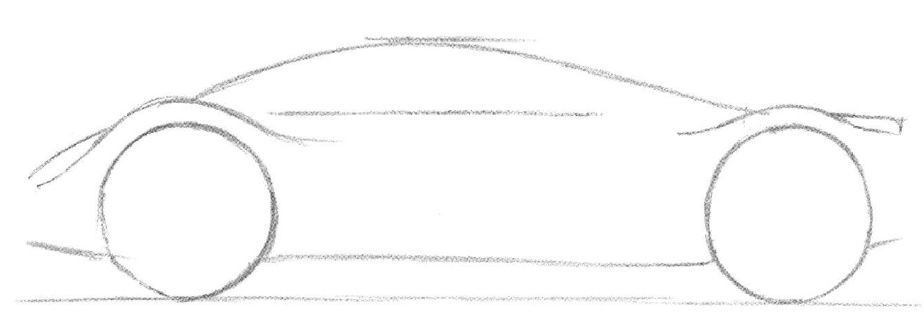

Complete the overall shape of the car.

Add:
- front and rear bumpers
- windows
- wheel wells
- lights
- rear view mirror
- tires and wheels

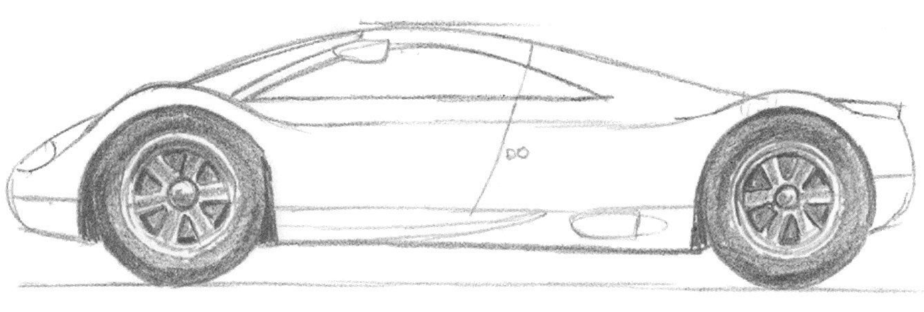

Draw other details you see (or want—hey, it's your drawing!). Add shading.

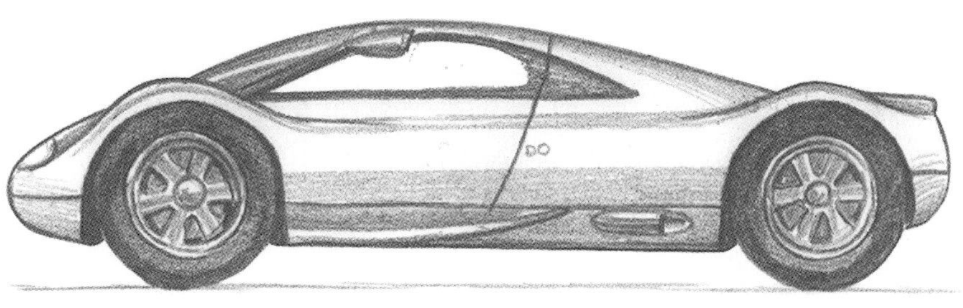

Remember:
- *Start out lightly!*
- *Turn your drawing as you work. Use a piece of scrap paper to keep your hand off finished parts.*
- *While your pencil is sharp, go over fine details and make lines cleaner. As it gets duller, add shading.*
- *Clean up any smudges with your eraser. Make sure all final lines are crisp and sharp.*

Dodge Viper

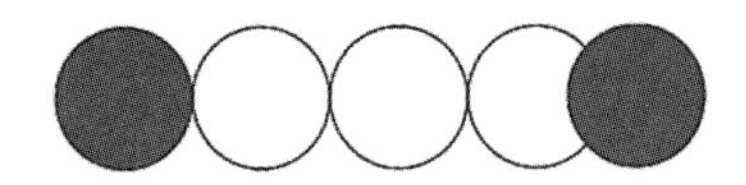

Before you start, look carefully at your ***reference material*** *(for now, my finished drawing).*

Draw the ground line. Using the wheel diagram above, draw the wheels the correct distance apart. Draw the basic body lines.

Complete the overall shape of the car.

Add:
- windows
- pillars A and B
- wheel wells
- side body seams
- radical side vent
- lights
- rear view mirror
- fuel cap

Draw other details you see (or want—hey, it's your drawing!). Add shading.

Remember:
- *Start out lightly!*
- *Turn your drawing as you work. Use a piece of scrap paper to keep your hand off finished parts.*
- *While your pencil is sharp, go over fine details and make lines cleaner. As it gets duller, add shading.*
- *Clean up any smudges with your eraser. Make sure all final lines are crisp and sharp.*

Always start out ***lightly***!

Corvette

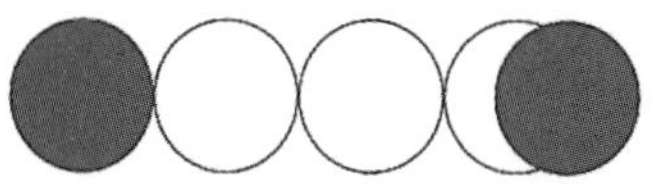

*Before you start, look carefully at your **reference material** (for now, my finished drawing).*

Draw the ground line. Using the wheel diagram above, draw the wheels the correct distance apart. Draw the basic body lines.

Complete the overall shape of the car.

Add:
- windows
- pillars A and B
- wheel wells
- side vent
- side lights
- rear view mirror
- fuel cap

Draw other details you see (or want—hey, it's *your* drawing!). Erase guide lines. Add shading.

Remember:
- *Start out lightly!*
- *Turn your drawing as you work. Use a piece of scrap paper to keep your hand off finished parts.*
- *While your pencil is sharp, go over fine details and make lines cleaner. As it gets duller, add shading.*
- *Clean up any smudges with your eraser. Make sure all final lines are crisp and sharp.*

BMW 318

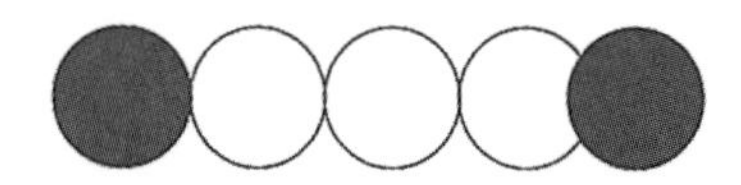

Before you start, look carefully at your ***reference material*** *(for now, my finished drawing).*

Draw the ground line. Using the wheel diagram above, draw the wheels the correct distance apart. Draw the basic body lines.

Complete the overall shape of the car.

Add:

- windows
- split rear window
- pillars A, B, and C
- wheel wells
- side trim
- lights
- rear view mirror
- steering wheel

Draw other details you see (or want—hey, it's *your* drawing!). Add shading.

Remember:

- *Start out lightly!*
- *Turn your drawing as you work. Use a piece of scrap paper to keep your hand off finished parts.*
- *While your pencil is sharp, go over fine details and make lines cleaner. As it gets duller, add shading.*
- *Clean up any smudges with your eraser. Make sure all final lines are crisp and sharp.*

Always start out ***lightly***!

Lamborghini Diablo Roadster

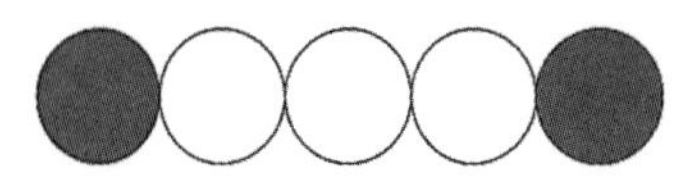

*Before you start, look carefully at your **reference material** (for now, my finished drawing).*

Draw the ground line. Using the wheel diagram above, draw the wheels the correct distance apart. Draw the basic body lines. Look carefully—they're unusual!

Complete the overall shape of the car.

Add:

- wheel wells
- side scoops
- running lights
- rear view mirror

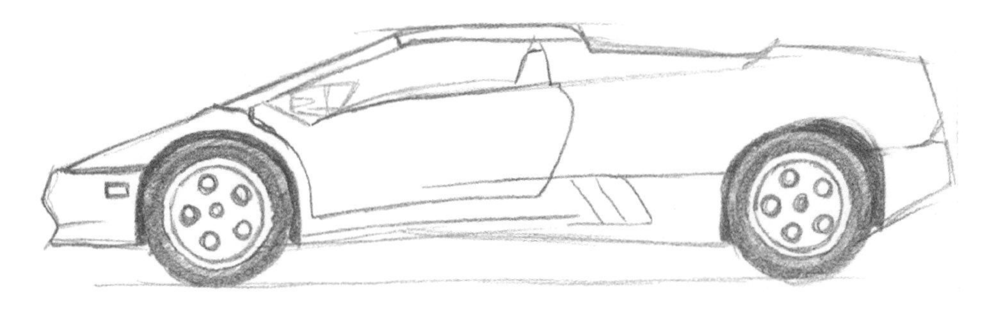

Draw other details you see (or want—hey, it's *your* drawing!). Add shading.

Remember:

- *Start out lightly!*
- *Turn your drawing as you work. Use a piece of scrap paper to keep your hand off finished parts.*

This little number costs more than many people's houses—a lot more. There's not much cargo room (!), so if you did own one of these, you'd probably drive it a lot. For example, grocery shopping: you'd need one trip for milk, another for bread, another for vegetables....

Volkswagen Beetle

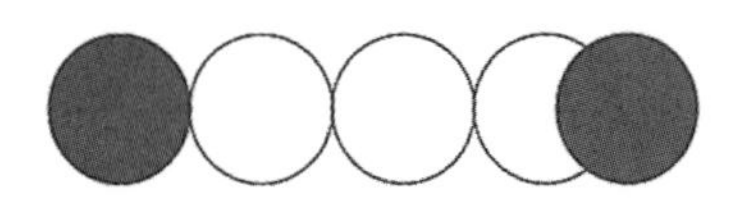

Before you start, look carefully at your ***reference material*** *(for now, my finished drawing).*

Draw the ground line. Using the wheel diagram above, draw the wheels the correct distance apart. Draw the basic body lines.

Complete the overall shape of the car, starting with the distinctive window shape.

Add:
- wheel wells
- blacked-out b-pillar
- door handle
- lights
- rear view mirror

Draw other details you see (or want—hey, it's *your* drawing!). Add shading.

Remember:
- *Start out lightly!*
- *Turn your drawing as you work. Use a piece of scrap paper to keep your hand off finished parts.*
- *While your pencil is sharp, go over fine details and make lines cleaner. As it gets duller, add shading.*

The one millionth VW beetle was built way back in 1955. Unlike the old beetle, this new design has the engine in front.

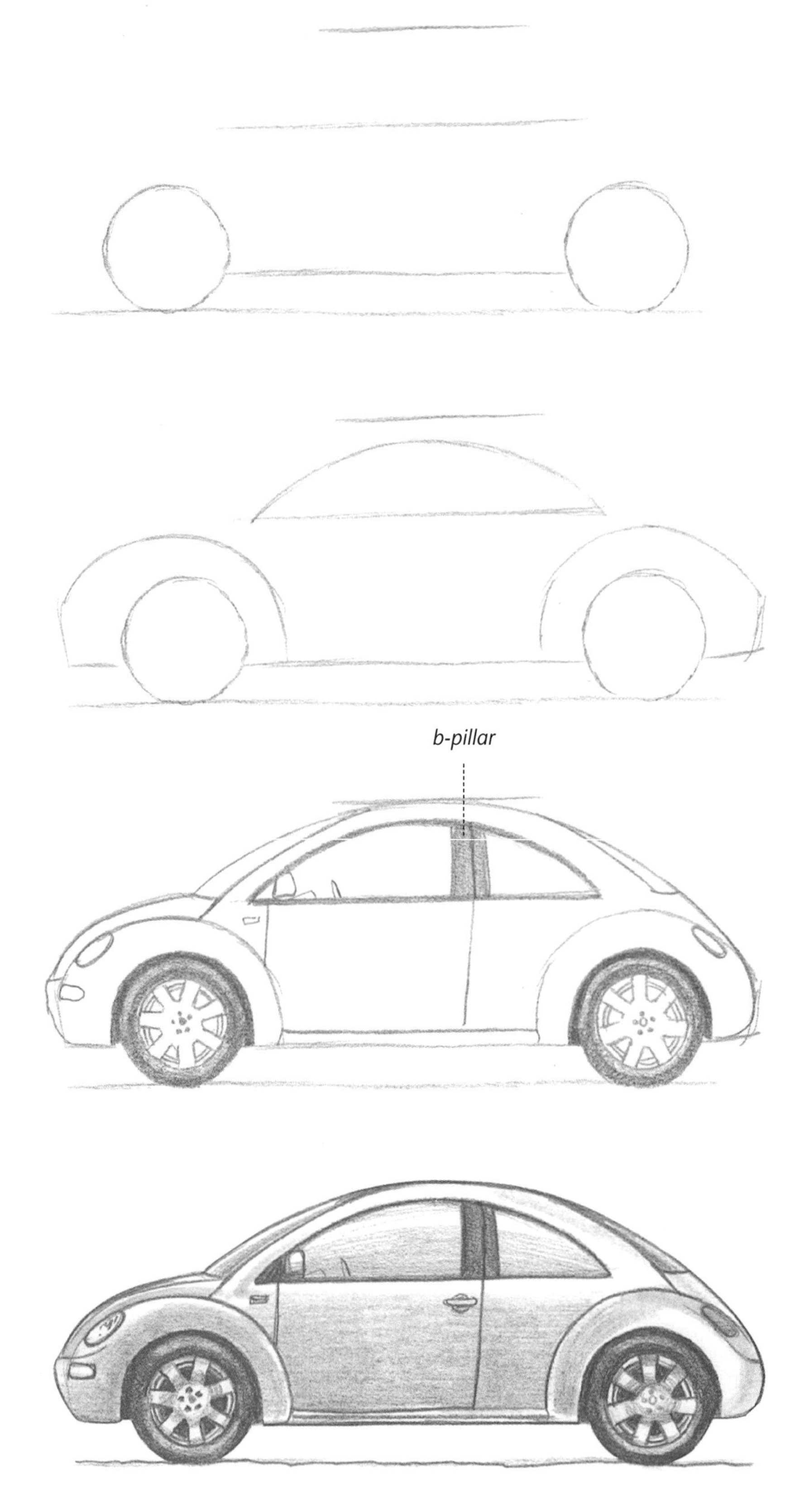

1906 Franklin

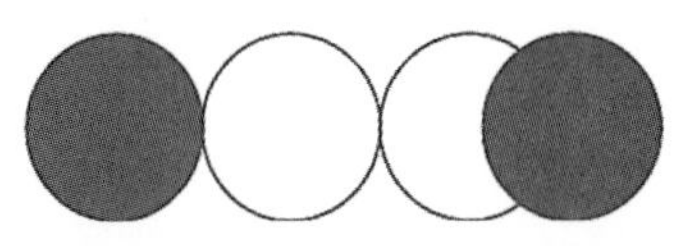

*Before you start, look carefully at your **reference material** (for now, my finished drawing).*

Always start out ***lightly***!

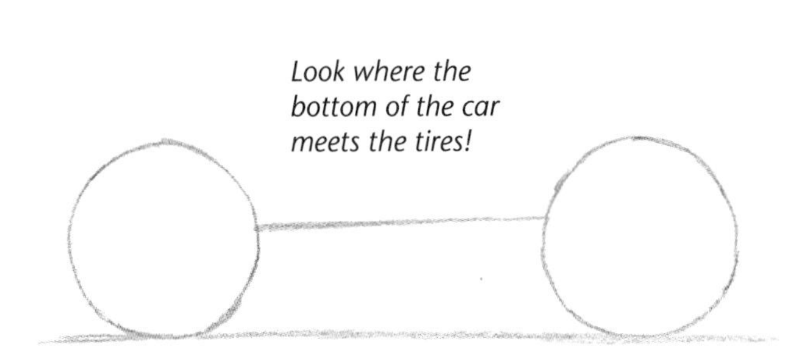

Look where the bottom of the car meets the tires!

Draw the ground line. Using the wheel diagram above, draw the wheels the correct distance apart. Draw the basic body lines.

Complete the overall shape of the car.

Look where the front and rear meet the tires!

Add:

- windows
- pillars A, B, and C
- fenders
- side trim
- wheel spokes
- head light, side lantern
- rear view mirror*

**I-don't-think-soooo…*

Draw other details you see (or want—hey, it's *your* drawing!). Add shading.

Remember:

- *Start out lightly!*
- *Turn your drawing as you work. Use a piece of scrap paper to keep your hand off finished parts.*
- *While your pencil is sharp, go over fine details and make lines cleaner. As it gets duller, add shading.*
- *Clean up any smudges with your eraser. Make sure all final lines are crisp and sharp.*

1934 Ford Model A

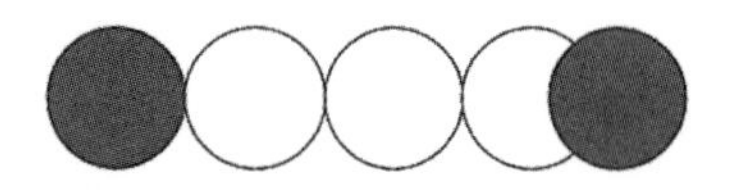

*Before you start, look carefully at your **reference material** (for now, my finished drawing).*

Draw the ground line. Using the wheel diagram above, draw the wheels the correct distance apart. Notice where the bottom of the car meets the tires! Draw the basic body lines.

Complete the overall shape of the car. Notice where the front and rear meet the tires!

Add:

- windows
- pillars A, B, and C
- fenders
- side vents
- lights
- rumble seat
- bumpers
- spare tire

Draw other details you see (or want—hey, it's *your* drawing!). Add shading.

Remember:

- *Start out lightly!*
- *Turn your drawing as you work. Use a piece of scrap paper to keep your hand off finished parts.*
- *While your pencil is sharp, go over fine details and make lines cleaner. As it gets duller, add shading.*
- *Clean up any smudges with your eraser. Make sure all final lines are crisp and sharp.*

Always start out ***lightly***!

1946 Chrysler Town and Country

*Before you start, look carefully at your **reference material** (for now, my finished drawing).*

Draw the ground line. Using the wheel diagram above, draw the wheels the correct distance apart. Draw the basic body lines.

Complete the overall shape of the car.

Add:

- windows
- pillars A, B, and C
- wheel wells, fenders
- side paneling
- lights
- rear view mirror
- luggage rack
- hood ornament

Draw other details you see (or want—hey, it's *your* drawing!). Add shading.

Remember:

- *Start out lightly!*
- *Turn your drawing as you work. Use a piece of scrap paper to keep your hand off finished parts.*
- *While your pencil is sharp, go over fine details and make lines cleaner. As it gets duller, add shading.*

1956 Chevy

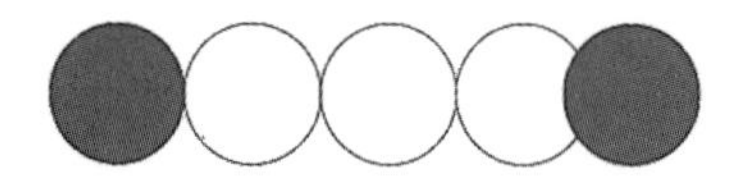

*Before you start, look carefully at your **reference material** (for now, my finished drawing).*

Draw the ground line. Using the wheel diagram above, draw the wheels the correct distance apart. Draw the basic body lines.

Complete the overall shape of the car.

Add:
- windows
- pillars A, B, and C
- wheel wells
- side trim
- rear view mirror
- hood ornament

Draw other details you see (or want—hey, it's your drawing!). Add shading.

Remember:
- *Start out lightly!*
- *Turn your drawing as you work. Use a piece of scrap paper to keep your hand off finished parts.*
- *While your pencil is sharp, go over fine details and make lines cleaner. As it gets duller, add shading.*
- *Clean up any smudges with your eraser. Make sure all final lines are crisp and sharp.*

Always start out ***lightly***!

Hummer

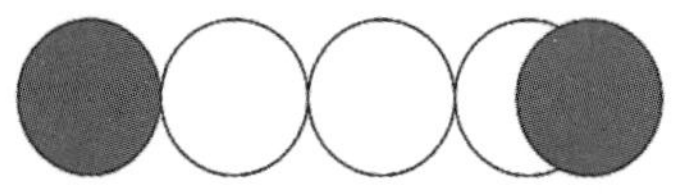

*Before you start, look carefully at your **reference material** (for now, my finished drawing).*

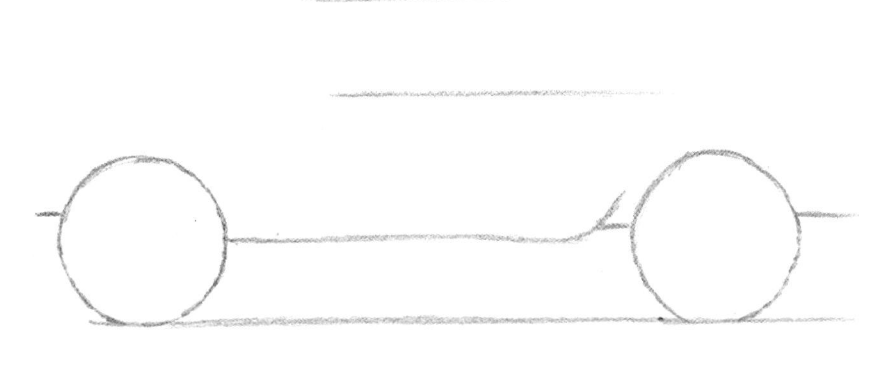

Draw the ground line. Using the wheel diagram above, draw the wheels the correct distance apart.

Draw the basic body lines. Notice where the bottom of the car meets the tires!

Complete the overall shape of the car.

Add:

- windows
- pillars A, B, and C
- wheel wells
- side details
- lights
- fuel caps

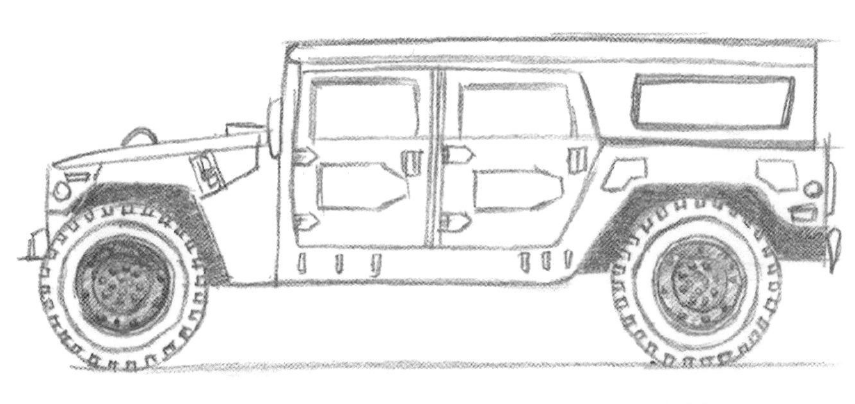

Draw other details you see (or want—hey, it's *your* drawing!). Add shading.

Remember:

- *Start out lightly!*
- *Turn your drawing as you work. Use a piece of scrap paper to keep your hand off finished parts.*
- *While your pencil is sharp, go over fine details and make lines cleaner. As it gets duller, add shading.*
- *Clean up any smudges with your eraser. Make sure all final lines are crisp and sharp.*
- *When you see it coming, this vehicle has the right of way.*

About Perspective

Perspective comes into play every time you draw a car from an angle.

Sometimes—as in the case of this 1959 Cadillac—the effects are very noticeable. If you draw the basic body lines, you'll see they extend back to a single *vanishing point.**

The wide-angle lens on the camera makes this photograph more dynamic.

Here you can see a Mercedes-Benz sport utility vehicle with a similar "wide-angle" view. This customized vehicle appeared in a certain dinosaur movie. Because of the dramatic wide-angle view, it looks as though it's ready to leap into action, perhaps chasing a *Pachycephalosaurus.***

The basic lines converge *(get closer together) as they go toward the background.*

With a telephoto lens, this advertising photo gives a different impression: the vehicle looks much less wild.

(Which is probably just as well; most people don't buy cars to chase dinosaurs.)

* for more on perspective, see *Learn To Draw 3-D*

** for more on Pachycephalosaurus, see *Draw Dinosaurs*

Always start out ***lightly***!

BMW Z3

*Before you start, look carefully at your **reference material** (for now, my finished drawing).*

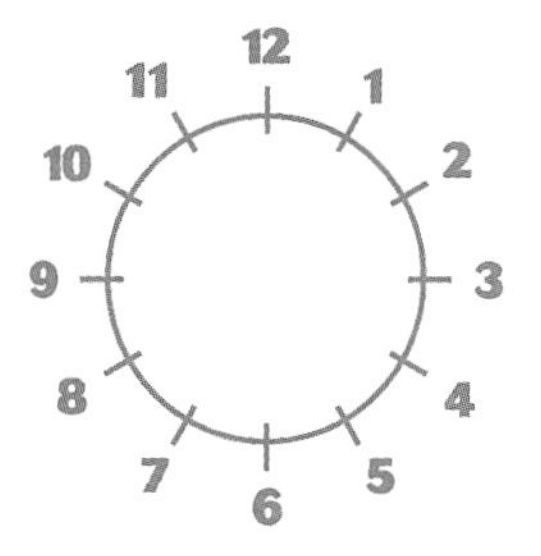

What are the angles formed by the wheels, on the side, and—if you could see them—the two front wheels? Compare these basic angles with the clock face if you need to. Pay special attention to perspective: how much do the lines converge *toward the background? How much smaller is the rear wheel?*

Draw the side ground line and the wheels. Add the basic body lines.

Draw lines to show depth, on the rear deck, front, and windshield. Look at the clock face if you find the angles confusing. Add the distinctive curves of the hood.

With all these lines in place, add more details.

Finishing the drawing takes the most effort, so make sure you're happy with your drawing so far.

Look at it in a mirror, or hold it up to the light and look at it through the back of the paper. Does everything look correct, forward and backward? If not, what can you fix to make the drawing look better? Start over if you need to.

When you're satisfied with the angles and proportions, add more details. Add details while your pencil is sharp.

Add shading when your pencil is dull. If you have more than one pencil, use a softer one (3B) for shading and a harder one (HB) for details.

Look again at the final drawing. Add any details you've missed.

Remember:

- *Start out lightly!*
- *Turn your drawing as you work. Use a piece of scrap paper to keep your hand off finished parts.*
- *While your pencil is sharp, go over fine details and make lines cleaner. As it gets duller, add shading.*
- *Clean up any smudges with your eraser. Make sure all final lines are crisp and sharp.*

Stand back and admire your creation!

Always start out ***lightly***!

Ruf CTR-2

*Before you start, look carefully at your **reference material** (for now, my finished drawing).*

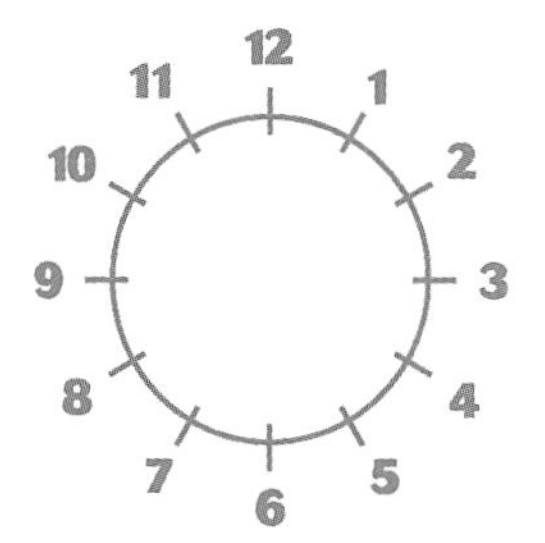

What are the angles formed by the wheels, on the side, and—if you could see them—the two front wheels? Compare these basic angles with the clock face if you need to. Pay special attention to perspective: how much do the lines converge *toward the background? How much smaller is the rear wheel?*

Draw the ground line, the wheels and the bottom body line.

Draw guide lines for adding depth. Notice how they converge toward a distant vanishing point, because of perspective.

Add curved lines for the fender and roof. Draw the other headlight, the window pillars and the rear view mirror.

When is a Porsche not a Porsche? When it's a Ruf, so completely altered that it actually has a new serial number. Built with a Porsche body shell, this Ruf costs slightly more than a Lamborghini Diablo Roadster. It goes from 0-60 MPH (0-100 KMH) in 3.6 seconds. Which is fast.

Extremely fast.

Finishing the drawing takes the most effort, so make sure you're happy with your drawing so far.

Look at it in a mirror, or hold it up to the light and look at it through the back of the paper. Does everything look correct, forward and backward? If not, what can you fix to make the drawing look better? Start over if you need to.

When you're satisfied with the angles and proportions, add more details. Add details while your pencil is sharp.

Add shading when your pencil is dull. If you have more than one pencil, use a softer one (3B) for shading and a harder one (HB) for details.

Look again at the final drawing. Add any details you've missed.

Remember:

- *Start out lightly!*
- *Turn your drawing as you work. Use a piece of scrap paper to keep your hand off finished parts.*
- *While your pencil is sharp, go over fine details and make lines cleaner. As it gets duller, add shading.*
- *Clean up any smudges with your eraser. Make sure all final lines are crisp and sharp.*

Stand back and admire your creation!

Always start out ***lightly***!

Formula 1 Racer

*Before you start, look carefully at your **reference material** (for now, my finished drawing).*

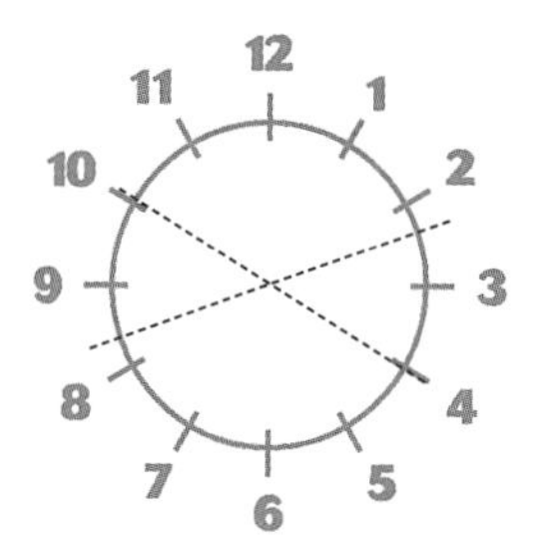

What angles do the wheels form, on one side, and between the two front wheels? Compare these basic angles with the clock face if you need to. Pay special attention to perspective: how much do the lines converge toward the background? How much smaller is the rear wheel?

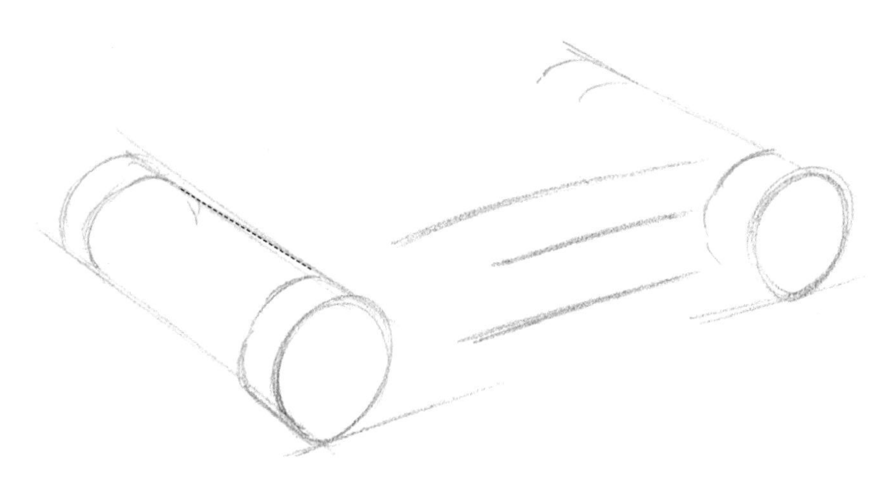

Draw the ground lines, the wheels, the basic body lines, and in this case the top of the air scoop.

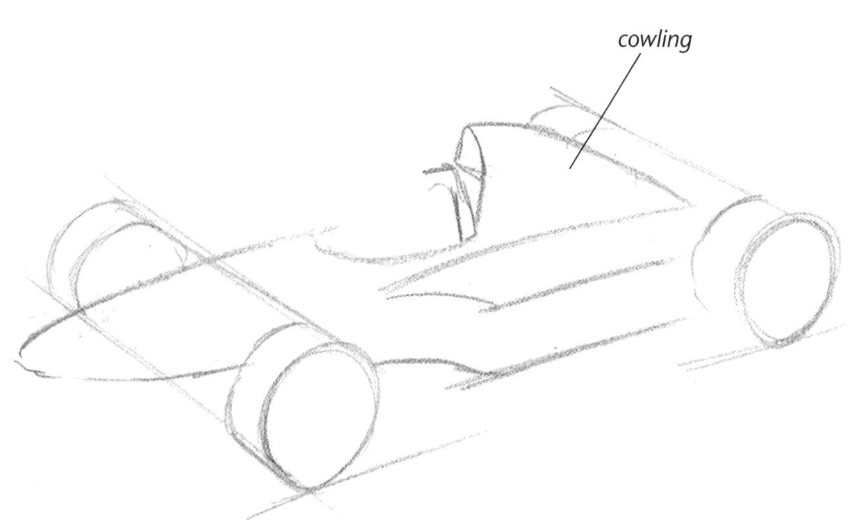

Draw depth guide lines to find the correct placement of the other wheels. Again, look at the clock face if you find the angles confusing.

Add the rounded point of the front of the car, the rim of the cockpit, and the cowling that covers the engine.

Finishing the drawing takes the most effort, so make sure you're happy with your drawing so far.

Look at it in a mirror, or hold it up to the light and look at it through the back of the paper. Does everything look correct, forward and backward? If not, what can you fix to make the drawing look better? Start over if you need to.

When you're satisfied with the angles and proportions, add more details. Add details while your pencil is sharp.

Add shading when your pencil is dull. If you have more than one pencil, use a softer one (3B) for shading and a harder one (HB) for details.

Look again at the final drawing. Add any details you've missed.

Remember:

- *Start out lightly!*
- *Turn your drawing as you work. Use a piece of scrap paper to keep your hand off finished parts.*
- *While your pencil is sharp, go over fine details and make lines cleaner. As it gets duller, add shading.*
- *Clean up any smudges with your eraser. Make sure all final lines are crisp and sharp.*

Stand back and admire your creation!

Always start out ***lightly***!

1957 Chevy

Before you start, look carefully at your ***reference material*** *(for now, my finished drawing).*

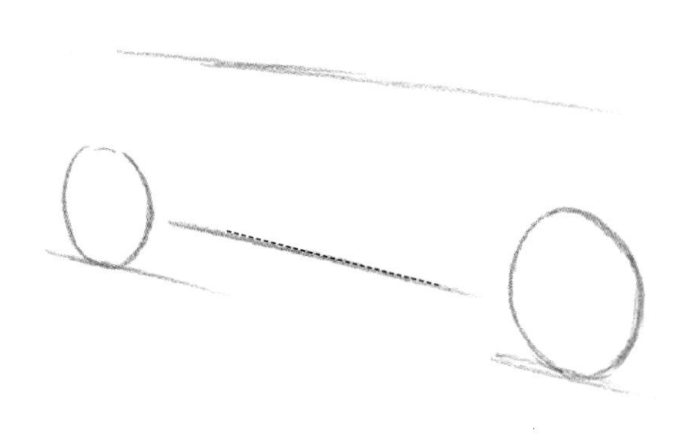

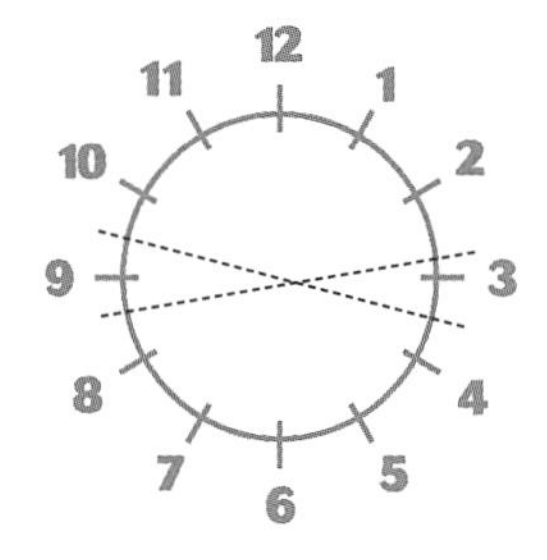

What angles are formed between the wheels on the side, and—if you could see it—between the two front wheels? Compare these basic angles with the clock face if you need to. Pay special attention to perspective: how much do the lines converge toward the background? How much smaller is the rear wheel?

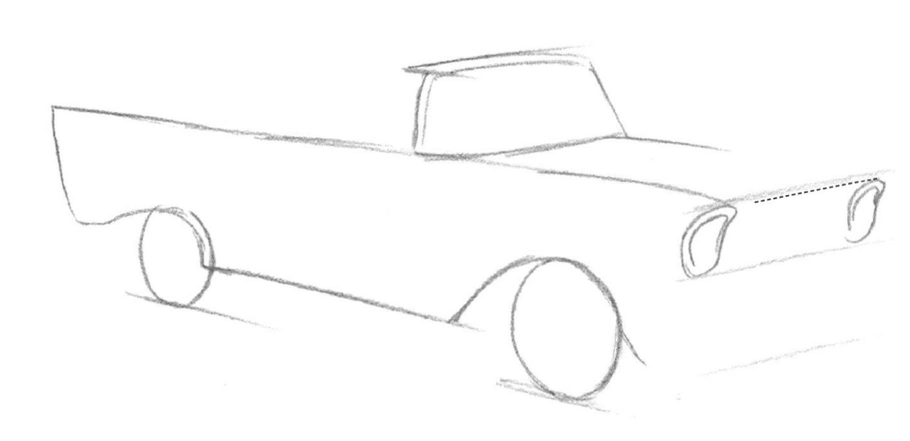

Draw the ground lines, the wheels, and the basic body lines.

Draw lines showing depth on the front of the car and windshield. Look at the clock face if you find the angles confusing. Add the distinctive headlights, rear end line and flaring wheel wells.

Add the curves of the windshield, side trim, front bumper, and other details you see.

Finishing the drawing takes the most effort, so make sure you're happy with your drawing so far.

Look at it in a mirror, or hold it up to the light and look at it through the back of the paper. Does everything look correct, forward and backward? If not, what can you fix to make the drawing look better? Start over if you need to.

When you're satisfied with the angles and proportions, add more details. Add details while your pencil is sharp.

Add shading when your pencil is dull. If you have more than one pencil, use a softer one (3B) for shading and a harder one (HB) for details.

Look again at the final drawing. Add any details you've missed.

Remember:

- *Start out lightly!*
- *Turn your drawing as you work. Use a piece of scrap paper to keep your hand off finished parts.*
- *While your pencil is sharp, go over fine details and make lines cleaner. As it gets duller, add shading.*
- *Clean up any smudges with your eraser. Make sure all final lines are crisp and sharp.*

Stand back and admire your creation!

Introduction

The deserts, or dry places, of the world hold plenty of surprises for those who explore them. Let's do that with a pencil! *Draw Desert Animals* shows you how to draw fascinating creatures, step by step. You may find some of the drawings quite easy. Others will be challenging.

First

LOOK carefully at the desert animal you wish to draw! See the shapes and pieces and how they fit together.

Then, **lightly sketch** the shapes in the right place.

When you sketch lightly, you can easily correct any mistakes before they ruin your drawing.

Second

Make sure you have all the shapes and pieces in the right place:
- **adjust** lines
- **redraw** pieces that don't look right
- **erase** sketch lines you no longer need.

Third

Spend as much time as you need to make your drawing jump off the page:
- **darken** lines at emphasis points: joints, feet, points of claws, horns, spikes, eyes…
- add **fur**, **feathers**, or **scales**…
- add **shading**…
- **clean up** any smudges with your eraser...
- **date and save** your drawing in a portfolio.

Supplies

- **pencil** (2B or 3B will work well)
- **pencil sharpener**
- **eraser** (I like the kneadable type)
- **paper** (drawing paper erases best)
- **blending stump** if you want to do smooth shading (you can use your finger, too, but it's a bit messy)
- **place to draw** (good light, no distractions)
- **POSITIVE ATTITUDE!**

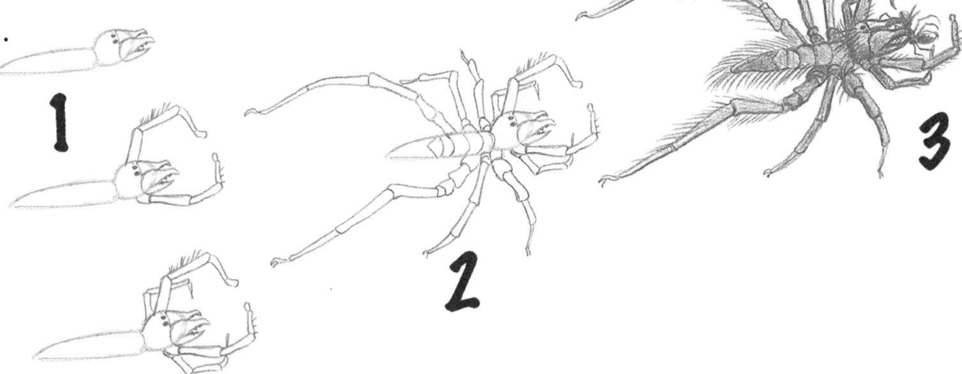

Just so you know

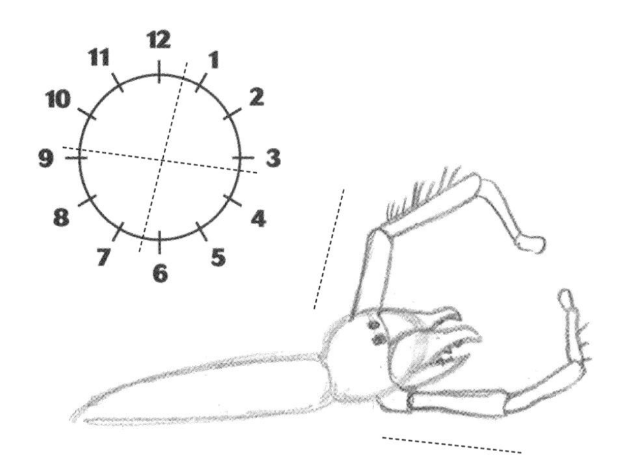

CLOCK FACES appear from time to time. Use them as a reference to see the tilt of ovals, legs, and other angles in the drawing.

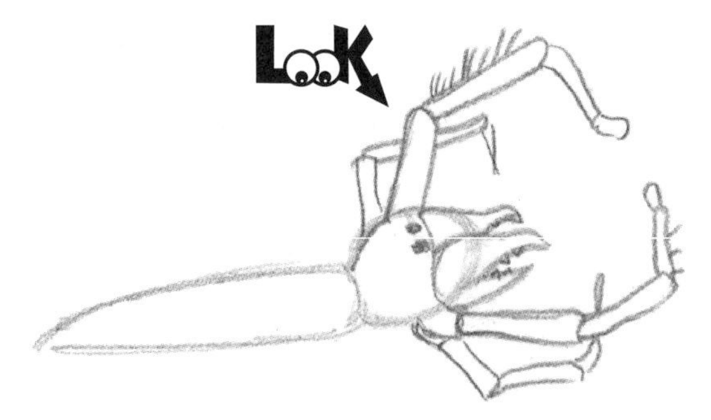

LOOK signs point out visual elements of the drawing–in this example, where one part overlaps another.

LABELS will help you identify the parts of the animal mentioned in the text.

DESERT ANIMALS

Drawing Tips

Start out loose and light

You've seen it enough times in this book: *Always sketch lightly at first.*

Sketching means trying out ideas, trying out variations, and basically not worrying too much whether the finished product is perfect.

Sketching can vastly improve your drawing skill. Try to do a number of quick sketches to get a feel for the animal: from life, from pictures, or from videos or TV. Then, using your sketch as a guide, carefully put together your final drawing.

You may find–as perhaps all illustrators and artists do–that your lightly drawn sketches have more energy, and capture more of the spirit of the animal, than your final drawing.

So save every drawing, always with the date you drew it!

Timed Drawings

Here's a challenge: pick a subject, and do timed drawings: first, ***five seconds*** (really, it's possible!). Next, do a 30-second drawing. One more: give yourself two minutes. Now take as long as you need–ten minutes, a half an hour, a day… feel the difference in each? Which is the most fun?

Drawing

Lines make a difference

Lines are not all created equal. Some lines can make your animal come to life. Try making your lines interesting. Learn to use lines to capture the feel of the animal you're drawing. Here are some suggestions.

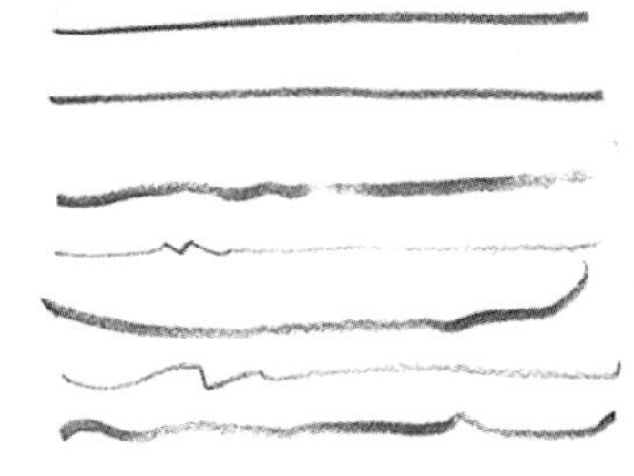

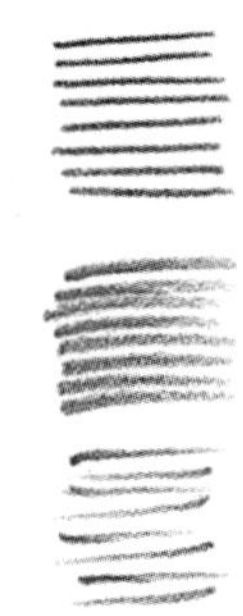

Make outlines expressive

How is the outline *of the animal different in each camel? Do you see a technique you can use to make your own drawing more lifelike?*

Create texture with lines

What about texture–which drawing gives you an idea what the camel might feel like if you touched it?

Use lines to show form

In addition to showing texture, how do lines help show the form (three-dimensional shape)? Can you see how lines on one of these two Bactrian camels make the drawing look more three-dimensional?

Addax antelope

Addax nasomaculatus

Africa. Height: .9 – 1.2 m (3 – 4 ft)

An addax never drinks, getting all the moisture it needs from its food. Its large, wide-spreading hooves are adapted to walking on soft sand. Addax are nomads, traveling in herds of 20 to 200. They seem to have a special ability to locate the patches of desert vegetation that suddenly sprout after a downpour. Color varies from animal to animal, but they all have a patch of dark brown hair on the forehead.

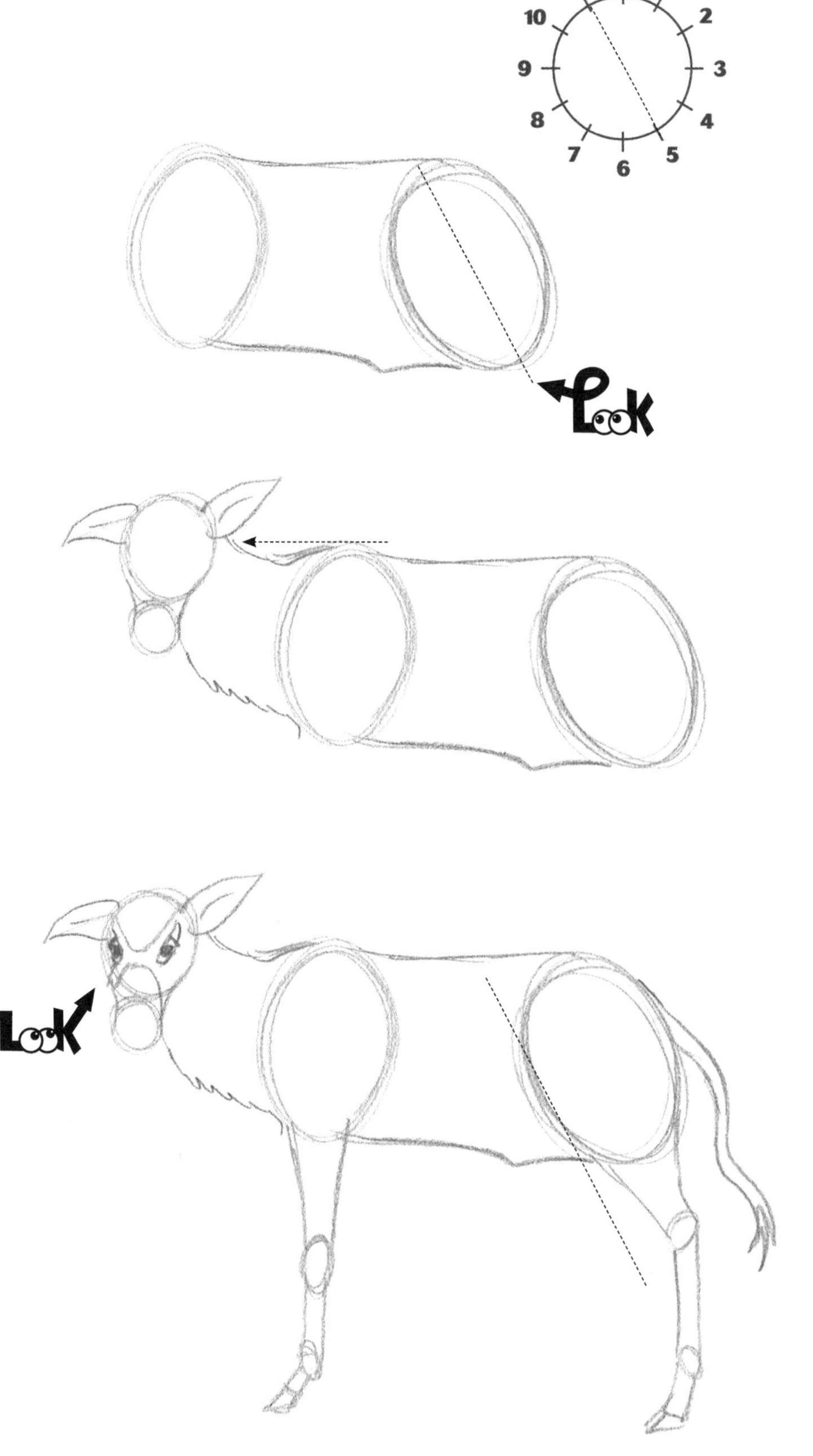

1. Begin the addax by lightly sketching two ovals. Compare the tilt of the back leg oval to the clock face. Draw lines to connect the ovals, top and bottom.

2. Sketch a circle for the head, centered at the top of the shoulder. Sketch a smaller circle for the nose and mouth. Add ears.

   Draw jagged lines to connect the head to the body.

3. Draw the eyes–**look** at the way one sits on the edge of the circle, and one doesn't. Add curved guide lines for the facial pattern.

   Sketch small, light circles for the leg joints. Draw the front and rear legs. Notice how the tilt of the oval shows you the angle of the top of the rear leg.

   Add the tail.

4. Lightly draw the graceful, spiralling horns. Once you have them right, begin to add small curved lines for the ridges on them. Add nostrils and the mouth. Shade the darker area of the face and ear.

   Lightly sketch the joints and limbs of the other two legs. Note where each line intersects the overlapping lines of the body or leg.

   Carefully erase "leftover" ovals before moving to the final step. If they're too dark–as in this example–you may want to start again, using what you've learned to make the second drawing even better.

5. Because the addax is light colored, you don't need to shade the whole body. Make your pencil strokes get lighter toward highlight areas. In the lightest areas, you don't need to shade at all.

   Starting with the darkest areas of the body, add light, short pencil strokes for fur. Leave the belly and side lighter.

   Clean up any smudges with your eraser. Put today's date on your drawing and save it in your portfolio!

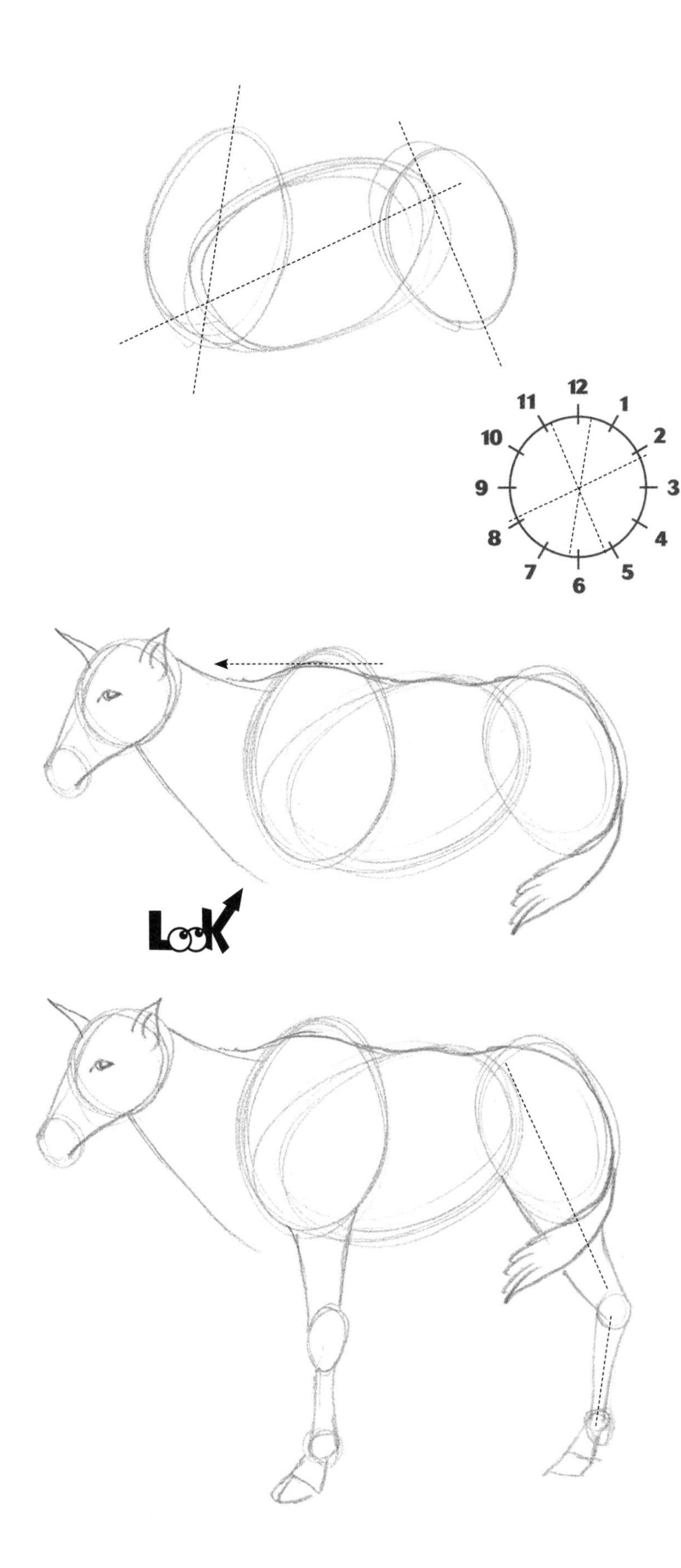

Arabian Oryx

Oryx leucoryx

SE Saudi Arabia.
Size: 2 m (6½ ft) long

The only oryx found outside Africa, this small, rare animal travels widely in extreme desert conditions to find grass and shrubs to eat. It shelters from the sun by scraping a hollow under a bush or on the side of a sand dune. This oryx has been over hunted for its hide, meat and horns. Protected by law, it may be extinct in the wild (the last wild one seen was in 1972). It lives in captivity, though, and hopefully can be reintroduced to its native habitat.

1. This drawing starts out with three ovals tilting in all different directions. The tilt of the ovals will capture the way the animal stands, or moves. The ovals also remind you of the underlying anatomy as you draw. Draw the ovals.

2. Notice the height of the head in relation to the shoulder (just a little bit above). Make a light circle for the head, a smaller one for the nose, and lines to connect them. Add the eye, halfway up the head circle and off to the left. Draw the ears. Draw a line to connect the head with the top of the body, and continue your line along the top—connecting all body ovals. Add the swishing tail. Draw the bottom of the neck.

3. Starting with small circles for the joints, draw the two closest legs. Note the angles of the rear leg.

4. Starting with light circles for the joints, draw the other two legs. Notice how the bottom of the neck meets the front leg. Connect the belly and the rear leg.

5. Draw the long, curved horns–lightly at first *(of course!)*.

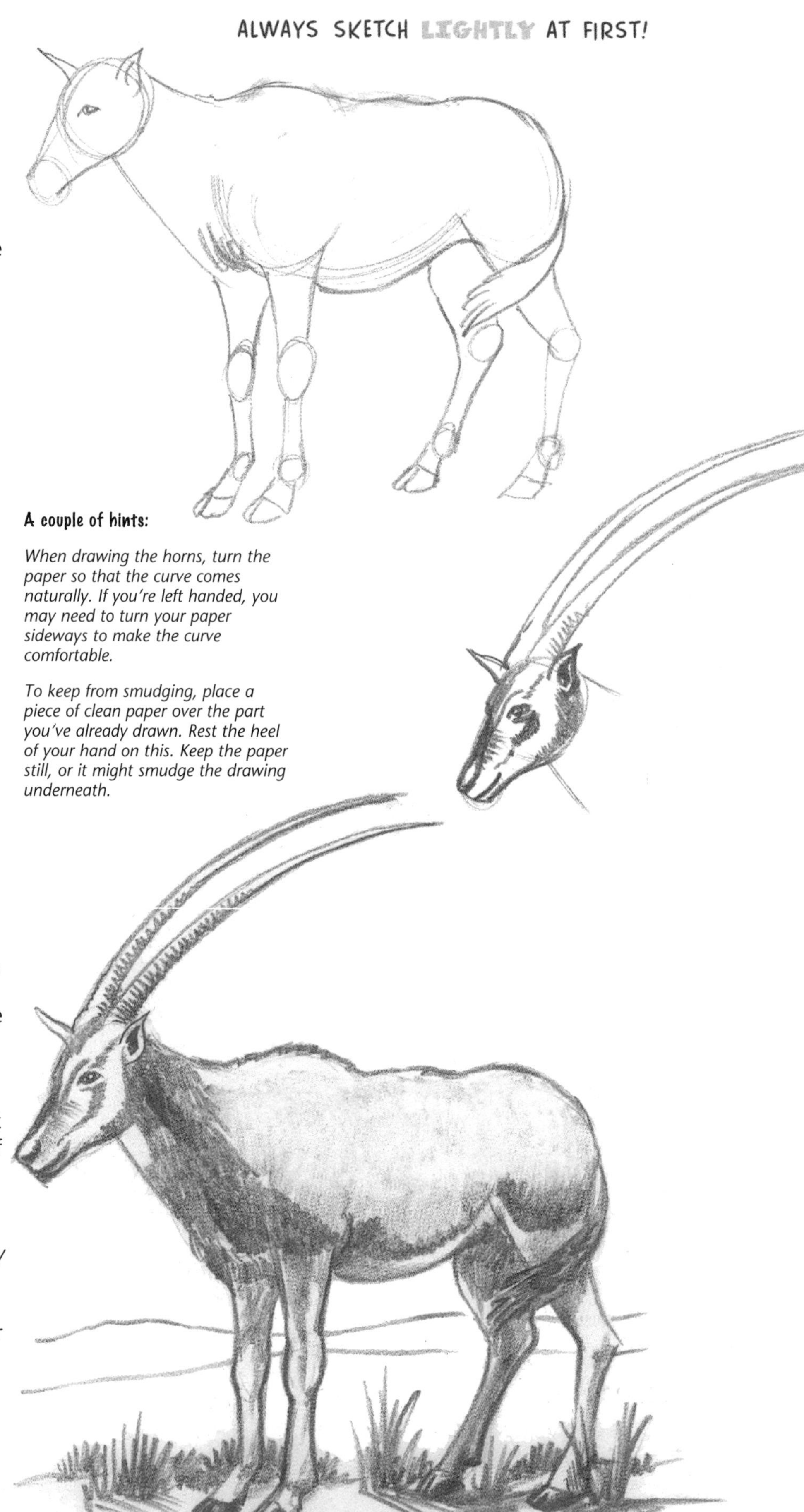

A couple of hints:

When drawing the horns, turn the paper so that the curve comes naturally. If you're left handed, you may need to turn your paper sideways to make the curve comfortable.

To keep from smudging, place a piece of clean paper over the part you've already drawn. Rest the heel of your hand on this. Keep the paper still, or it might smudge the drawing underneath.

Add the mouth and nose. Carefully shade the face to make the facial patterns.

6. Using short pencil strokes, continue shading the body. Pay attention to the direction of the lines and their darkness. Leave the belly light. Darken the hooves and add a little bit of grass. Make a couple of lines for distant sand dunes behind the oryx.

   Orsome Oryx! Clean up any smudges with your eraser, put today's date on your drawing and save it in your portfolio!

Bactrian camel

Camelus ferus

Central Asia, Northern Africa, Middle East. Size: 3 m (10 ft) long, 2 m (7 ft) high at shoulder

Bactrian camels have two humps–think of the letter B turned on its side. The humps store fat to help them survive when food is scarce. They eat grass, and foliage of bushes and trees. Their long, shaggy hair keeps them warm in the winter, but they shed it in the summer. They move slowly with a rolling gait, able to lift two legs on the same side at the same time.

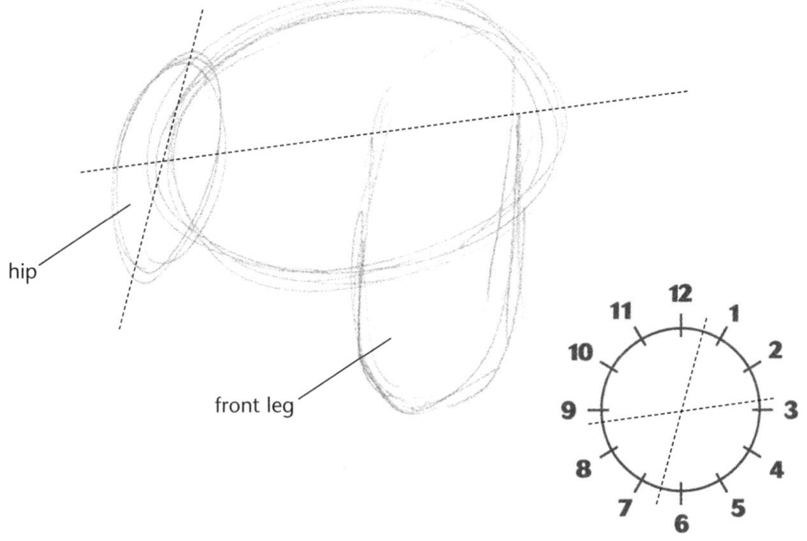

1. Start out by lightly sketching the large, slightly tilted oval of the body. *Intersecting* it, draw the small, narrow oval of the hip. Notice how it tilts. Add a U shape for the shaggy front leg, dropping down below the body.

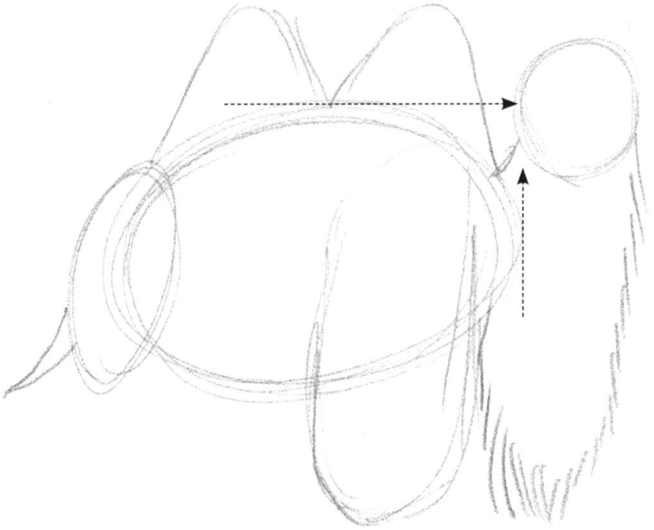

2. Add two humps on the back. Sketch a circle for the head. Where does it lie in relation to the first oval you drew? Add a short line connecting it to the back, and draw a long, shaggy, U shape for the neck. Draw the tail.

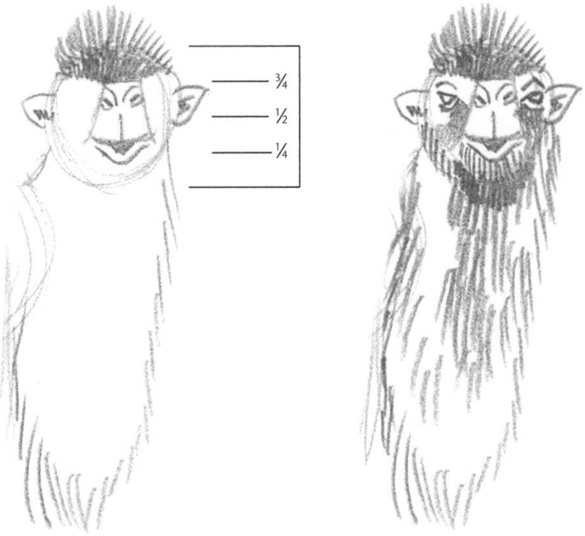

Where does the head lie in relation to the first oval you drew?

3. Three-fourths of the way up the head, draw a horizontal line. Fill in, above the line, with spiked hair. *(Nice hair!).* Halfway up the head, draw an ear on either side. Level with the top of the ears, draw the nostrils. Level with the bottom of the ears, draw the top of the mouth. Add more lines on the nose and mouth.

   Draw the eyes between the nostrils and ears, and use short pencil strokes to make the shaggy hair on the face and neck.

4. At the bottom of the front leg U, draw small ovals for the leg joints. Draw wide, low ovals for the hooves, and curving lines connecting them to the top part of the leg. Notice how one leg overlaps part of the other. Add toes.

   Using similar ovals and lines, complete the rear legs. Add the tail.

   Look: *where the camel kneels, thick callus builds up on the legs. On your body, the calluses on the rear leg would be on your knees; the ones in front on the back of your wrists.*

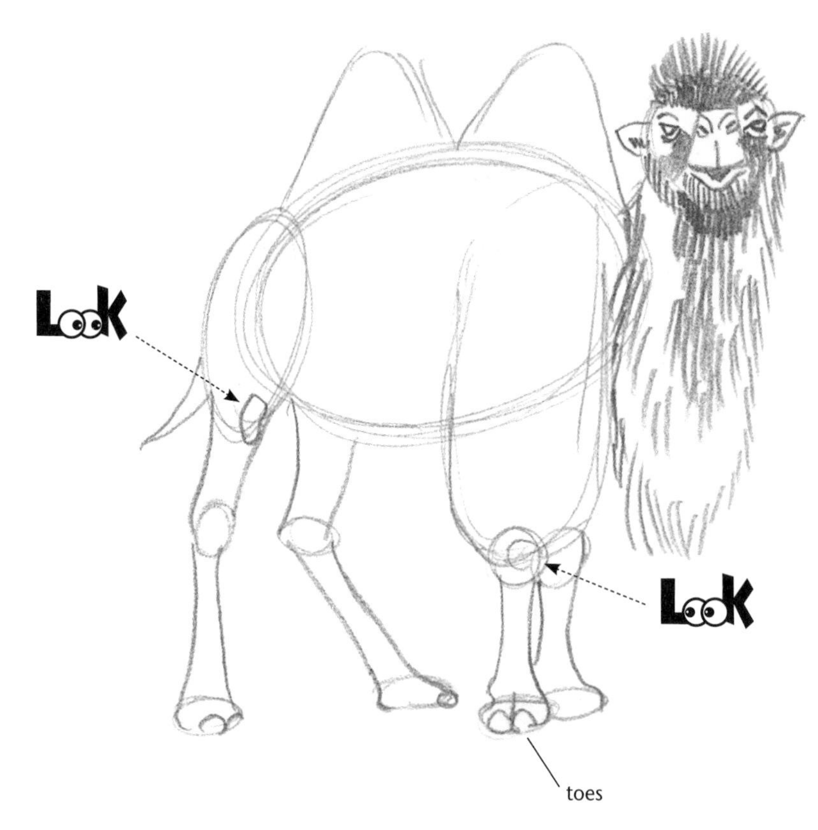

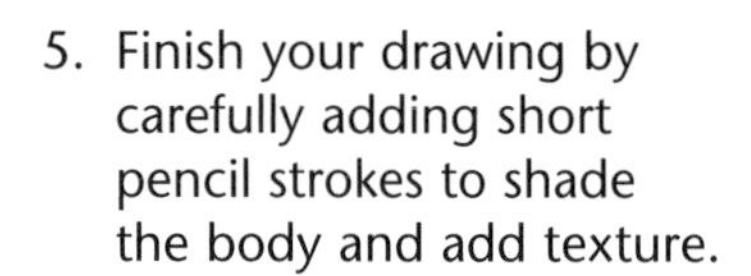

5. Finish your drawing by carefully adding short pencil strokes to shade the body and add texture.

   Take your time. Which parts are darkest? Which are lightest? What direction do the lines run on each part of the body? You'll improve quickly if you get in the habit of asking these questions often as you draw.

   Add a small *cast shadow* under the camel. Clean up any smudges with your eraser.

   Oh, by the way, camels spit. Does your camel look like it's spitting at you? Whether or not, put today's date on your drawing and save it in your portfolio!

Caracal

Felis caracal

Africa, Middle East to India.
Size: .8 – 1.2 m (33 – 47 in) including tail

The solitary caracal patrols a home range, preying on mammals from mice to medium-sized antelopes, including birds, reptiles, and smaller domestic animals. Females bear litters of 2-3 young, who don't become independent until they've reached the age of 9-12 months.

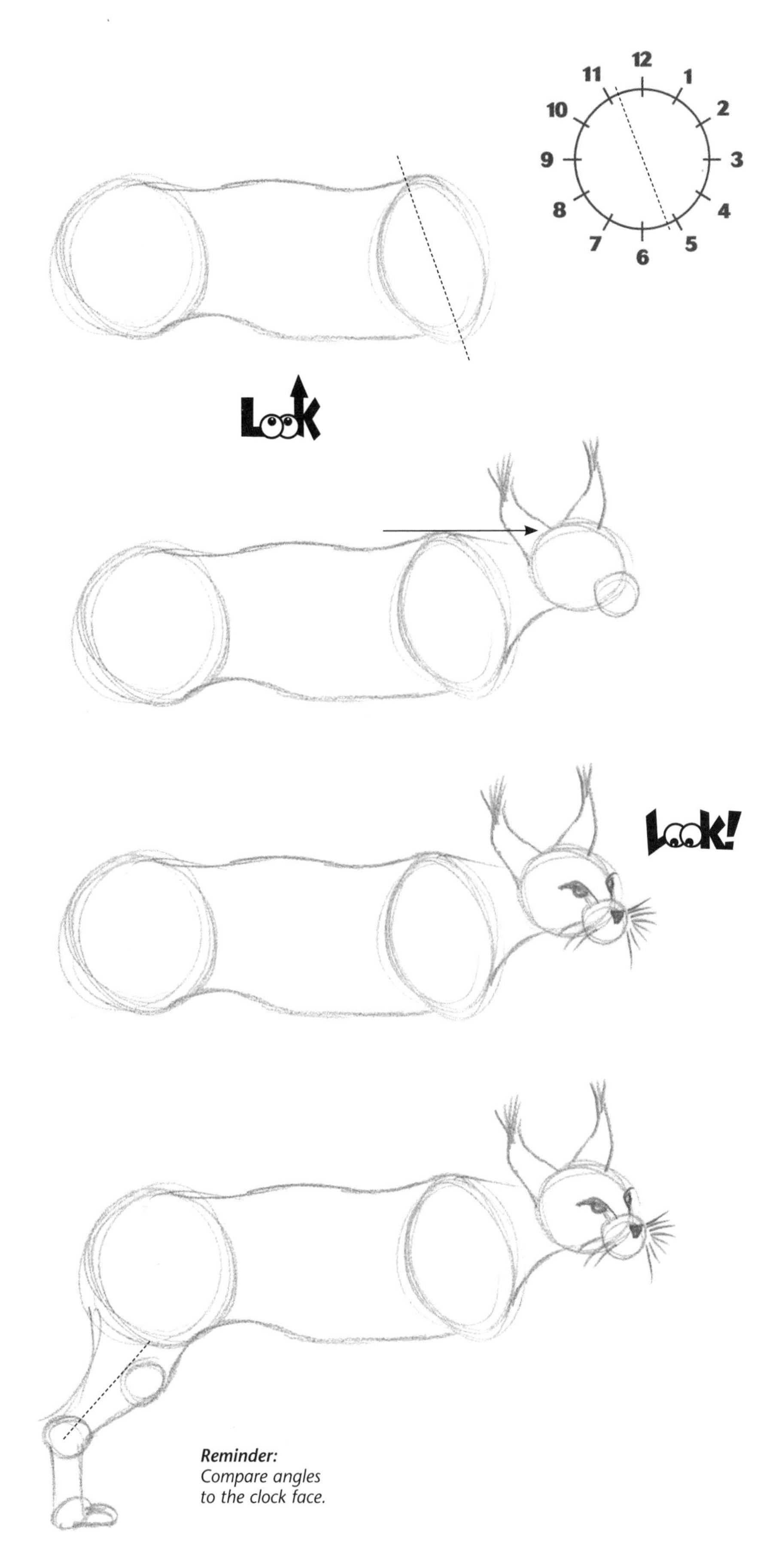

Reminder: *Compare angles to the clock face.*

1. Before you draw, **look** at how much room divides the two ovals of the cat's body. Now sketch one round oval; make the other narrower and slightly tilted. Add the curving lines for the top and bottom of the body.

2. Sketch a small circle for the head, level with the top of the shoulder. Draw the ears with their tufts of hair at the end. Connect the head to the body with short, curved neck lines. Sketch a smaller circle for the nose.

3. In the upper right of the small nose circle, draw the dark triangle of the nose, with whiskers sticking out either side. **Look** at the difference between the two eyes. Add a line curving up and back, with the round eye underneath. Draw the small visible bit of the other eye.

4. Sketch small circles to locate the joints on the back leg. Draw the leg, paying careful attention to the angle of each section.

5. Sketch the front leg ovals, then draw the front leg.

   You'll find it very helpful in your drawing if you get in the habit of lightly sketching those little circles for the joints. For one thing, it forces you to figure out where the limb bends. A second reason: it also helps you draw the limbs in different positions if you need to.

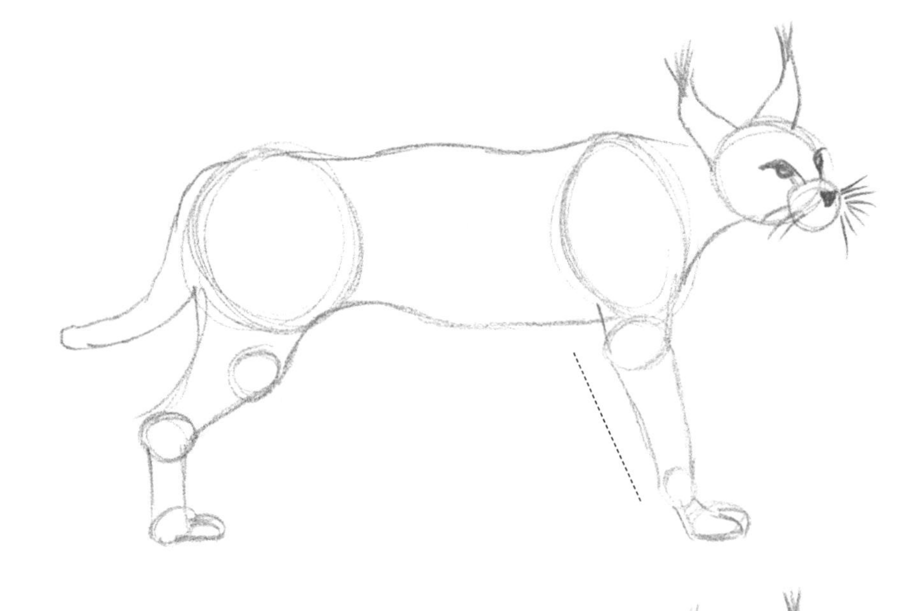

6. Now, in a similar manner, add the other legs.

7. To complete the caracal, make short pencil strokes—in the direction of the fur—over the entire body. Note lighter and darker areas. Take your time.

   Go over the outline with a sharpened pencil, and clean up any smudges with your eraser. Put today's date on your drawing and save it!

Desert Cottontail

Sylvilagus audubonii

North America.
Size: 35 – 45 cm (9 – 11 in) incl. tail

Desert cottontails make their shelter in a burrow or shallow depression in the ground. Most active in the late afternoon and evening, they stay close to cover. When alarmed, they dart away quickly, flicking up their tails as they run, showing the white underside. The young are born blind and helpless after a gestation period of 26-30 days.

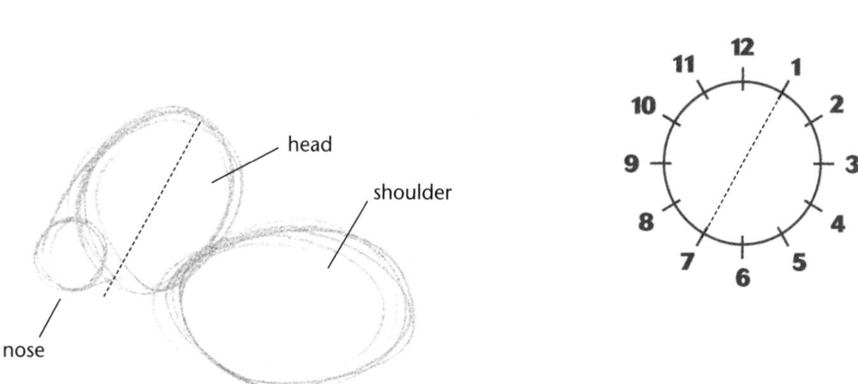

1. Sketch a horizontal oval for the rabbit's shoulder, and a tilted oval for the head. Sketch a small circle for the nose and connect it to the head with lines.

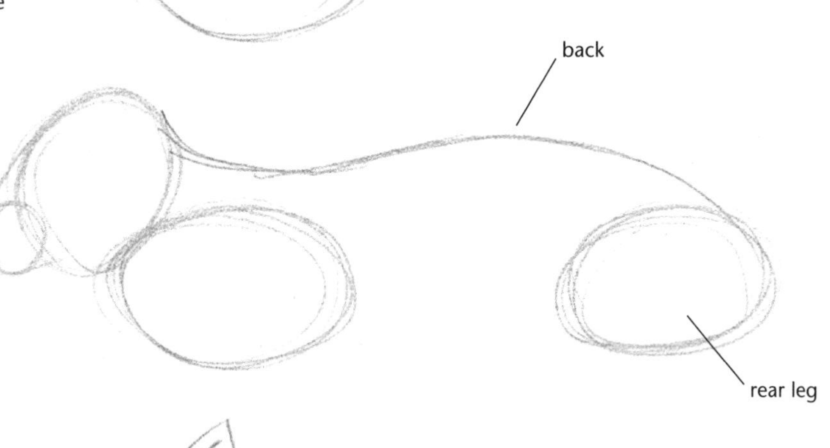

2. Sketch another horizontal oval to begin the rear leg. Connect it to the head with the long, swooping line of the back.

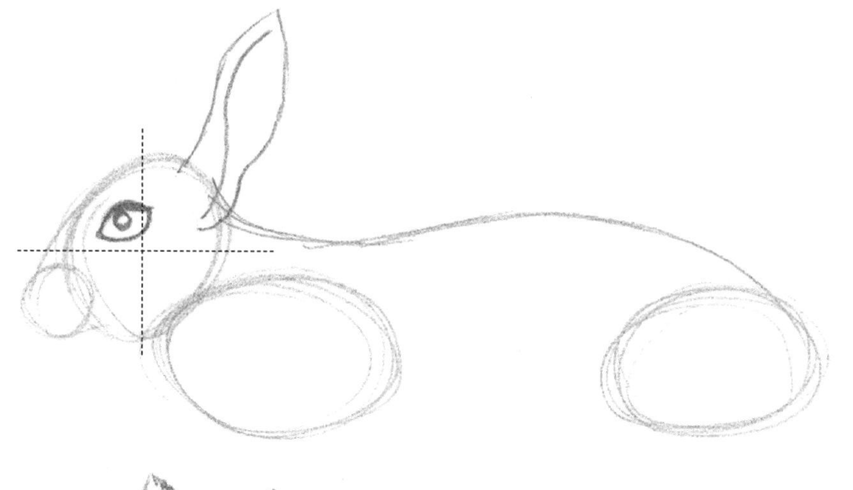

3. Notice where the eye appears in the head. Draw the eye with a circle for the highlight. Add the ear. Make it about as long as the rest of the head.

4. Draw the second ear. Darken the eye (except for the small circle). Add lines for the nostril and mouth, and lines for the chin and throat.

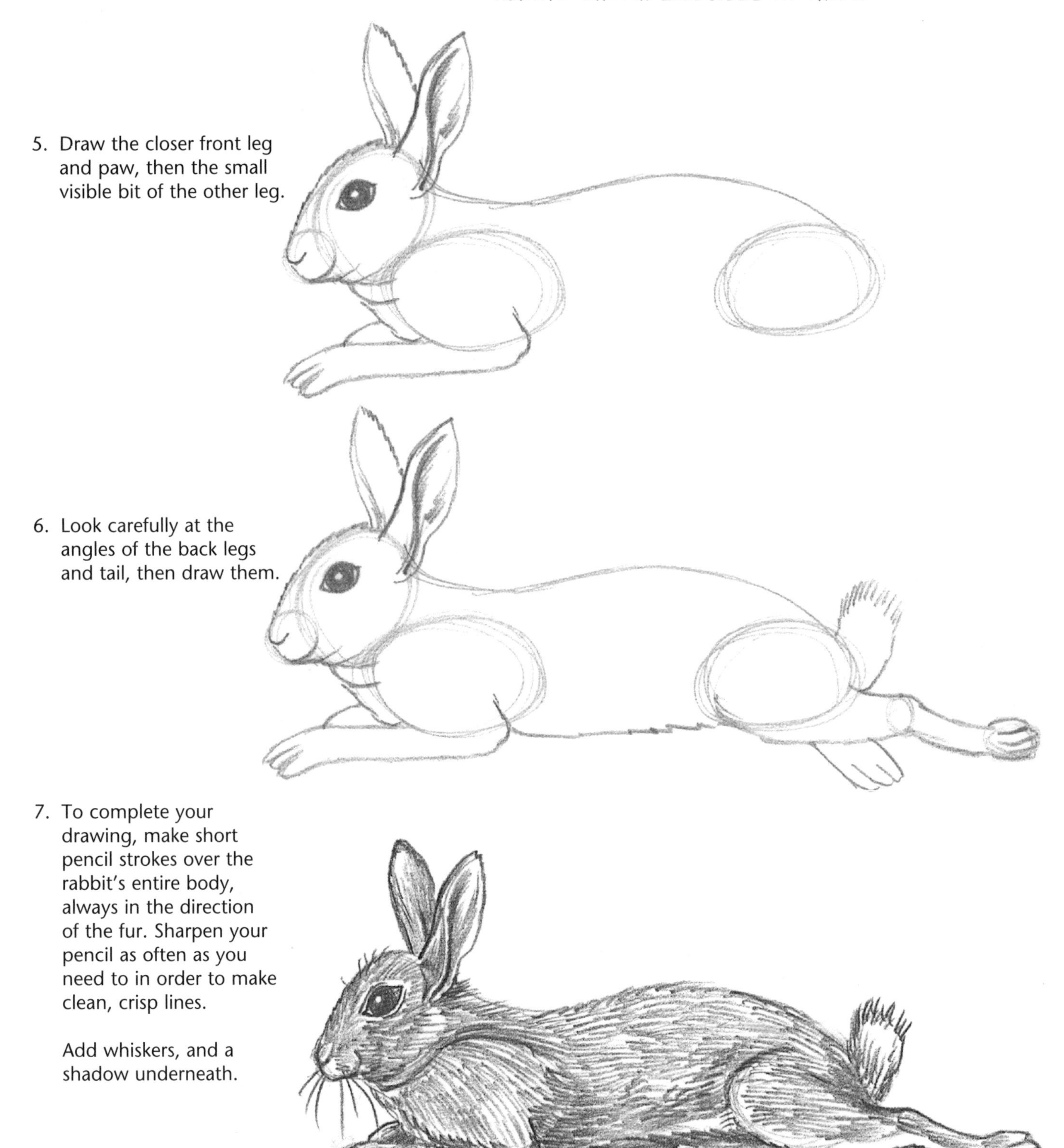

5. Draw the closer front leg and paw, then the small visible bit of the other leg.

6. Look carefully at the angles of the back legs and tail, then draw them.

7. To complete your drawing, make short pencil strokes over the rabbit's entire body, always in the direction of the fur. Sharpen your pencil as often as you need to in order to make clean, crisp lines.

   Add whiskers, and a shadow underneath.

Wonderful wabbit! Add today's date and save your drawing!

Desert Tortoise

Gopherus agassizi

SW United States.
Size: up to 51 cm (20 in) long

LOOK During the heat of the day, the desert tortoise stays in an underground burrow, which may be up to 9 m (30 ft) long. It gets all its water from plants it eats, such as cactus and succulents. A desert tortoise can exist an entire dry season without water!

1. Sketch an upward arc and a downward arc for the top and bottom of the shell. Note the straight section at the neck.

2. Lightly sketch the front and rear legs, and the lower part of the shell, including the point behind the rear leg.

3. Sketch an oval for the head. Add the neck, eye, and the part of the shell underneath the head, and the visible portion of the other front leg. Draw the feet. Don't forget claws!

4. Carefully lay out the row of hexagons (six-sided shapes) on the top of the shell.

5. Continue laying out the hexagon pattern on top of the shell, above the row of hexagons, and the rectangle shapes on the bottom of the shell.

6. Shade the bottom part of the shell. Add shadows to create the folds on the neck. Darken the eye, leaving a small white area. Draw small scaly patterns on the head, front leg, and feet.

7. Light and dark contrasts make the tortoise drawing come to life. Look at the dark areas; see which areas stay light.

   Add lots and lots and lots of small lines in the patterns of the shell–some lighter, some darker. Add more small scaly patterns on the head, neck, legs and feet.

   Draw a shadow on the ground, and a few small marks for pebbles.

Torrific tortoise! Clean up any smudges with your eraser, put today's date on your drawing and save it in your portfolio!

Diamondback Rattlesnake

Crotalus atrox

Southwest US & northern Mexico.
Size: .76 – 2.25 m (2½ – 7½ ft)

The markings on the western diamondback aren't as distinct as you'd think from the name: on the back you'll see diamond-shaped or hexagonal markings, but you may have to look carefully *(and by the time you get that close, the snake is probably rattling its tail at you in warning!).* Overall, the snake has a speckled or dusty appearance. The tail is set off by broad black and white rings. When rattlesnakes strike, their fangs pierce the victim just for a split second, enough time to inject poison. Then they retreat to their hiding place. Later they look for their kill.

Have fun with this drawing. Enjoy practicing the swooping curves!

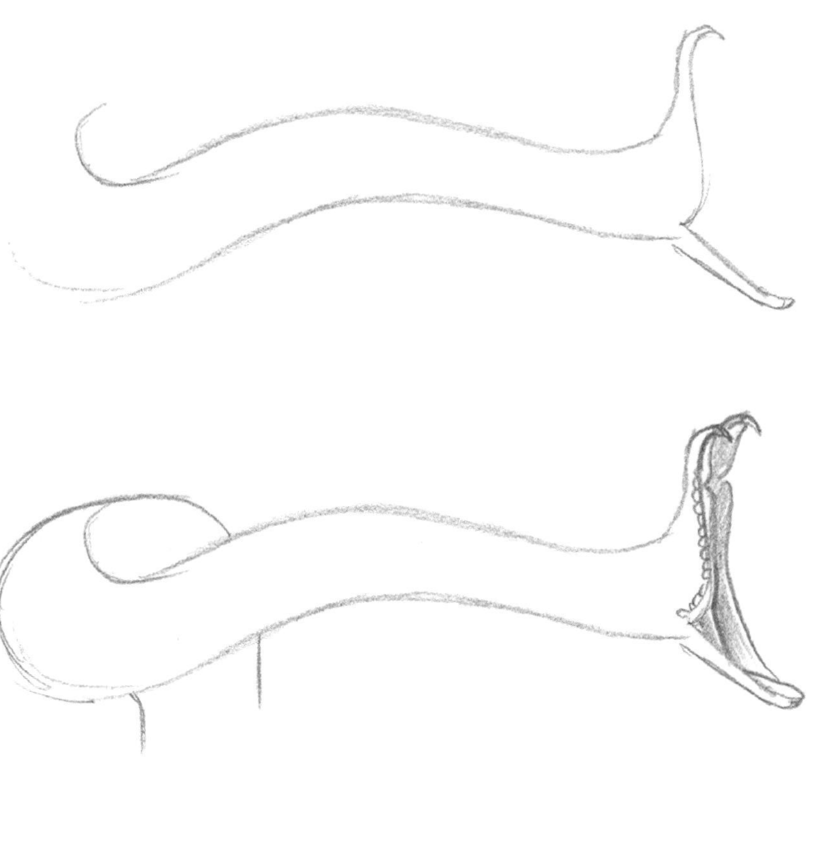

1. Sketch gentle, curving lines for the top and bottom of the snake's body. Join them in an upward curve for the fang, and add an extending lower jaw.

2. Look at the rear portion—then carefully draw it. Add the other fang, and mouth details.

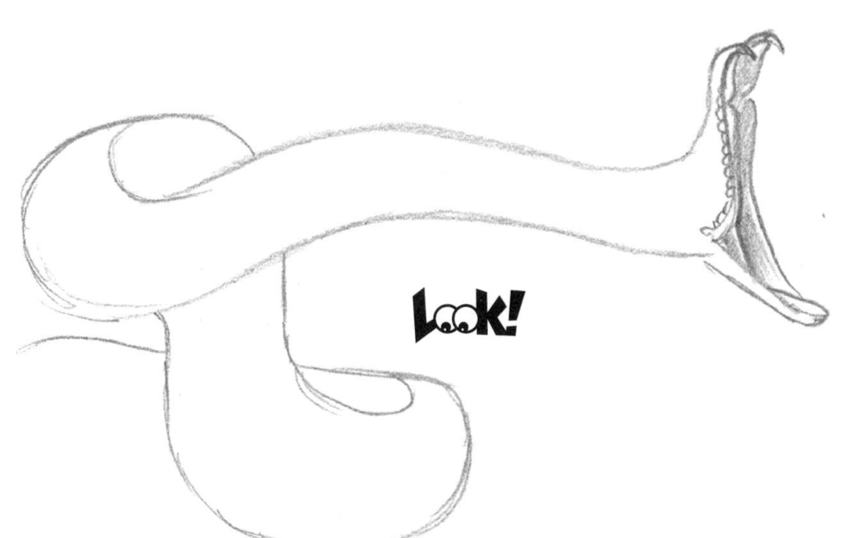

3. Extend the body downward. Study how each line curves. Two of them even run into each other **(look)**.

4. Draw curving lines to finish the body and the tail. Draw small ovals for the rattles.

   Before you go on, look at your drawing. Is your snake shape smooth and flowing? If not, try again, practicing nice, smooth, connecting curves. Get comfortable with drawing the snake before you spend time adding scales and shading. Save your sketches (with today's date!) in your portfolio!

5. Add *crosshatching* (crisscrossing lines), curving around the *contour* to create guide lines for scales. Use short pencil strokes to darken the shadows.

6. Shade the whole body—except, of course, for highlights **(look)** and the faint pattern on the back. Continue shading and adding scales. Go over the outline with a sharpened pencil. Add the distinct light and dark bands on the tail.

   Draw a *cast shadow* on the ground. Soften it by rubbing it with your finger or a piece of paper.

   Clean up any smudges with your eraser. Put today's date on your drawing and save it in your portfolio!

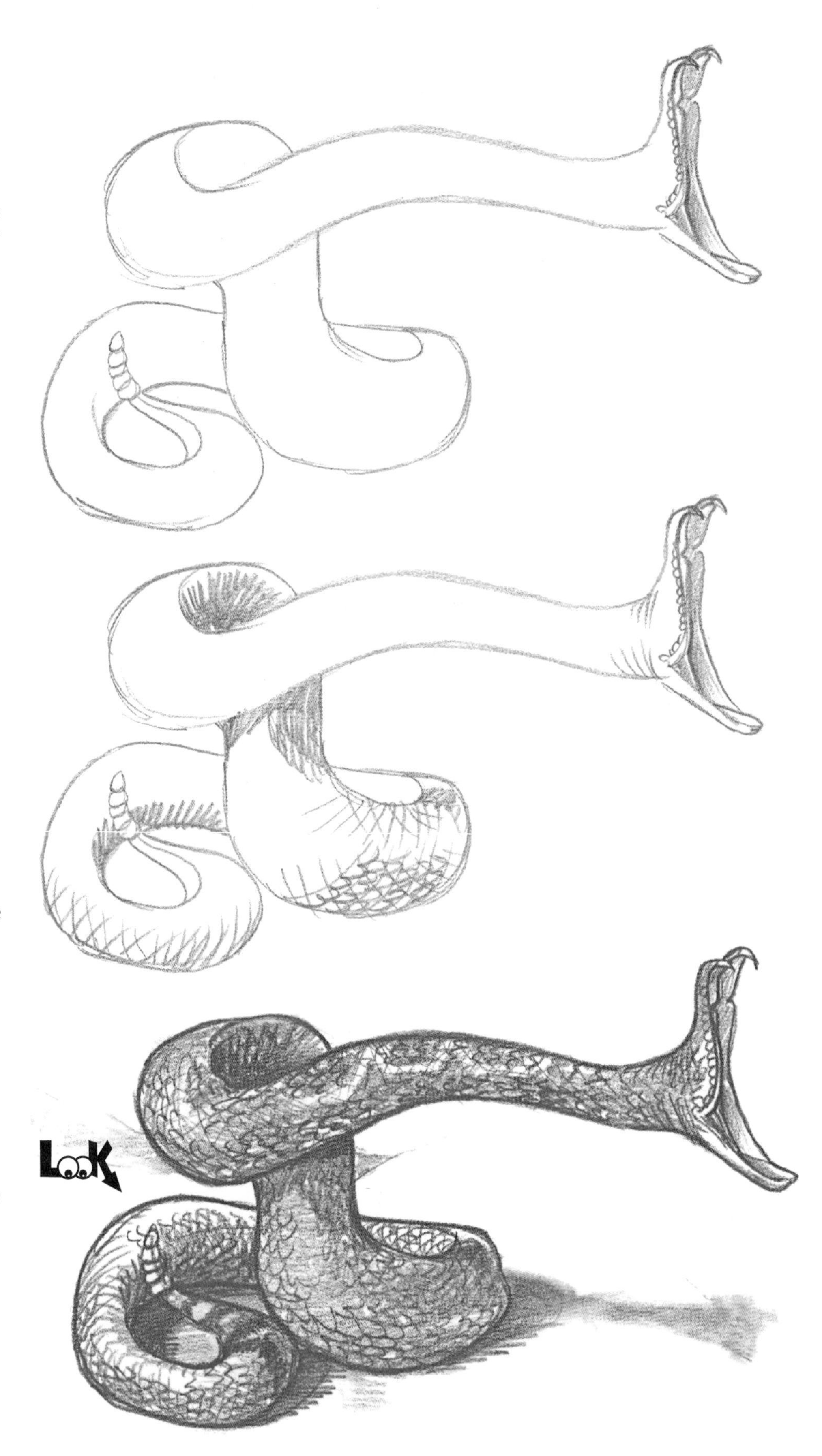

Dromedary

Camelus dromedarius

North Africa, Middle East.
Size: body 2.2 – 3.4 m (7¼ – 11 ft); tail 50 cm (19¾ in)

Not a wild animal! People who know think the one-humped camel has been domesticated since 4,000 BC. Today, you'll find two types: heavy, slow-moving beasts of burden, and graceful, fast racers used for riding. They feed on grass and other available plants, and can withstand long periods in areas of tough, sparse vegetation without drinking, thanks to adaptations in their stomach linings and kidneys. In one experiment, a thirsty camel drank 104 liters (27 US gallons) of water in ten minutes! The hump stores fat, not water. Females breed every other year. The long gestation period (365-440 days) results in a single young that can walk after a day.

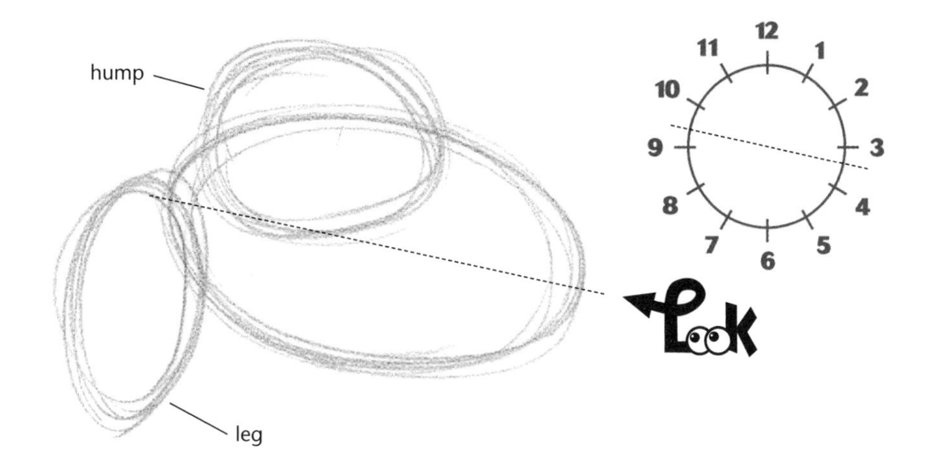

1. Sketch a large, slightly tilted, oval. Sketch a smaller oval, off-center, for the hump. Add a vertical oval for the rear leg.

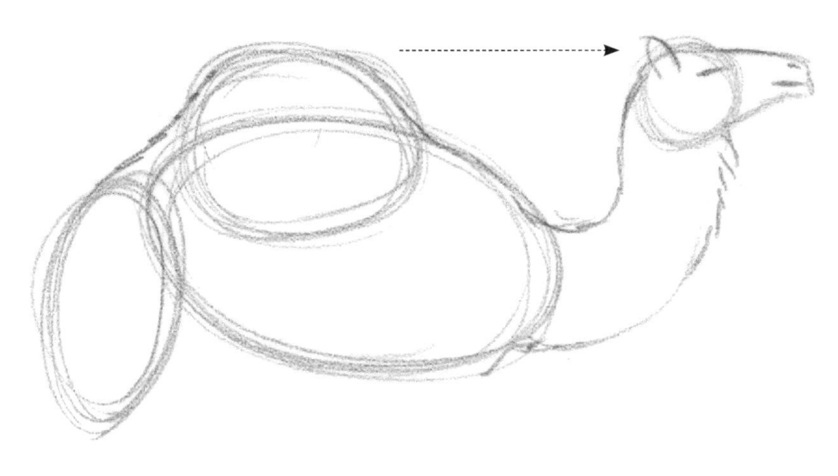

2. Level with the top of the hump, sketch a small circle for the head. Add lines to form the front of the head. Draw the mouth and nostril. Add the eye and the ear. Draw the gently curving (and slightly shaggy) lines for the neck.

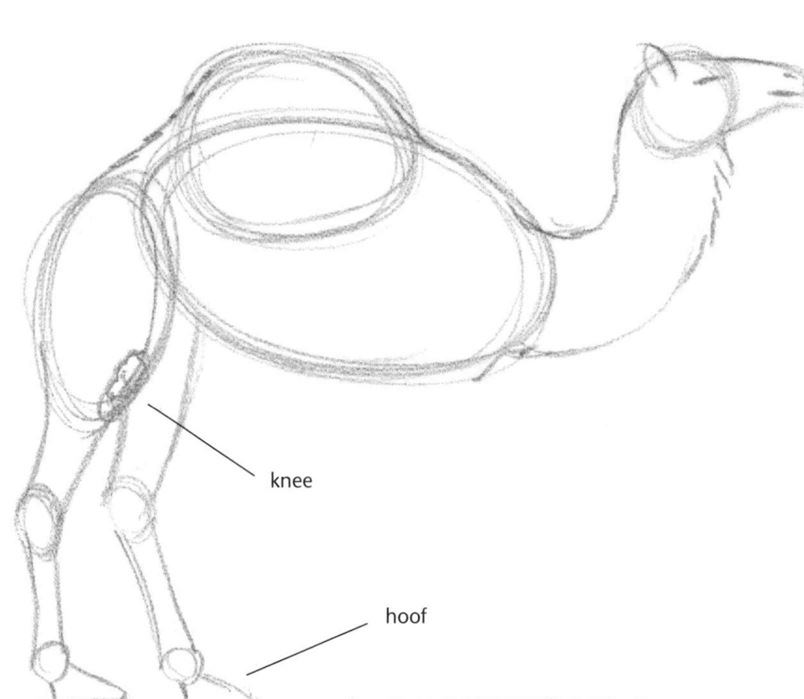

3. Draw the callused knee at the bottom front of the leg oval. Sketch circles for the leg joints. Add curving lines to complete the rear legs. Draw wide, almost triangular shapes for the camel's spreading hoofs.

4. Next, add the front legs. Notice the callus on the front of the front leg. The callused areas on the front and rear legs are from kneeling, to lie down and get up again.

   A camel folds its legs underneath to reduce exposure to the hot desert sun. Also, the camel's food store–the fat-filled hump on its back–helps insulate the body underneath from the sun's heat.

5. Using your eraser, carefully clean up sketch lines you no longer need.

   Add pencil strokes—always in the direction of the hair and contours of the body—to shade *just* the shadow areas.

   Go over the outline with a sharpened pencil. Add a *cast shadow* beneath, and *(why not?)* a couple of pyramids in the distance.

   Dazzling dromedary! Clean up any smudges with your eraser, put today's date on your drawing and save it in your portfolio!

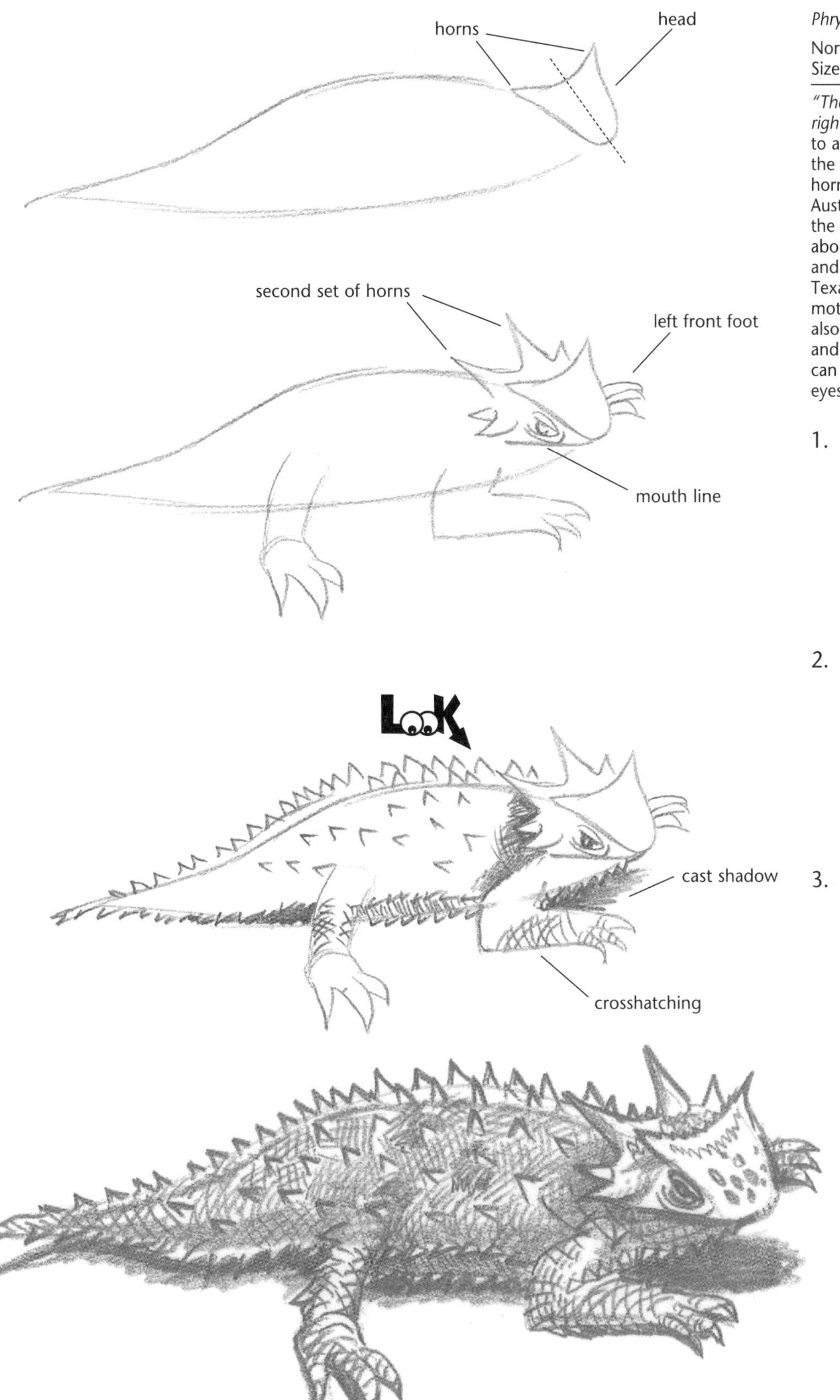

Horned Toad

Phrynosoma douglasii

North America.
Size: 4 – 13 cm (1.6 – 5.2 in)

"That's not a toad!" you say. You're right. The name horned toad is given to a lizard, with horns or spikes on the back of the head (the only other horned lizard is the Thorny Devil of Australia). At night, it wriggles below the sand, during the day it moves about slowly and feeds on insects and ants. Horned toads (also called Texas horned lizards) lie very flat and motionless when disturbed, but can also inflate themselves, jump forward and hiss. And–who knows how–they can even squirt blood from their eyes!

1. Lightly sketch curved lines for the top and bottom of the body. Add the tilted shape that makes the top of the head—rounded at the front and pointed at the back for the horns.

2. Add the second set of horns. Draw the eye and the mouth line. Lightly sketch the two visible legs, with claws. Draw the claws of the left front foot.

3. *Now look at the details!* Add a row of spikes along the back and scattered on the body. Add a *cast shadow* for contrast under the chin and behind the horns. Use *crosshatching* to create scales.

   Following this example, add more shading, shadows, and *crosshatching*. Leave the head lighter than the body. This makes the head, eye, and spikes, the focal point of the drawing.

   Put today's date on your drawing and save it!

Fennec fox

Vulpes zerda

North Africa, Arabia.
Size: body 36 – 40 cm (14½ – 16 in); tail 20 – 20 cm (8 – 12 in)

Fennec foxes live in groups of up to ten, and feed at night on small animals and insects. Small and agile, they live in burrows. In soft sand, they dig so quickly it can look like they're just sinking into the ground!

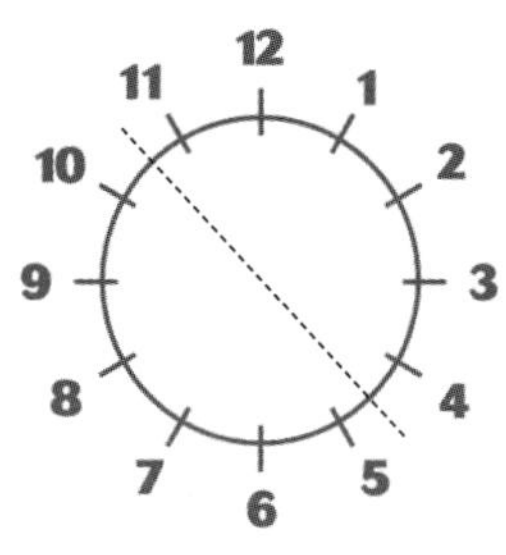

Compare the tilt of ovals and other angles with the clock face.

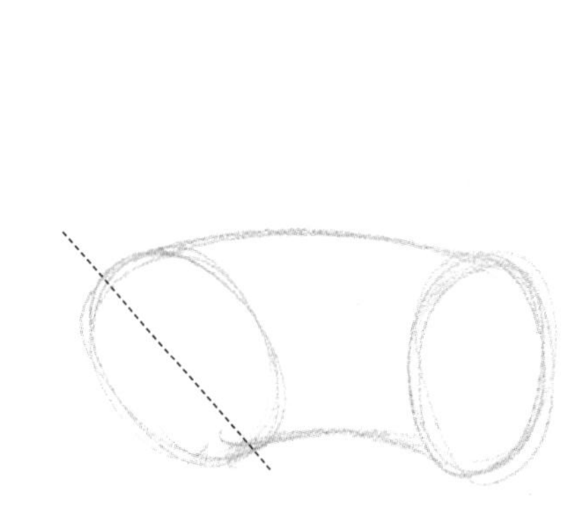

1. Begin by sketching the body of the fox—two tall ovals connected with curving lines.

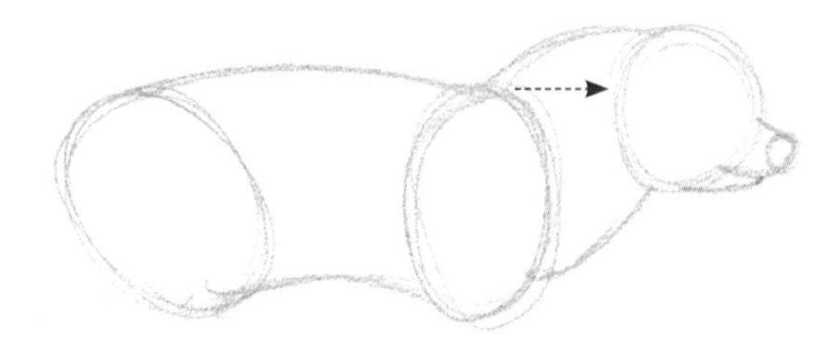

2. Sketch a light circle for the head, noting where it lies in relationship to the shoulder (arrow). Add the nose and mouth. Notice that the neck lines curve outward on both top and bottom. Draw lines for the neck.

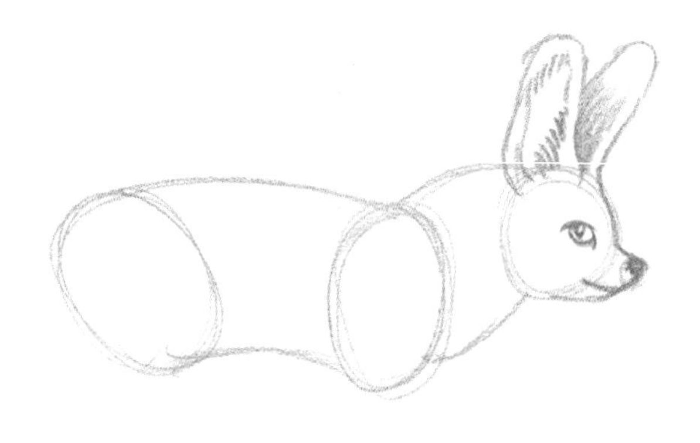

3. Darken the nose and mouth. Add the eye, with a small circle that will remain white. Draw the distinctive large ears.

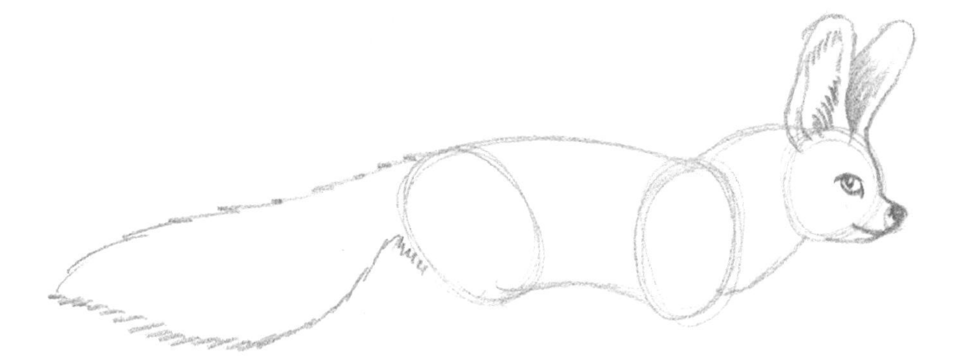

4. Draw squiggly lines to form the bushy tail.

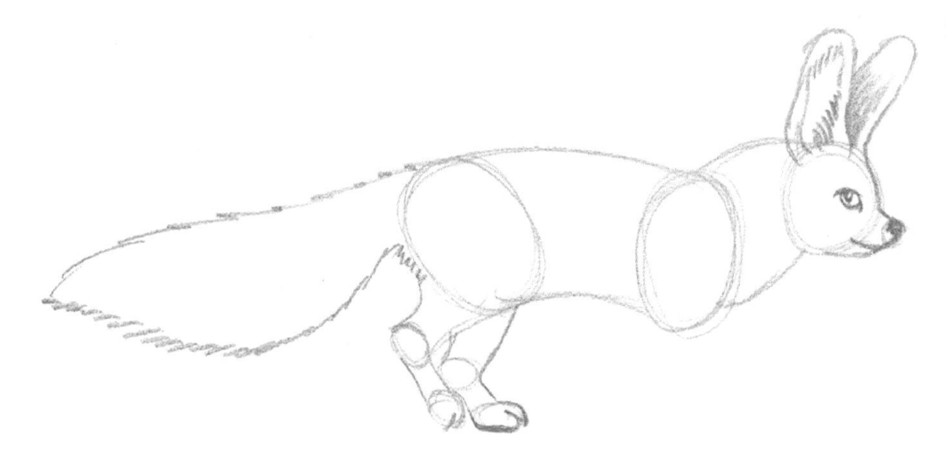

5. Sketch small circles for the leg joints. Draw the rear legs and feet. Add emphasis to the farther one, which is supporting the fox's entire weight.

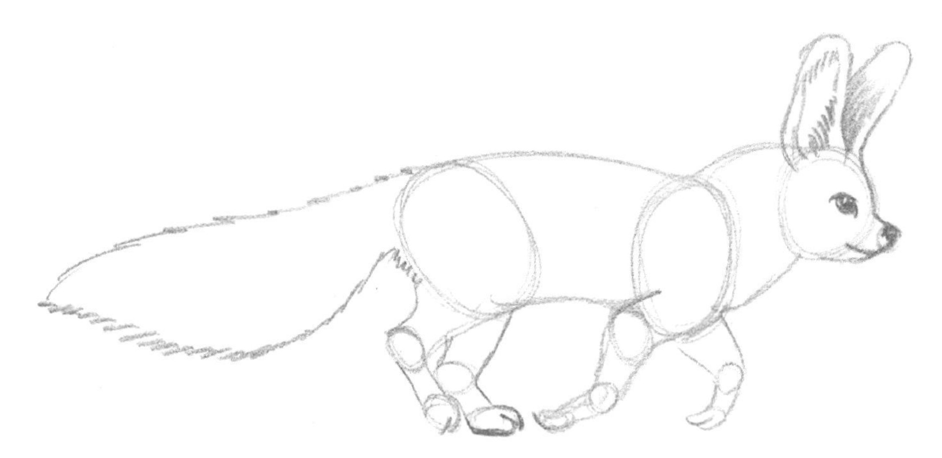

6. Likewise, draw the front legs and feet. Notice that neither is completely on the ground.

7. Look at the variations in the tones (light and dark). Use short pencil strokes to create the fur of the fennec fox. Leave some areas light. Go over the outline, adding emphasis at points you think need it.

   Add a slight *cast shadow* underneath the fox. Draw whiskers! Clean up any smudges with your eraser.

Fine fox! Put today's date on your drawing and save it!

Scorpion

order *Scorpiones*
Size: body 3 mm – 8 cm (⅛ in – 3 in)

About 600 different species of scorpion are known. They have one main part of their body, then five segments forming the "tail," at the end of which is the poisonous stinger. Scorpions live in cracks, but can dig their own resting places as well. At night, they eat beetles, cockroaches, and other arthropods. With their pincers (pedipalps) they bring prey to their chelicerae (jaws), which they use to tear it apart. They only sting when they need to subdue large or struggling prey. American and North African desert scorpions have the worst sting – one Sahara scorpion's sting can kill a dog in a few seconds.

1. Sketch the two main parts of the body at an angle (compare with clock face).

2. Sketch five connected ovals for the tail, and the stinger at the end.

3. Notice the three main sections of the pedipalp, with smaller connecting sections. Carefully observe the angle of each section *before drawing.*

   Draw the first of the two pedipalps, with the large pincers at its end.

4. Add the other pedipalp, and the first of the walking legs.

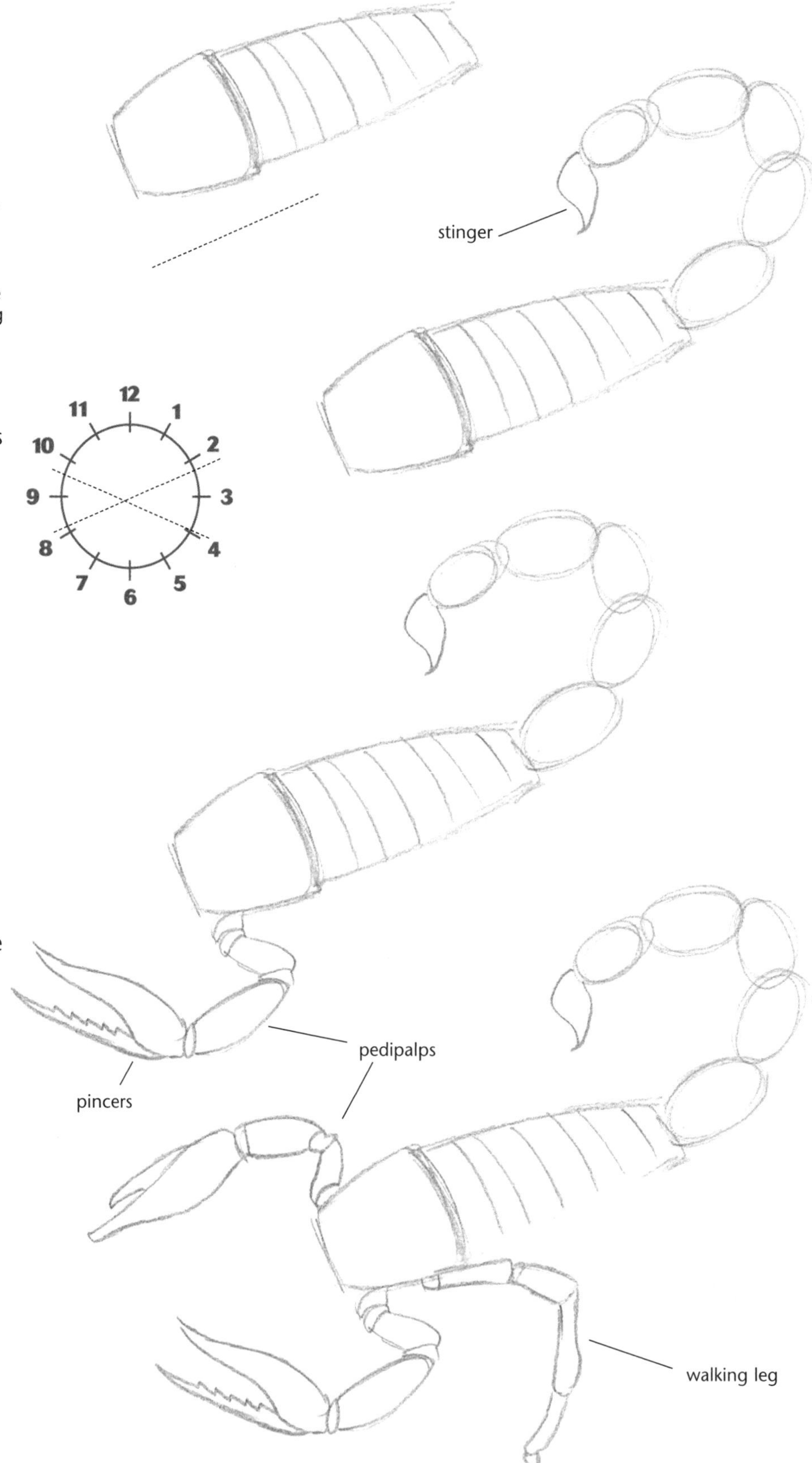

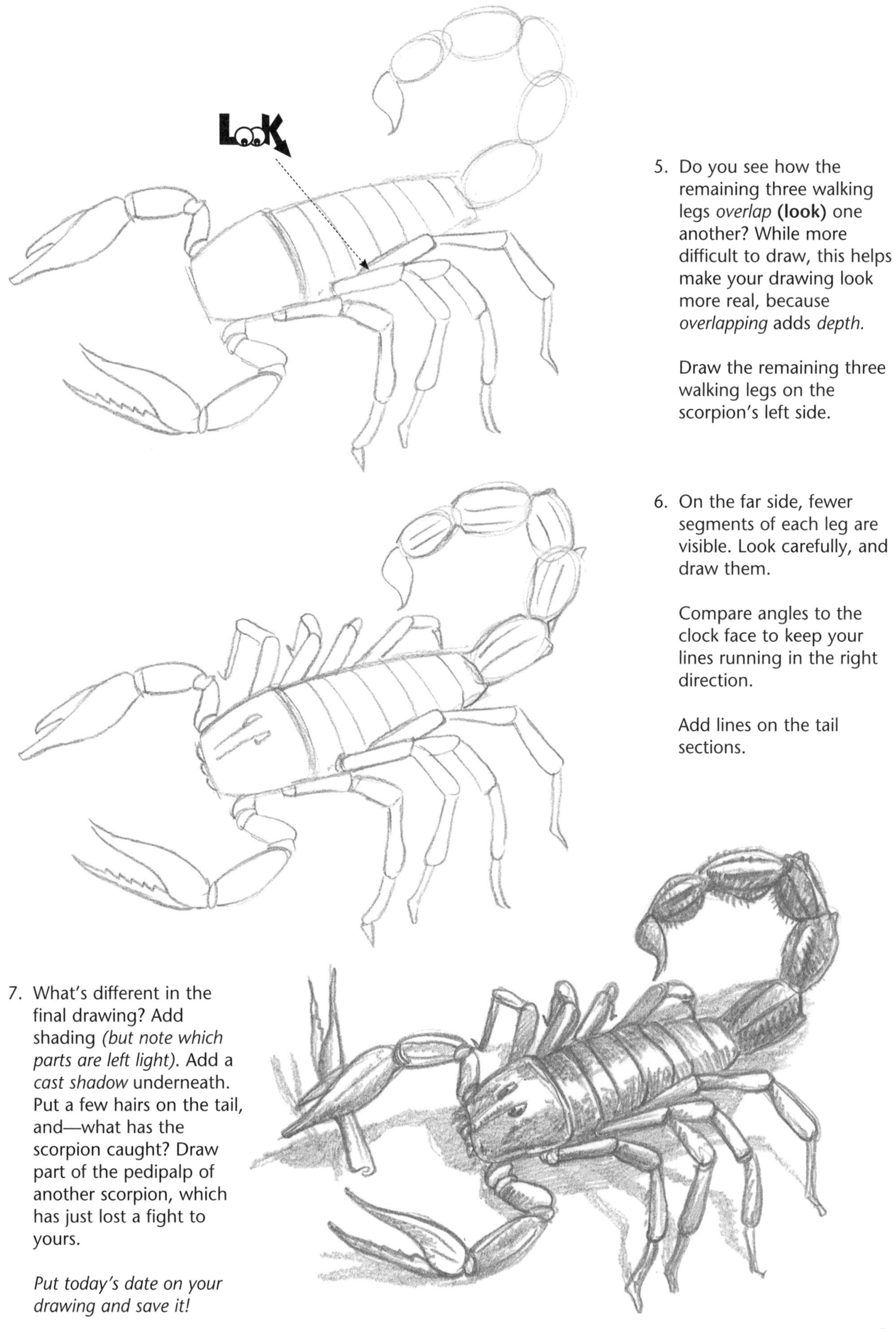

5. Do you see how the remaining three walking legs *overlap* **(look)** one another? While more difficult to draw, this helps make your drawing look more real, because *overlapping* adds *depth.*

   Draw the remaining three walking legs on the scorpion's left side.

6. On the far side, fewer segments of each leg are visible. Look carefully, and draw them.

   Compare angles to the clock face to keep your lines running in the right direction.

   Add lines on the tail sections.

7. What's different in the final drawing? Add shading *(but note which parts are left light)*. Add a *cast shadow* underneath. Put a few hairs on the tail, and—what has the scorpion caught? Draw part of the pedipalp of another scorpion, which has just lost a fight to yours.

   Put today's date on your drawing and save it!

Tarantula

North America.
Size: body up to 7.5 cm (3 in) long; leg span to 30 cm (12 in)

The tarantula is a kind of wolf spider *(Lycosa)*. When threatened, a tarantula might rear up on its hind legs and make a hissing noise. Unlike other spiders, the jaws of the tarantula move up and down instead of sideways. While it is a big, scary looking spider, the tarantula's bite is not as bad as people sometimes think: it's similar to a wasp sting.

ALWAYS SKETCH LIGHTLY AT FIRST!

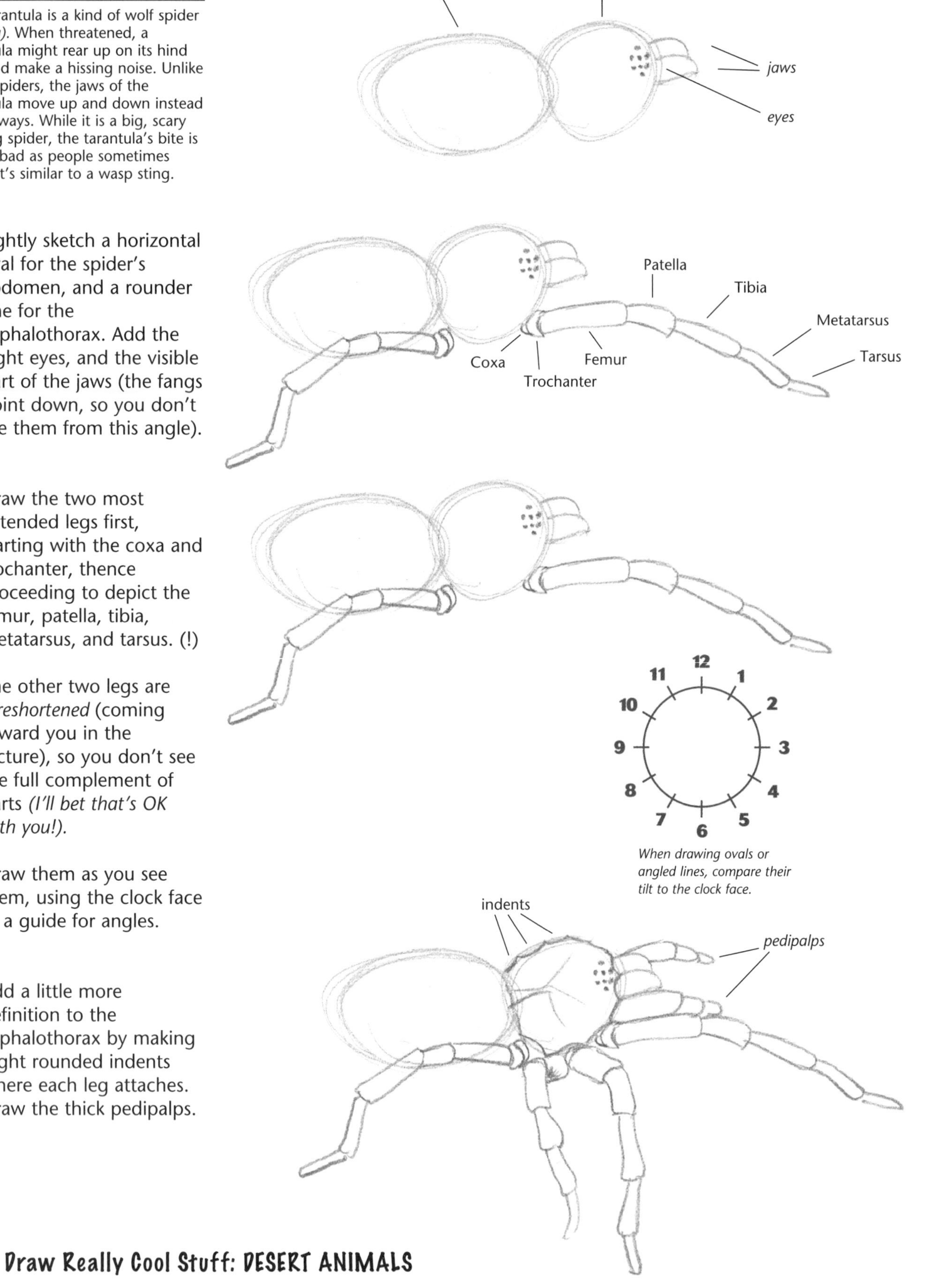

When drawing ovals or angled lines, compare their tilt to the clock face.

1. Lightly sketch a horizontal oval for the spider's abdomen, and a rounder one for the cephalothorax. Add the eight eyes, and the visible part of the jaws (the fangs point down, so you don't see them from this angle).

2. Draw the two most extended legs first, starting with the coxa and trochanter, thence proceeding to depict the femur, patella, tibia, metatarsus, and tarsus. (!)

3. The other two legs are *foreshortened* (coming toward you in the picture), so you don't see the full complement of parts *(I'll bet that's OK with you!)*.

   Draw them as you see them, using the clock face as a guide for angles.

4. Add a little more definition to the cephalothorax by making slight rounded indents where each leg attaches. Draw the thick pedipalps.

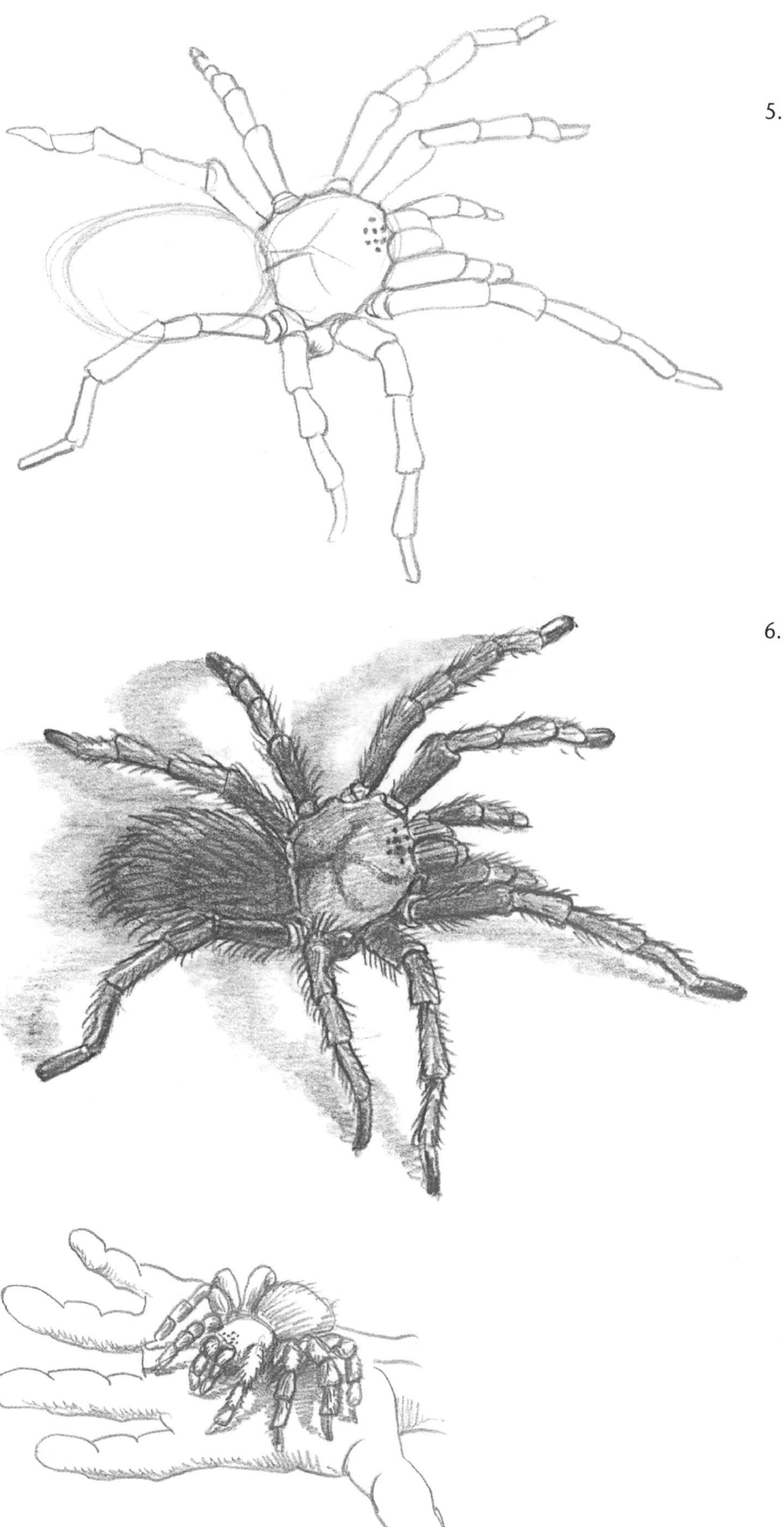

5. You'll find the legs on the other side easier to draw, since there is little *foreshortening.* Add them one segment at a time.

As you can see, the last step involves some time. Are you ready to keep going on this drawing, or do you want to keep it as a practice sketch and start another? Your choice. Put the date on this drawing and save it if you do decide to start over.

6. Finish your tarantula by shading the body parts with a dull pencil, then adding short pencil strokes for hairs when the pencil is sharp.

   With a dull pencil (and perhaps smearing it a bit with your finger or a small wad of paper), add the *cast shadow* beneath.

You can have fun adding a hand to your drawing to show scale. Don't know how to draw a hand? Maybe you want to practice on a separate sheet, and draw it before you draw the spider!

Tantalizing tarantula! Clean up any smudges with your eraser, put today's date on it and save it in your portfolio!

Thorny devil

ALWAYS SKETCH LIGHTLY AT FIRST!

Moloch horridus

Australia. Size: 15 cm (6 in)

This small desert lizard (also known as the *Australian moloch)* looks larger because of the points all over its body. The points keep predators away (would *you* eat something that thorny?). It moves slowly, and likes to eat ants–one at a time, sitting for hours by an ant nest. At night, dew drops form on the lizard's skin: this is how the Thorny Devil gets water to drink!

1. Sketch a long, slightly tilted oval for the body. Sketch a smaller oval for the head, tilting the opposite way. Connect them with lines for the neck.

2. Add lines for the legs and claws. Draw the tail.

   Add a line underneath for the ground.

3. Look at this thorny devil! At the front of the head, draw the eye and mouth. Add spikes on the chin and top of the head.

   Add a jagged edge to the bottom of the tail. Draw spikes on the front and rear leg. Make smaller spikes on each of the claws.

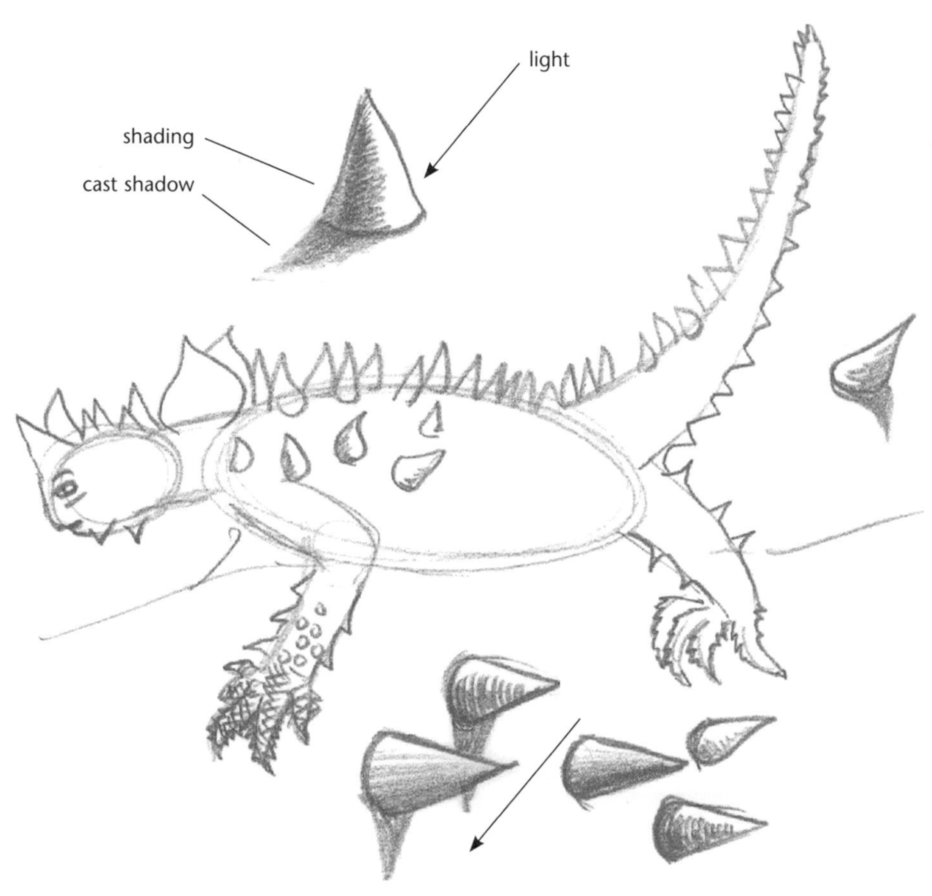

4. Before you start going wild with spikes, take a moment to study the various cones you see here. The rounded spikes on the Moloch's back are really little cones; you don't have to draw them as carefully as these examples, but you'll find it helpful to see how the shadows of the cones look.

   Draw more spikes along the lizard's back, and start adding those little cone-shaped spikes.

   On the legs, make small circles, tightly packed together, for scales.

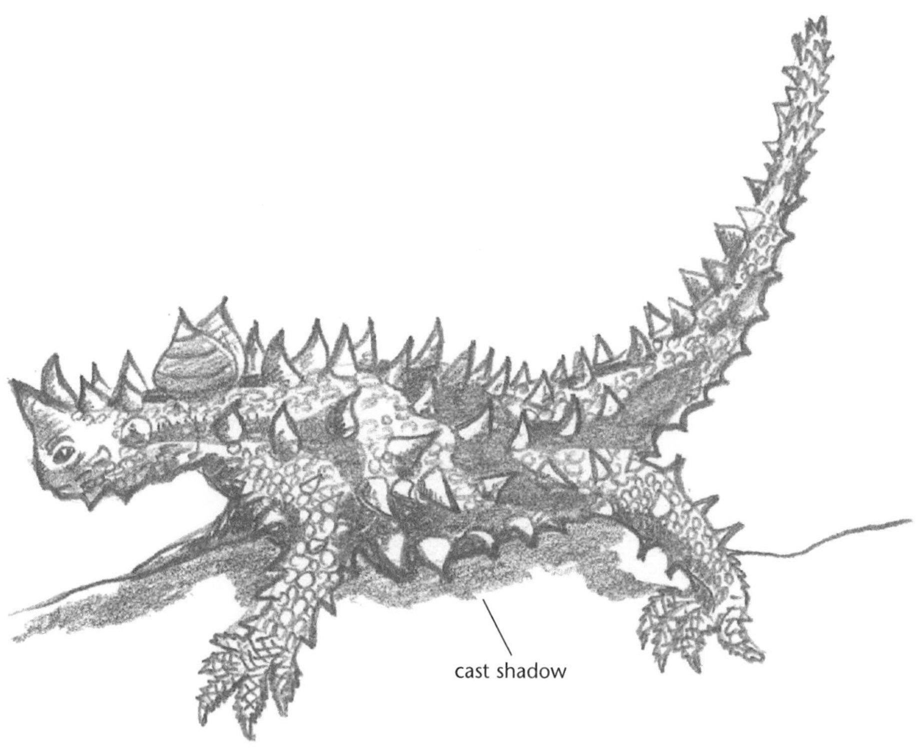

5. Go wild with spikes! Then add shading and the darker areas of the lizard's camouflage pattern. Make a *cast shadow* beneath.

Mahvelous Moloch! Clean up any smudges with your eraser. Put the date on your drawing and save it!

Trapdoor Spider

family Ctenizidae

Worldwide.

Trap-door spiders dig burrows, covering the opening with a hinged flap made from silk and dirt. Then they sit and wait until an unwary insect wanders close to the door, and ZIP!–they push the door open, jump on the insect, and drag it back into the tunnel to kill and eat it.

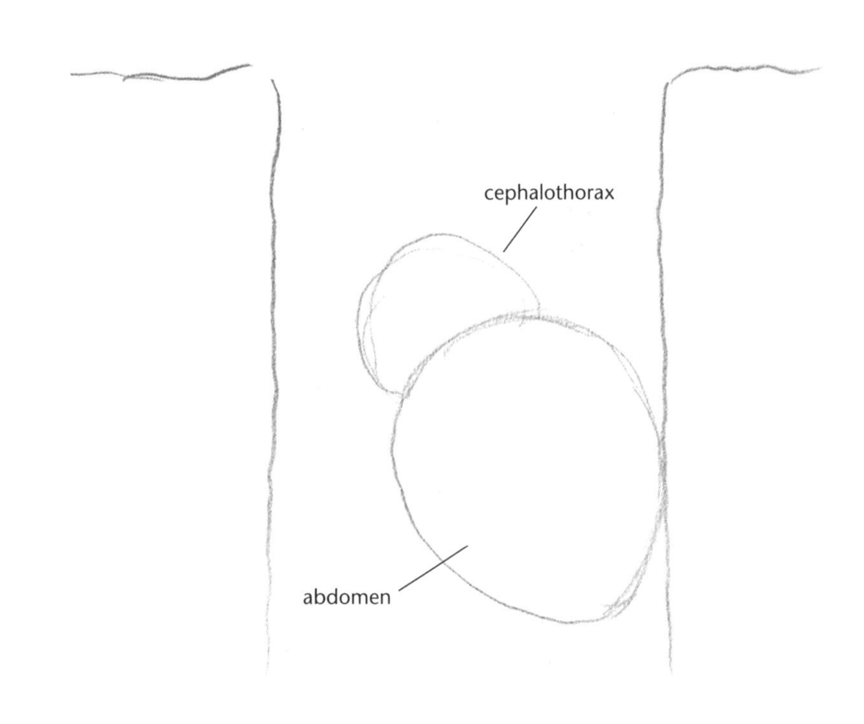

1. Start your drawing with two upside-down L shapes for the tunnel. Lightly draw the two ovals of the spider's body—the abdomen and cephalothorax.

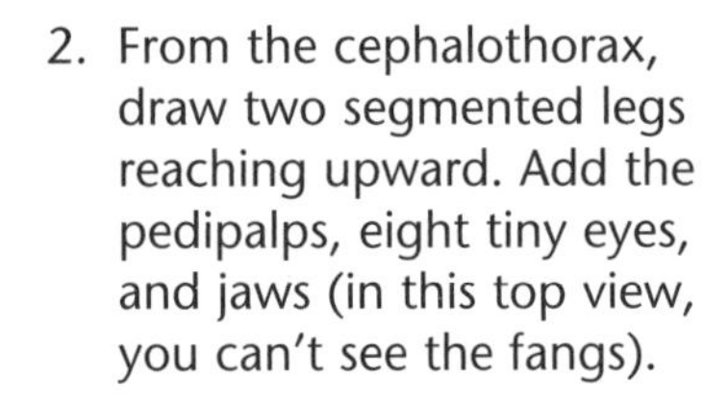

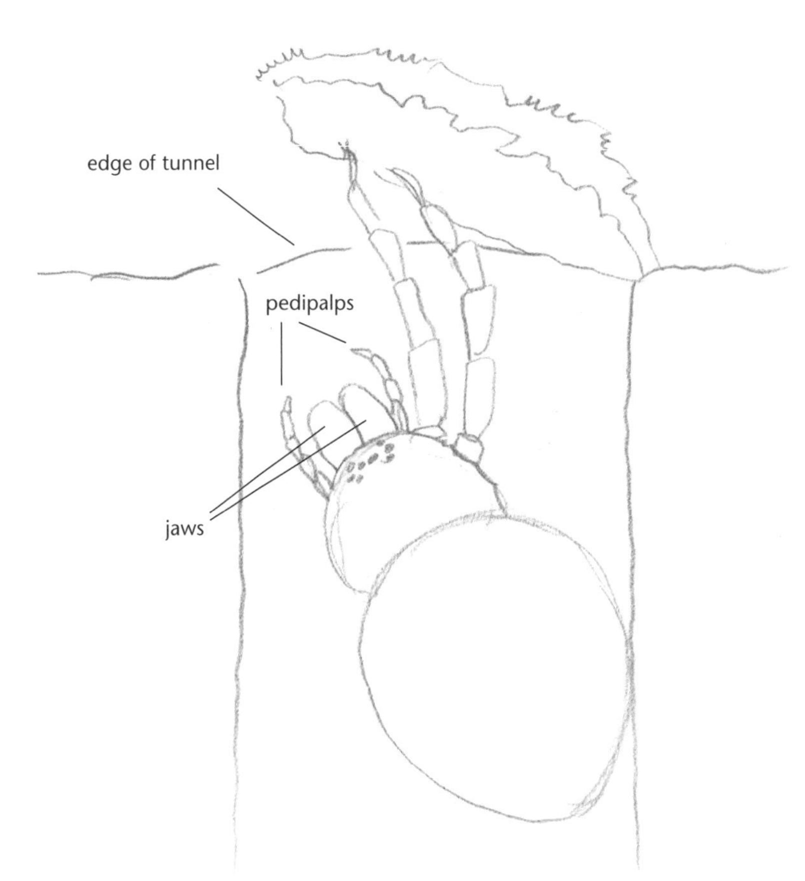

2. From the cephalothorax, draw two segmented legs reaching upward. Add the pedipalps, eight tiny eyes, and jaws (in this top view, you can't see the fangs).

   Look at the squiggly shaped trap door. Draw the trap door and a line for the edge of the tunnel.

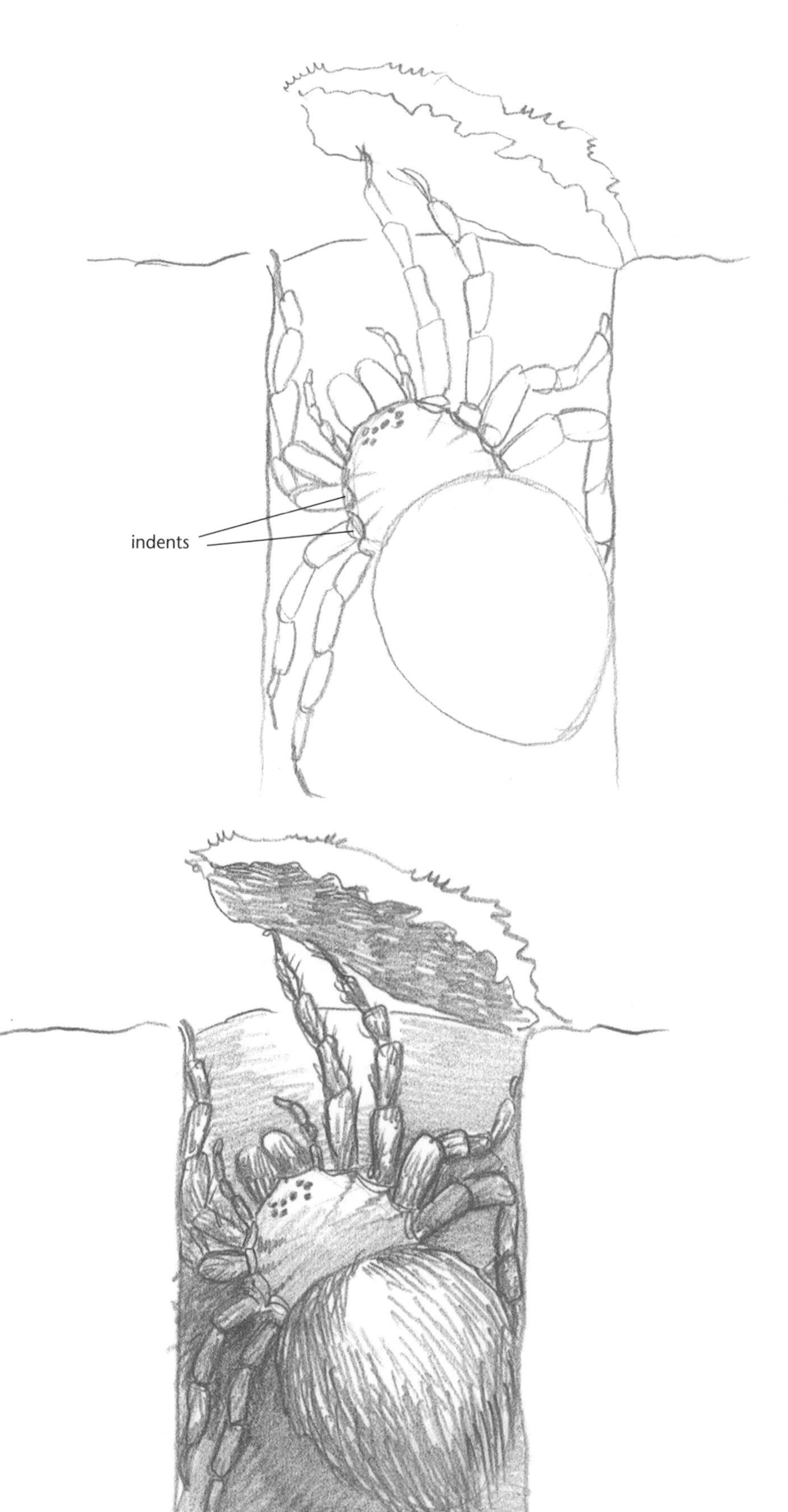

3. Add the remaining legs, one at a time. Draw indents on the cephalothorax at the point where each leg attaches.

4. With a sharp pencil, make short strokes to shade the hairy abdomen and legs. As your pencil gets dull, add to the softer shading of the tunnel and trap door.

   Go over outlines, darkening as necessary.

Clean up any smudges with your eraser. Put the date on your drawing and save it in your portfolio!

Knock knock.

Who's there?

A final thought

ALWAYS SKETCH LIGHTLY AT FIRST!

Save your work!

Whenever you do a drawing–or even a sketch–put your initials (or autograph!) and the date on it. Save it. You don't have to save it until it turns yellow and crumbles to dust, but do keep your drawings, at least for several months. Sometimes, hiding in your portfolio, they will mysteriously improve! I've seen it happen often with my own drawings, especially the ones I knew were no good at all, but kept anyway…

Do-it-yourself portfolio

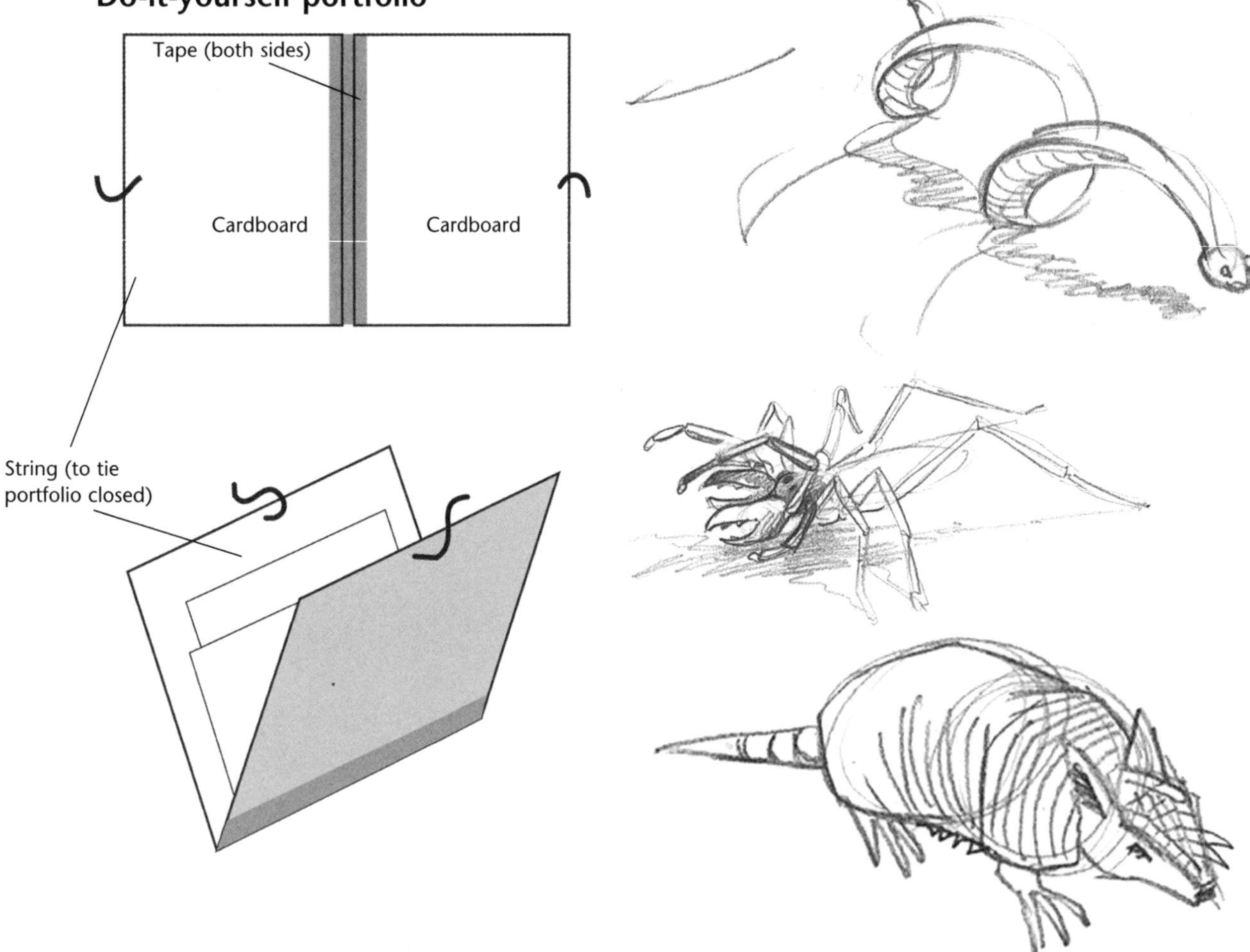

Introduction

Look carefully at this *Tyrannosaurus* skeleton.

Can you find the shoulder joint? The knee? Can you see where the legs and arms bend?

To make the legs of a dinosaur look good in your drawing, learn about the skeleton. Look at one whenever you can when drawing a dinosaur.

Draw *rods* (lines) to show parts of arms and legs. Draw *joints* (circles) where they bend.

From this angle, one hip joint lies directly behind the other, so you can only see one.

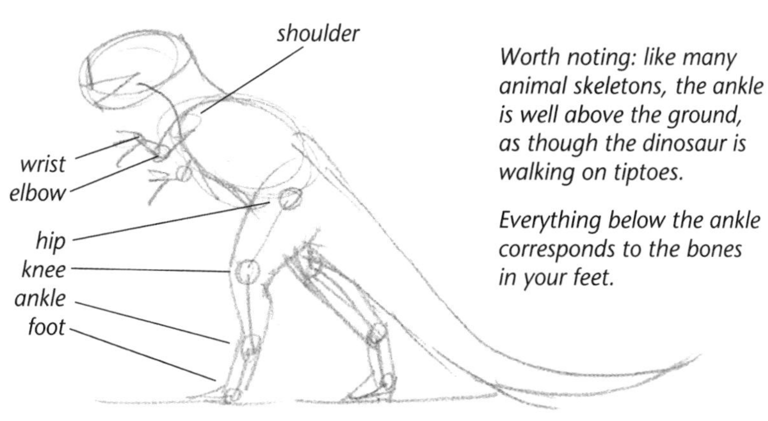

Worth noting: like many animal skeletons, the ankle is well above the ground, as though the dinosaur is walking on tiptoes.

Everything below the ankle corresponds to the bones in your feet.

Always draw rods and joints very lightly, so you can either erase them or cover them with shading. You don't want them as part of your final drawing, but they do give you a powerful tool to use along the way!

Always start out ***lightly***!

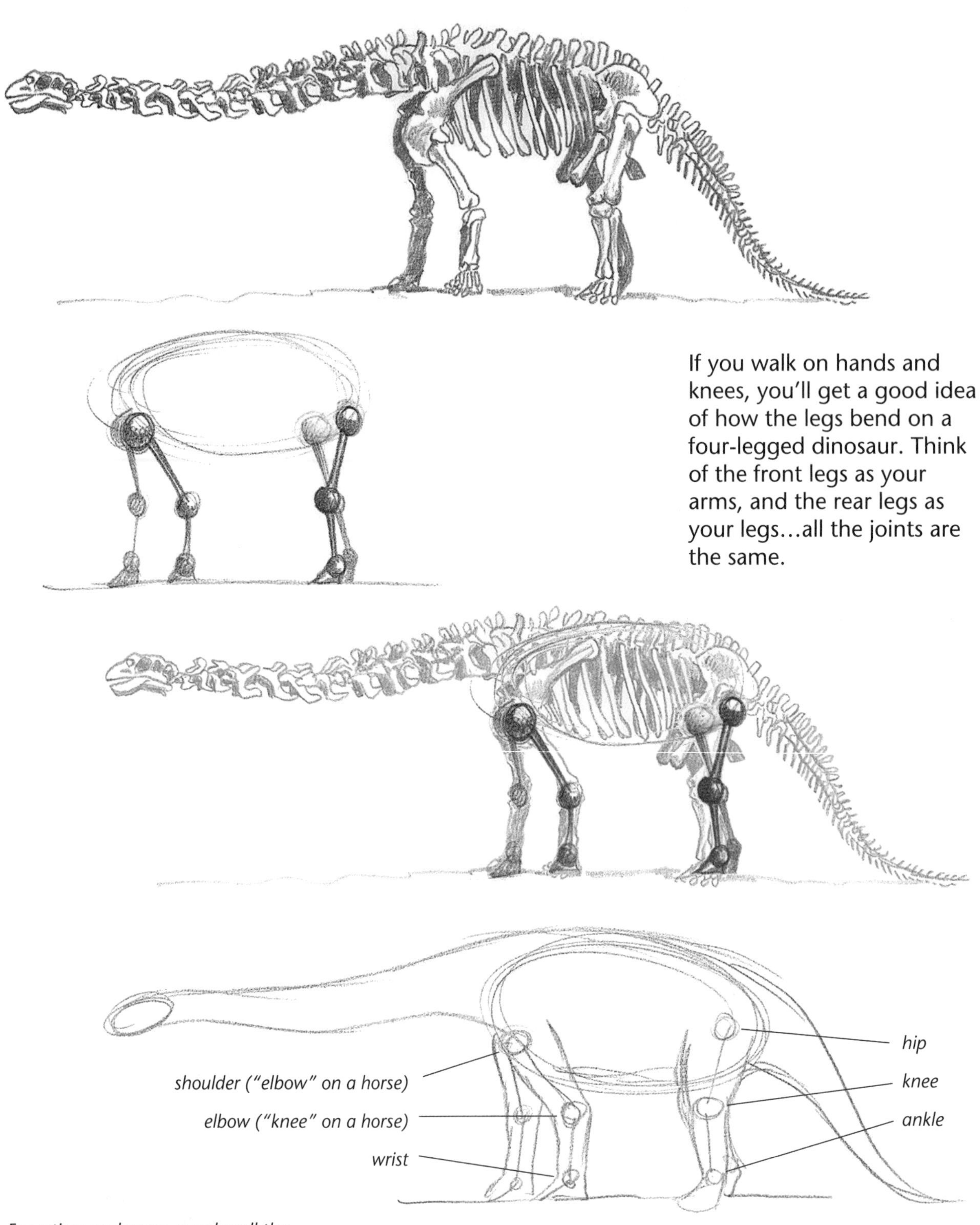

If you walk on hands and knees, you'll get a good idea of how the legs bend on a four-legged dinosaur. Think of the front legs as your arms, and the rear legs as your legs…all the joints are the same.

Exception: on horses, people call the shoulder the elbow, and the elbow the knee…even though they call the part between them the forearm! It makes no sense at all…(to me).

Supplies

You can draw with just about anything.

People in caves used dried clay and black stuff out of the fire pit, and we're still talking about their drawings 25,000 years later! But caves, charcoal, mud and torches do not make for an optimal drawing environment. So find a comfortable place to draw – with decent light, so you can see what you're doing.

Draw with a pencil that's longer than your finger.

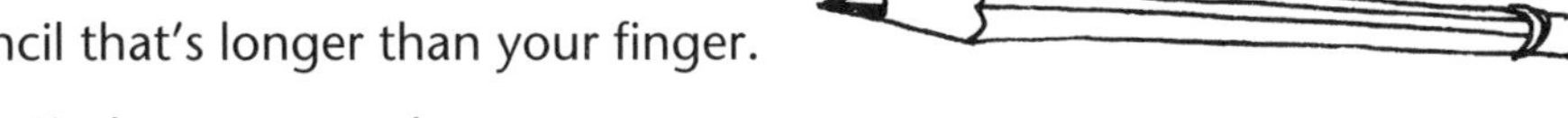

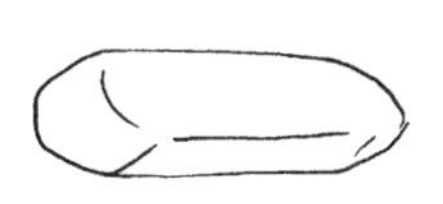

Find an eraser – the one on your pencil will disappear quickly.

For practice drawings, use recycled paper – for example, draw on the back of old photocopies or computer printouts.

Sharpen your pencil when it gets dull!

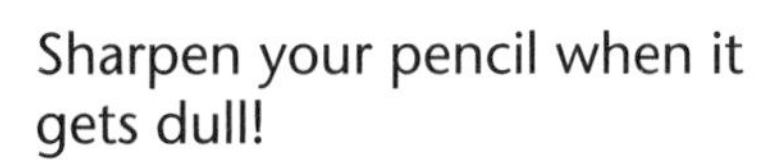

Allosaurus

AL-o-SAW-rus

"Other lizard." Late Jurassic; North America, Africa, Australia, perhaps Asia. Up to 39 ft (12 m) long; weighed 1-2 tons. Lived long before Tyrannosaurus, and had longer arms with strong claws to hold its prey while it tore at it with teeth serrated like steak knives.

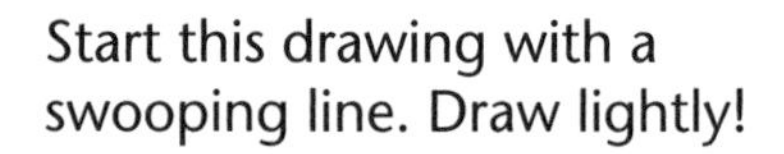

Start this drawing with a swooping line. Draw lightly!

Draw another line above the first, starting at one end and ending in the middle.

From the top line, add a smooth, curving line to complete the tail. At the other end, add lines for the neck and head. Make a bump where the eye will go. Leave room for the mouth.

Now lightly draw the leg. You may find it helpful to start with *rods and joints*.

The leg looks complex, but actually it bends just the way your own leg bends, at the knee and at the ankle.

back of knee

front of knee

Always start out ***lightly***!

Add the other leg. Now your dinosaur looks as though it's moving!

Draw the arm.

Draw the other arm. Now add nose, eye and mouth.

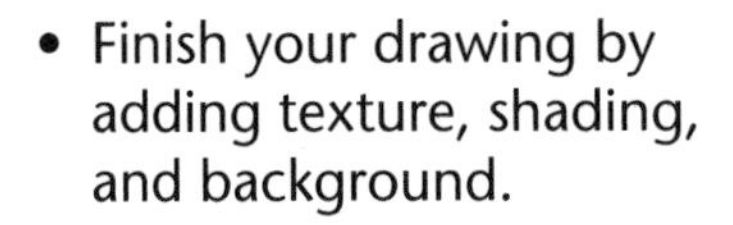

- Finish your drawing by adding texture, shading, and background.
- Look at your drawing in a mirror (or through the back of the paper) to spot areas you can improve.
- While your pencil is sharp, go over fine details and make lines cleaner. As it gets duller, add shading.
- Turn your drawing as you draw to avoid smudging it with your hand.
- Finally, clean up any smudges with your eraser.

Awesome Allosaurus!

Apatosaurus

A-PAT-O-SAW-RUS

"Deceptive reptile." Late Jurassic; Colorado, Oklahoma, Utah and Wyoming, USA. Ate plants. 70 ft (21 m) long; weighed 33 tons. One of the best-known dinosaurs. Has also been called *Brontosaurus* ("thunder reptile"). Shorter than *Diplodocus* but much heavier.

Lightly draw two overlapping ovals for the body.

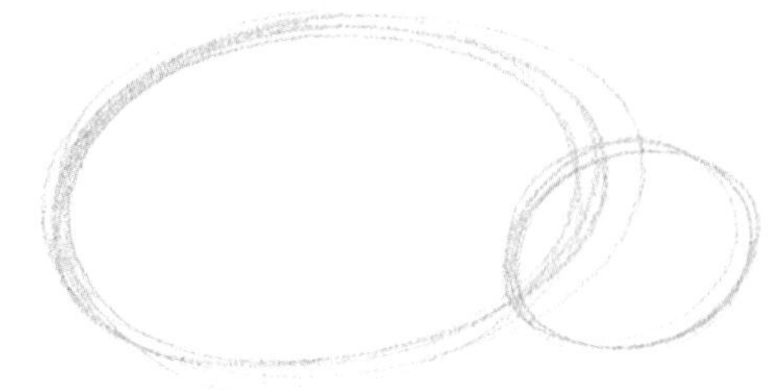

Make a much smaller, tilted oval for the head. Notice how far it is from the body.

From the top of the head, draw a smooth curving line touching the tops of larger ovals to make the back.

Add the line for the bottom of the neck. Add details to the face.

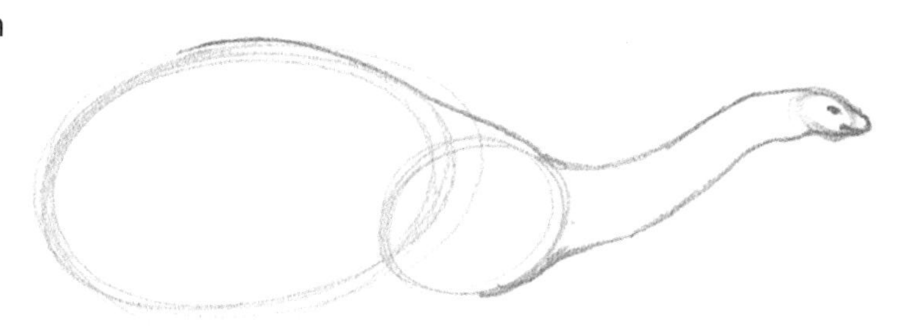

Always start out ***lightly***!

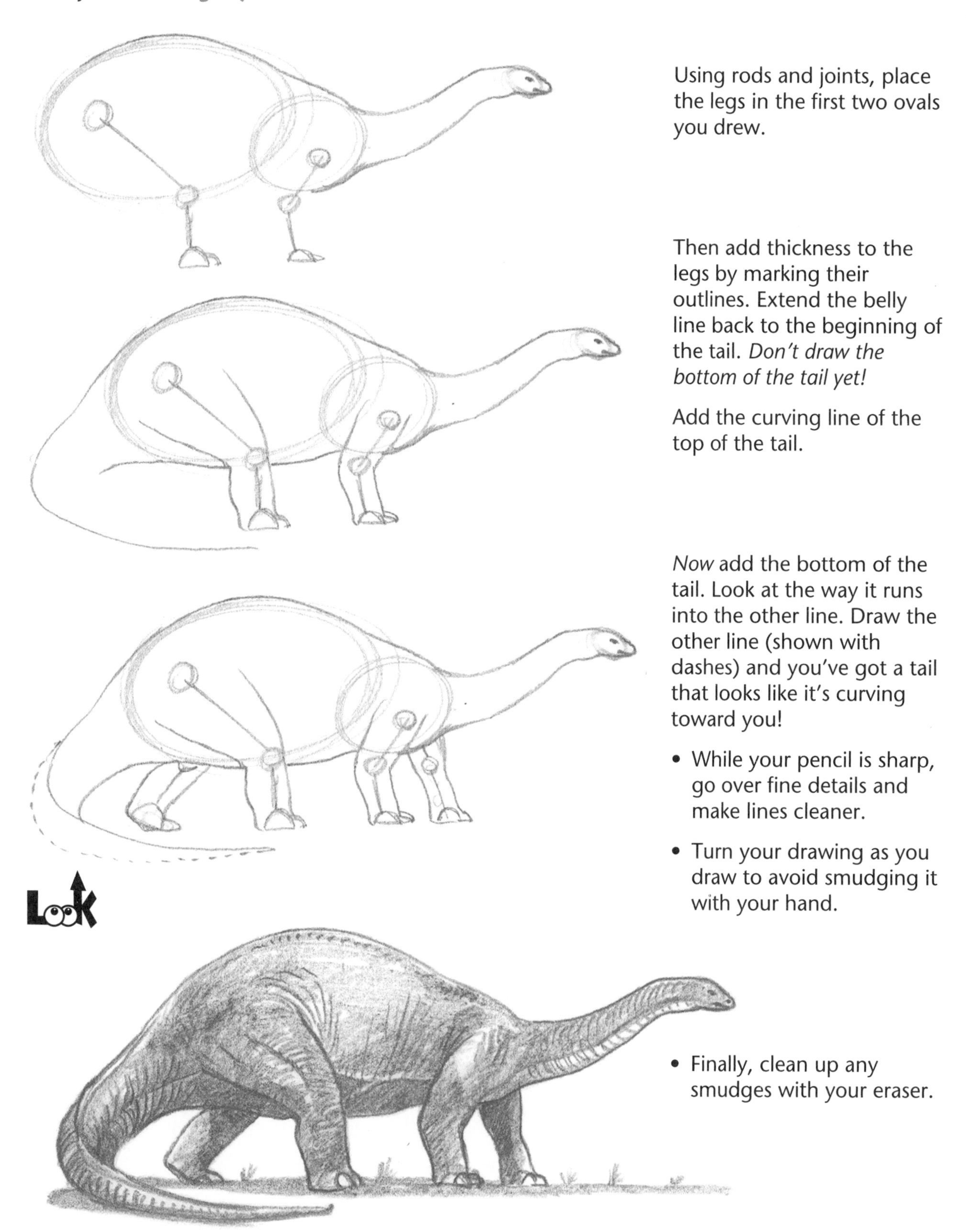

Using rods and joints, place the legs in the first two ovals you drew.

Then add thickness to the legs by marking their outlines. Extend the belly line back to the beginning of the tail. *Don't draw the bottom of the tail yet!*

Add the curving line of the top of the tail.

Now add the bottom of the tail. Look at the way it runs into the other line. Draw the other line (shown with dashes) and you've got a tail that looks like it's curving toward you!

- While your pencil is sharp, go over fine details and make lines cleaner.
- Turn your drawing as you draw to avoid smudging it with your hand.

- Finally, clean up any smudges with your eraser.

Triceratops

TRI-CER-A-TOPS

"Three-horned face." Cretaceous; North America, from Alberta and Saskatchewan to Colorado and South Dakota. Up to 30 ft (9 m) long; weighed 6 tons. Cores of the horns measure up to 3 ft (90 cm); actual horns may have been much longer.

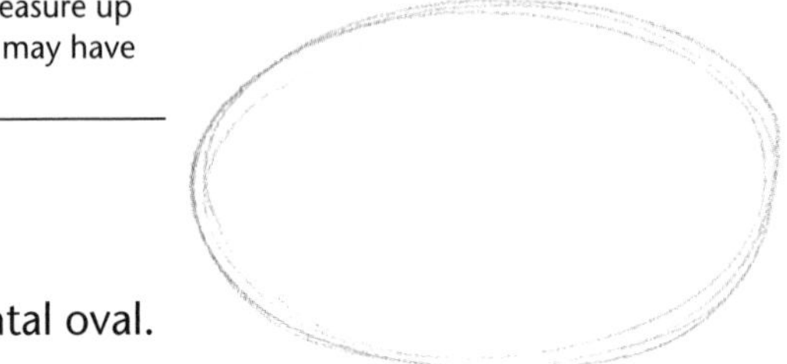

Draw a light, horizontal oval.

Using rods and joints, construct the front and rear leg. Make the hip higher than the shoulder. Notice how the legs bend toward each other.

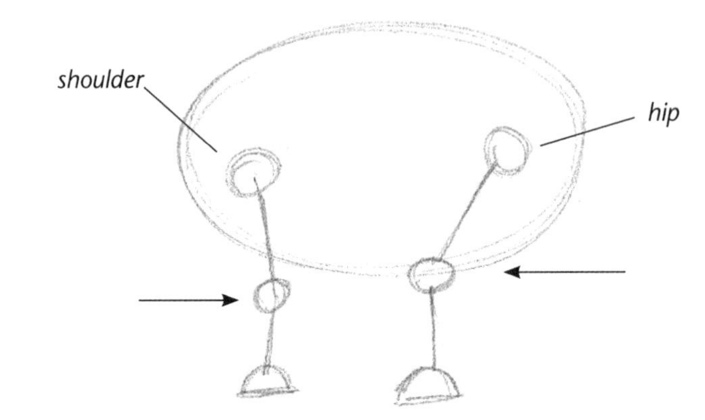

Carefully outline the legs and draw the toes. Then lightly erase the rods and joints.

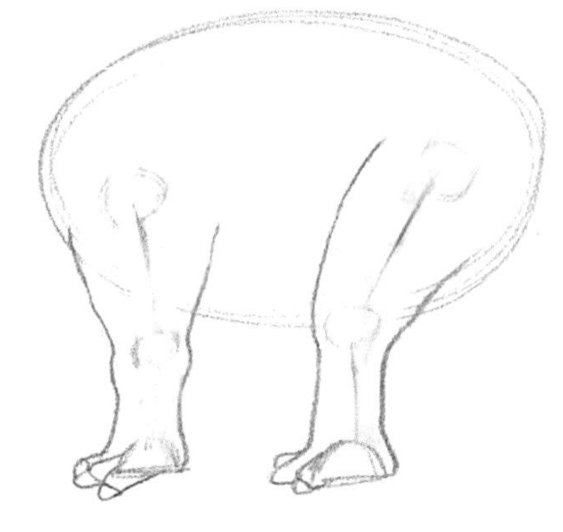

Now draw the other legs.

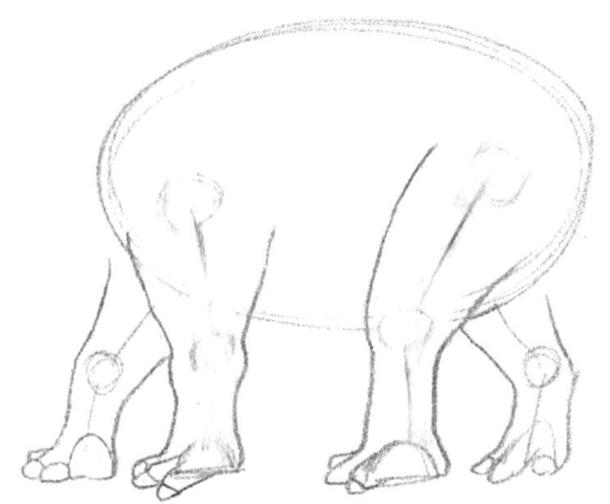

Always start out ***lightly***!

Draw the tail, making the top and bottom of it blend right into the oval. Draw the shape of the head—*very lightly!*

Add the eye, nose and mouth. Draw the three horns. Make the curved frill above the neck.

- Finish your drawing by adding texture, shading, and background.
- Look at your drawing in a mirror (or through the back of the paper) to spot areas you can improve.
- While your pencil is sharp, go over fine details and make lines cleaner. As it gets duller, add shading.
- Turn your drawing as you draw to avoid smudging it with your hand.
- Finally, clean up any smudges with your eraser.

Ankylosaurus

AN-KY-LO-SAW-RUS

"Fused lizard." Late Cretaceous; Alberta, Canada; Montana, USA. Up to 35 ft (10.7 m) long. Built like an army tank. Swung its tail as a weapon, but with its armor plating, could have done well to simply hunker down when things started to get ugly. Some ankylosaurs had spikes along the sides; others didn't.

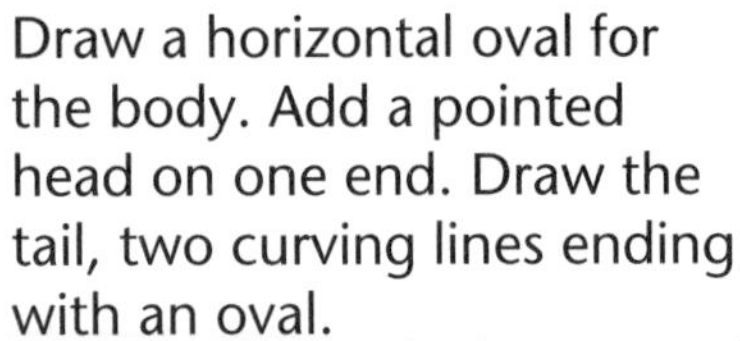

Draw a horizontal oval for the body. Add a pointed head on one end. Draw the tail, two curving lines ending with an oval.

Use rods and joints to draw the legs, then add their outlines. Don't forget the toenails!

Add the other two legs – notice where they join the body. Draw a line for the edge of the armor plating, all along the side. Draw eye and mouth, and horns on the face.

Carefully erase the rods and joints in the legs. Erase the main oval where the neck and tail join. Add a checkerboard pattern for the armor plates of the back, with a small bump in each square. Draw larger bumps on the neck and base of tail. Add a small row of bumps on the nose and tail.

Always start out ***lightly***!

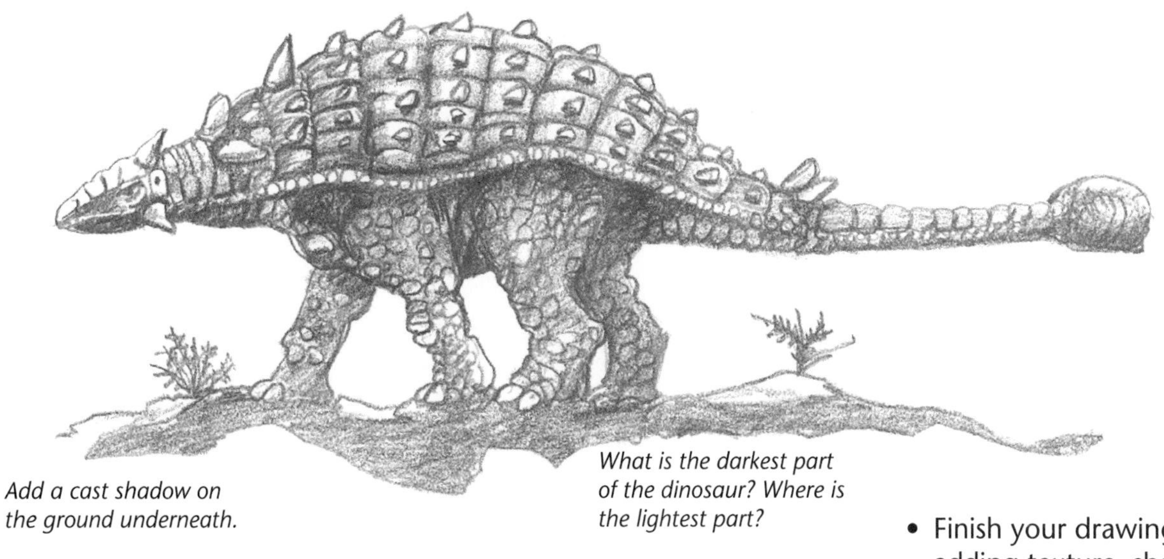

Add a cast shadow on the ground underneath.

What is the darkest part of the dinosaur? Where is the lightest part?

- Finish your drawing by adding texture, shading, and background.
- Look at your drawing in a mirror (or through the back of the paper) to spot areas you can improve.
- While your pencil is sharp, go over fine details and make lines cleaner. As it gets duller, add shading.
- Turn your drawing as you draw to avoid smudging it with your hand.
- Finally, clean up any smudges with your eraser.

Use your knowledge of ovals, rods and joints to make your ankylosaurus in different settings: perhaps using its tail as a weapon…

…or trying NOT to become someone's lunch!

Pachycephalosaurus

PAK-EE-SEF-O-LO-SAW-RUS

"Thick-headed lizard." Cretaceous; western North America. 15 ft (4.6 m) long. Scientists have decided that the extraordinarily thick (10 in/25 cm) skulls served as crash helmets, and that male dinosaurs would butt heads to establish dominance, as males of some species still do today.

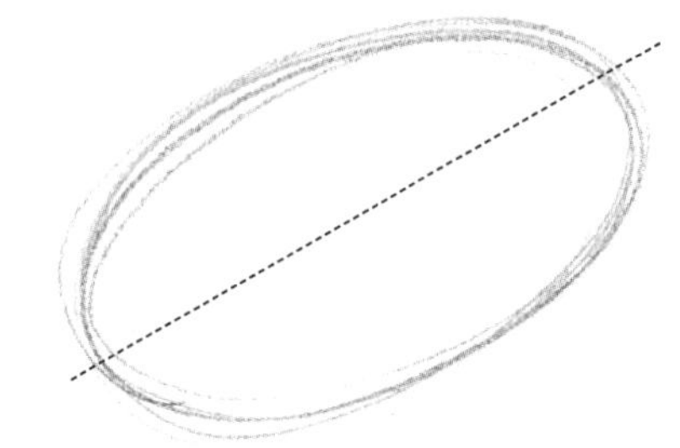

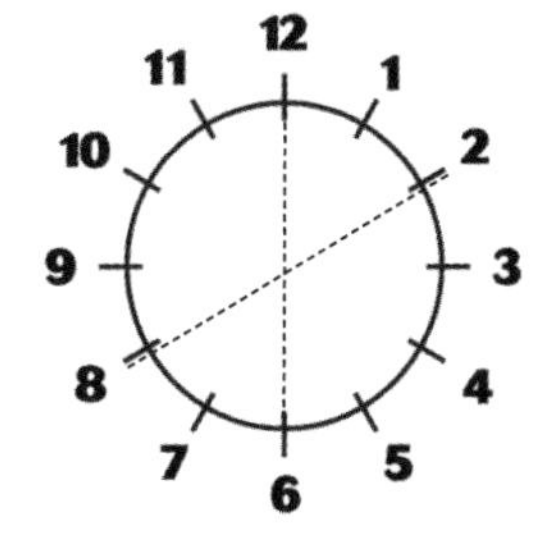

Use the clock face to compare angles of lines and ovals.

Begin by drawing a slanted oval for the dinosaur's body.

Add two swooping lines for the tail. Draw a vertical oval for the head, and two lines for the neck.

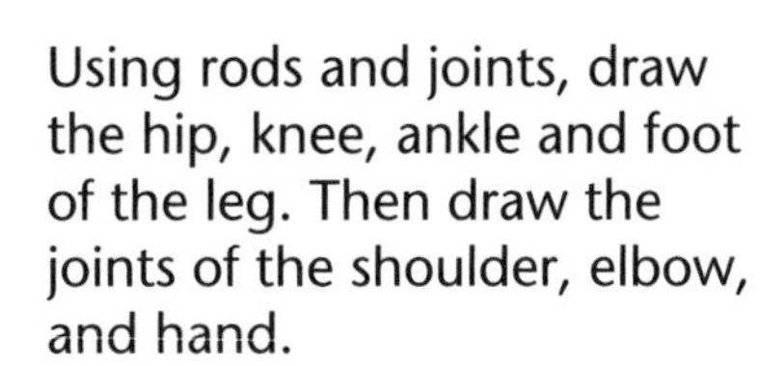

Using rods and joints, draw the hip, knee, ankle and foot of the leg. Then draw the joints of the shoulder, elbow, and hand.

Add a line for the ground.

Outline the leg and arm.

Always start out ***lightly***!

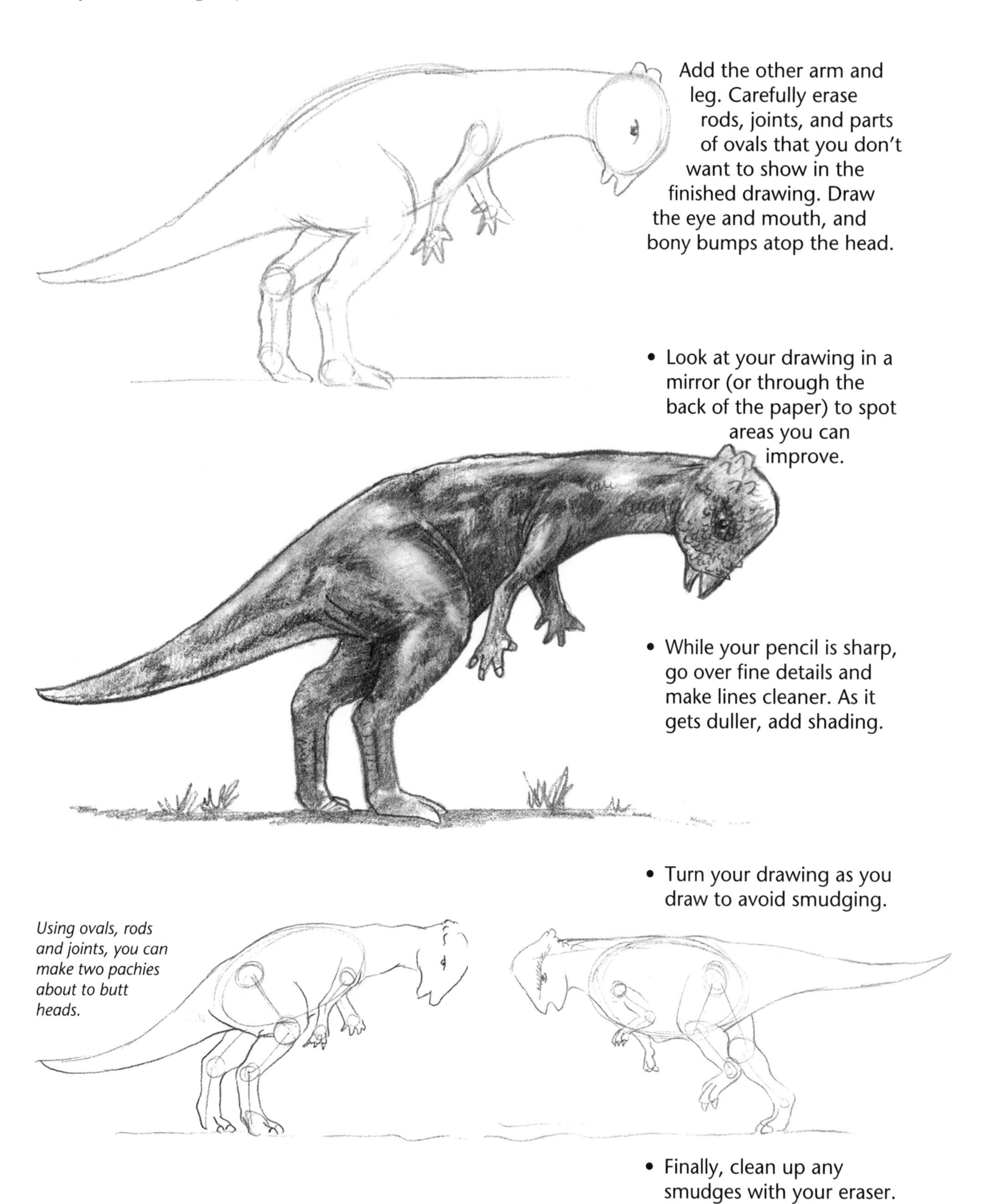

Add the other arm and leg. Carefully erase rods, joints, and parts of ovals that you don't want to show in the finished drawing. Draw the eye and mouth, and bony bumps atop the head.

- Look at your drawing in a mirror (or through the back of the paper) to spot areas you can improve.

- While your pencil is sharp, go over fine details and make lines cleaner. As it gets duller, add shading.

- Turn your drawing as you draw to avoid smudging.

Using ovals, rods and joints, you can make two pachies about to butt heads.

- Finally, clean up any smudges with your eraser.

Stegosaurus

STEG-O-SAW-RUS

"Roof lizard." Biggest known stegosaurid. Late Jurassic; Colorado, Oklahoma, Utah and Wyoming, USA. Up to 30 ft (9 m) long; weighed up to 2 tons. Spikes on end of tail for defense. Scientists still debate what those big plates did, and whether they were staggered or in even pairs.

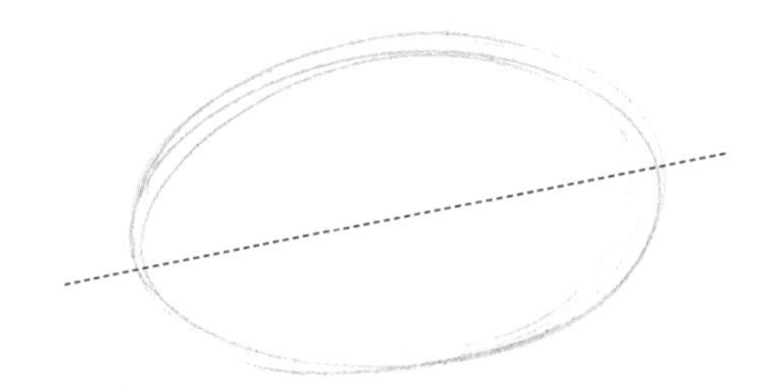

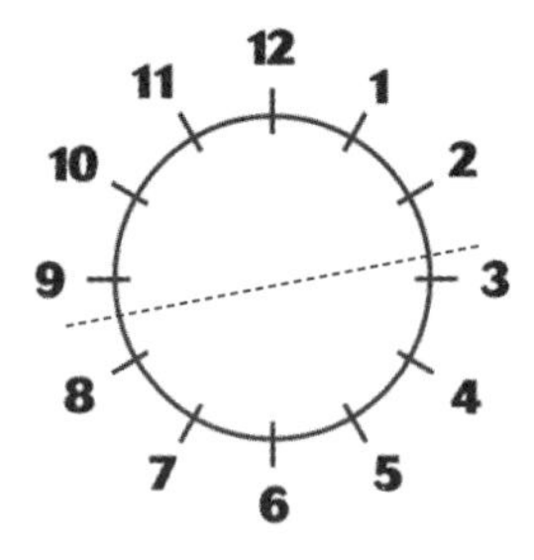

Use the clock face to compare angles of lines and ovals.

Draw a tilted, horizontal oval.

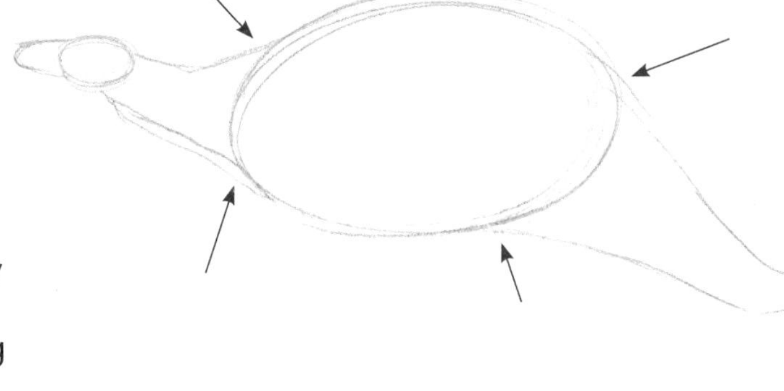

Draw a small, flat oval for the head, with a bump for the nose. Add two curving lines for the neck. Notice how the lines join the bottom of the big oval. They seem to flow right into it. Add lines for the tail, coming to a point at the end.

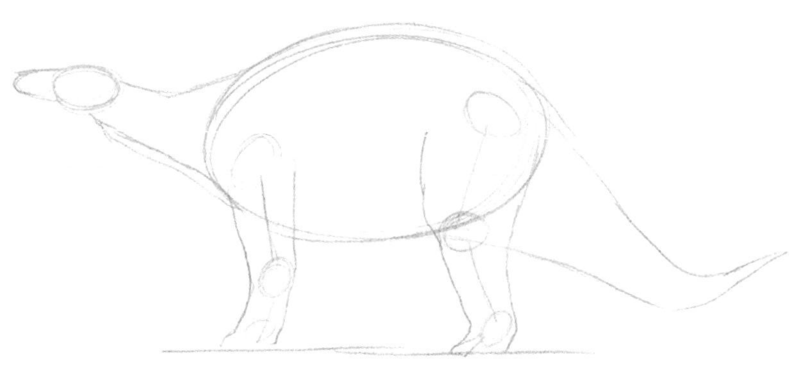

Using rods and joints, place the legs, then add outlines.

Add the remaining two legs. Draw the eye, nose and mouth. Carefully erase rods and joints, and parts of ovals that overlap. Darken the bottom outline.

Always start out ***lightly***!

Draw a line of diamond-shaped armor plates along the back. Draw two tail spikes.

Add another row of plates. Make vertical lines on them. Draw the remaining two spikes on the tail.

- Finish your drawing by adding texture and shading. Use your imagination! Did Stego have a camouflage pattern? Or perhaps stripes, like a zebra? And were those plates really bare, or perhaps supporting a fin on the back? *Who knows?*
- Look at your drawing in a mirror (or through the back of the paper) to spot areas you can improve.
- While your pencil is sharp, go over fine details and make lines cleaner. As it gets duller, add shading.
- Turn your drawing as you draw to avoid smudging it with your hand.
- Finally, clean up any smudges with your eraser.

Maiasaura

MY-A-SOR-A

"Good mother lizard." Cretaceous; Montana, USA. Up to 30 ft (9 m) long. In 1978 scientists discovered fossilized baby Maiasaura and eggs around a mound-shaped nest, the first evidence of dinosaurs with organized family structure.

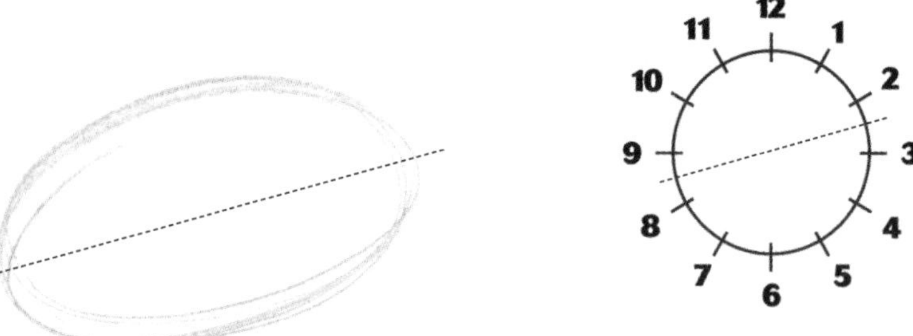

Use the clock face to compare angles of lines and ovals.

Start with a a tilted oval for the dinosaur's body.

LOOK

Look where the top of the tail joins the body. From that point, draw the line for the top of the tail. Then add the bottom of the tail, which flows smoothly into the bottom of the oval.

Notice the angle of the eye

Draw a circle for the head. Place the eye inside it. Add the curving lines of the neck, flowing into the ovals at either end.

Using rods and joints, draw the hip, knee, ankle and foot. Lightly add the outline of the leg.

Repeat for the arm. Make the hand higher than the foot. Draw lines for the inside and outside of the nest. Draw eggs in the nest.

outside of nest

inside of nest

You only see part of each egg.

Always start out ***lightly***!

Now add the other leg and arm. Draw the mouth and nostril.

Carefully erase rods and joints, and overlapping sections of the main oval. Then go over the outlines and begin to add details.

Finish your drawing by adding texture, shading, and background.

Clean up any smudges with your eraser.

Marvellous Maiasaura!

Plesiosaurus

PLEES-EE-O-SAW-RUS

"Ribbon reptile." Jurassic; Germany, England. 6-28 ft long (2-9 m). Swam by flapping front flippers up and down. Probably moved its neck very quickly to catch fish. Alas, not a dinosaur but a swimming reptile.

Draw a horizontal oval for the body, and a smaller one for the head.

Draw the swooping lines of the neck. Add the tail.

Draw the centerline of the back.

Add limbs, with flippers instead of feet.

Draw the mouth and eye. Carefully erase the original oval at neck and tail.

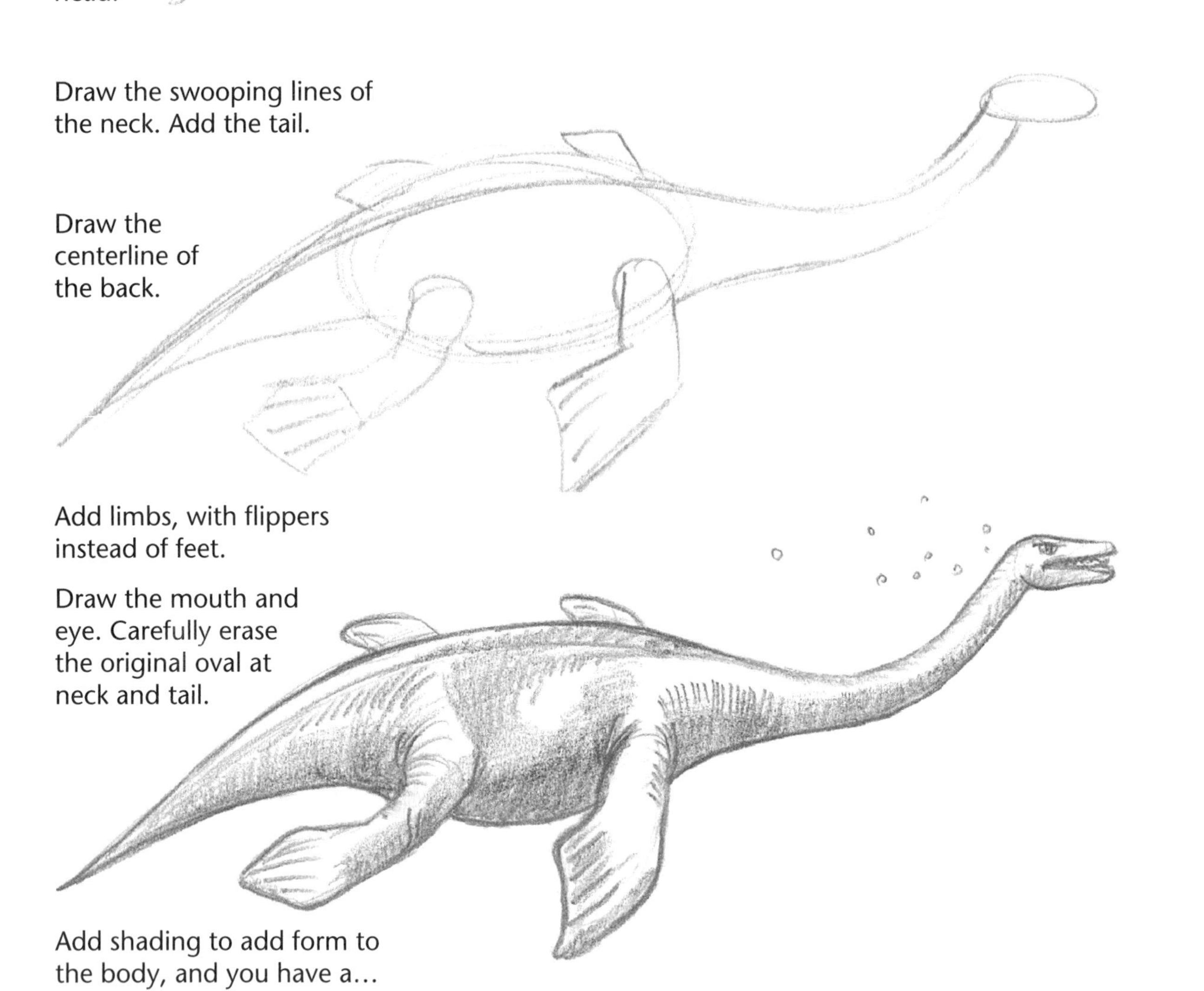

Add shading to add form to the body, and you have a...

pleasing Plesiosaurus!

Always start out ***lightly***!

Looking for Triangles

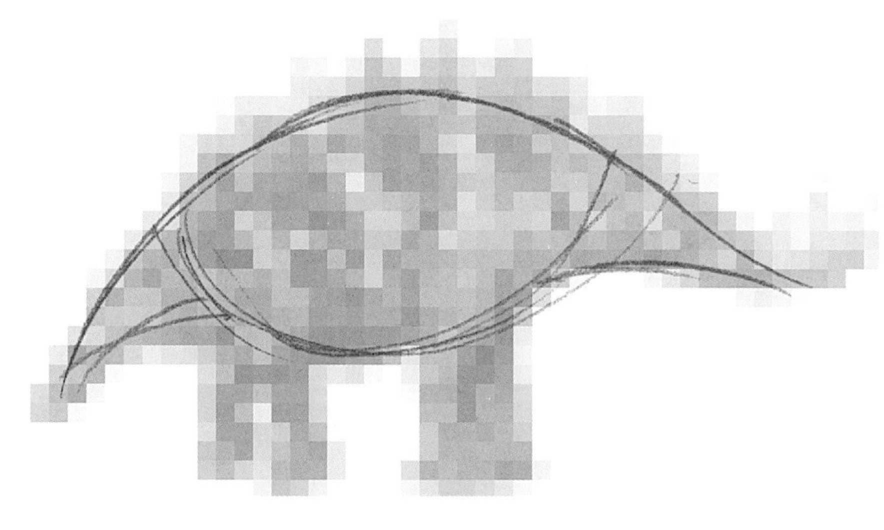

When artists and illustrators sit down to draw a realistic picture, they almost always have some sort of *reference material.* In other words, they look at something as they draw it.

But no people see things exactly alike.

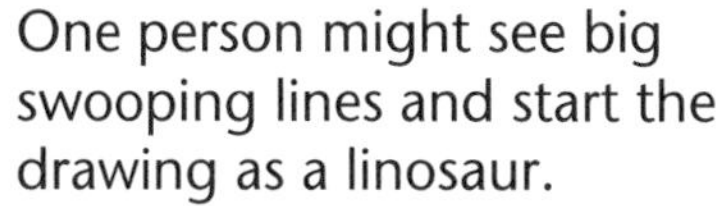

One person might see big swooping lines and start the drawing as a linosaur.

Another person might start with an oval for the body, making an ovalsaur.

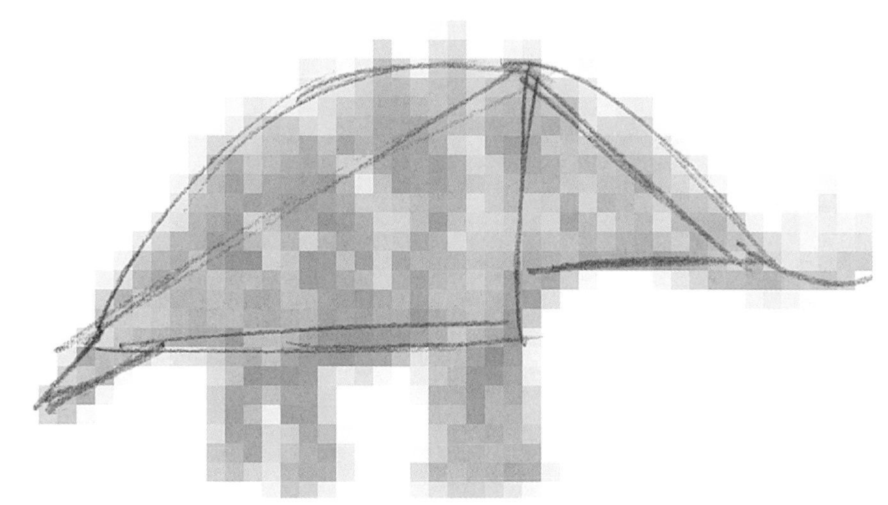

And a third person might see triangles, and use them to begin the drawing.

Triangles are everywhere. When you look at your subject, look for curving lines and look for ovals…but also look for triangles.

There are no rules to this type of drawing. Just keep looking until you find something – whether a line, an oval, or a triangle – that helps you get your drawing started. As with the other drawing techniques, you need to start out very lightly! Let's do a quick sketch to see how it works.

Draw a *right triangle.*

Add another right triangle for the tail. Draw a curve to round out the back. Add a round shape for the head.

Add the most obvious triangles of all – the plates on its back.

Draw triangles for feet, making them look very firmly planted on the ground. Use open triangles to connect with the knees, and you have the beginning of some solid-looking legs!

Can you figure out what to do next? Keep going!

Always start out ***lightly***!

Tyrannosaurus

TIE-RAN-O-SAW-RUS

"Tyrant lizard." Cretaceous; western North America, China. Ate meat. Lots of it. 39 ft (12 m) long; 18.5 ft (5.6 m) tall; weighed 7 tons—as much as an African elephant. Skull measured 4 ft (1.2 m). Saw-edged teeth could be 7 in (18 cm) long.

A right triangle has one angle that is square

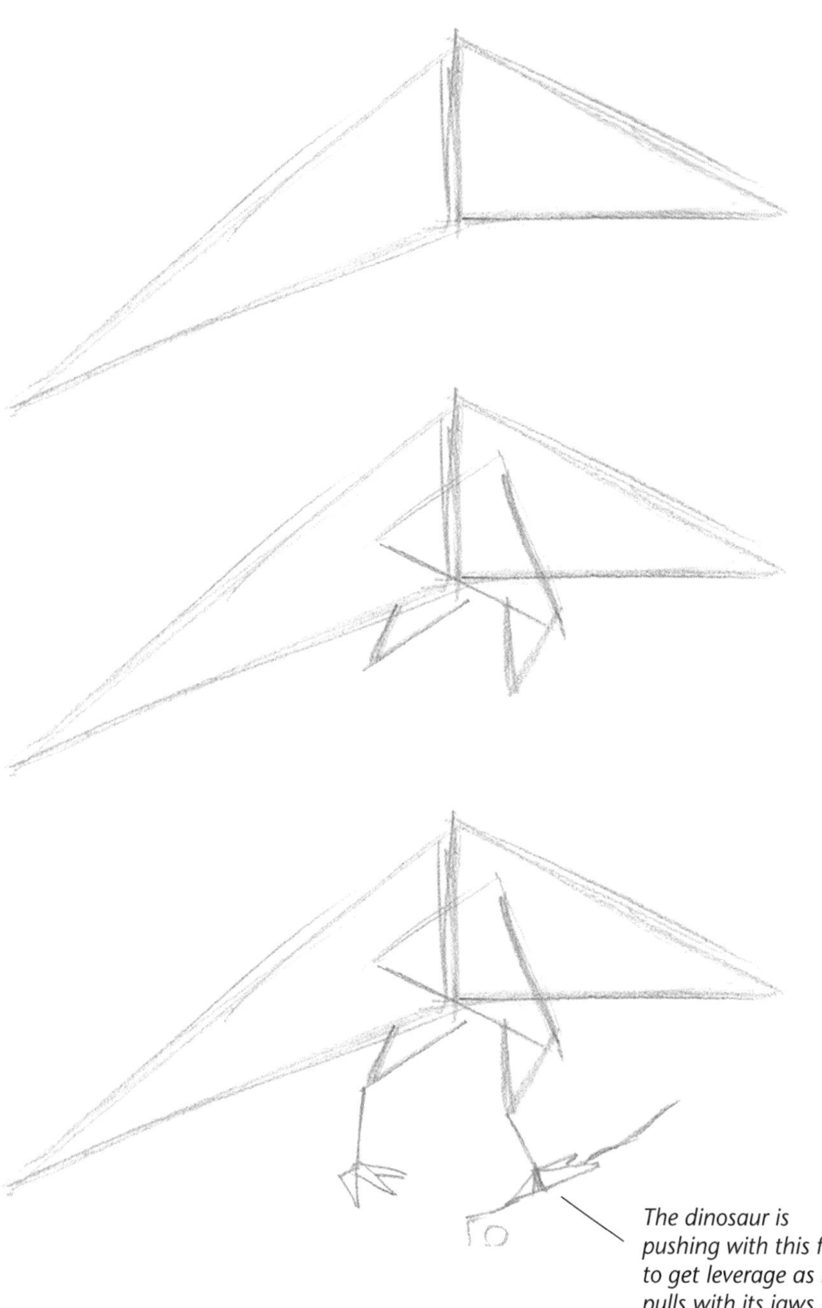

Start by drawing (very lightly!) a *right* triangle.

Draw another long triangle connecting to it and pointing downward.

Using more triangles, make the shape of the thigh and calf of the dinosaur. Add part of a triangle for the other leg. Notice how the triangles look like legs already!

Make single lines for the bottom part of the leg, and small triangles for the feet. Draw one foot at an angle and slightly higher.

The dinosaur is pushing with this foot to get leverage as it pulls with its jaws.

Add two triangles for the head. You now have a pattern of triangles that looks like Tyrannosaurus!

Looking at the finished example, round the triangles by making outlines of the tail, back, belly, legs, and head.

Add the arms.

If you drew your triangles very lightly, you can carefully use your eraser and make them disappear before finishing your drawing. If not, you may want to start over–making the triangles *very* light this time!

Add details to your finished drawing. Use your imagination!

- While your pencil is sharp, go over fine details and make lines cleaner. As it gets duller, add shading.
- Turn your drawing as you draw to avoid smudging it with your hand.
- Finally, clean up any smudges with your eraser.

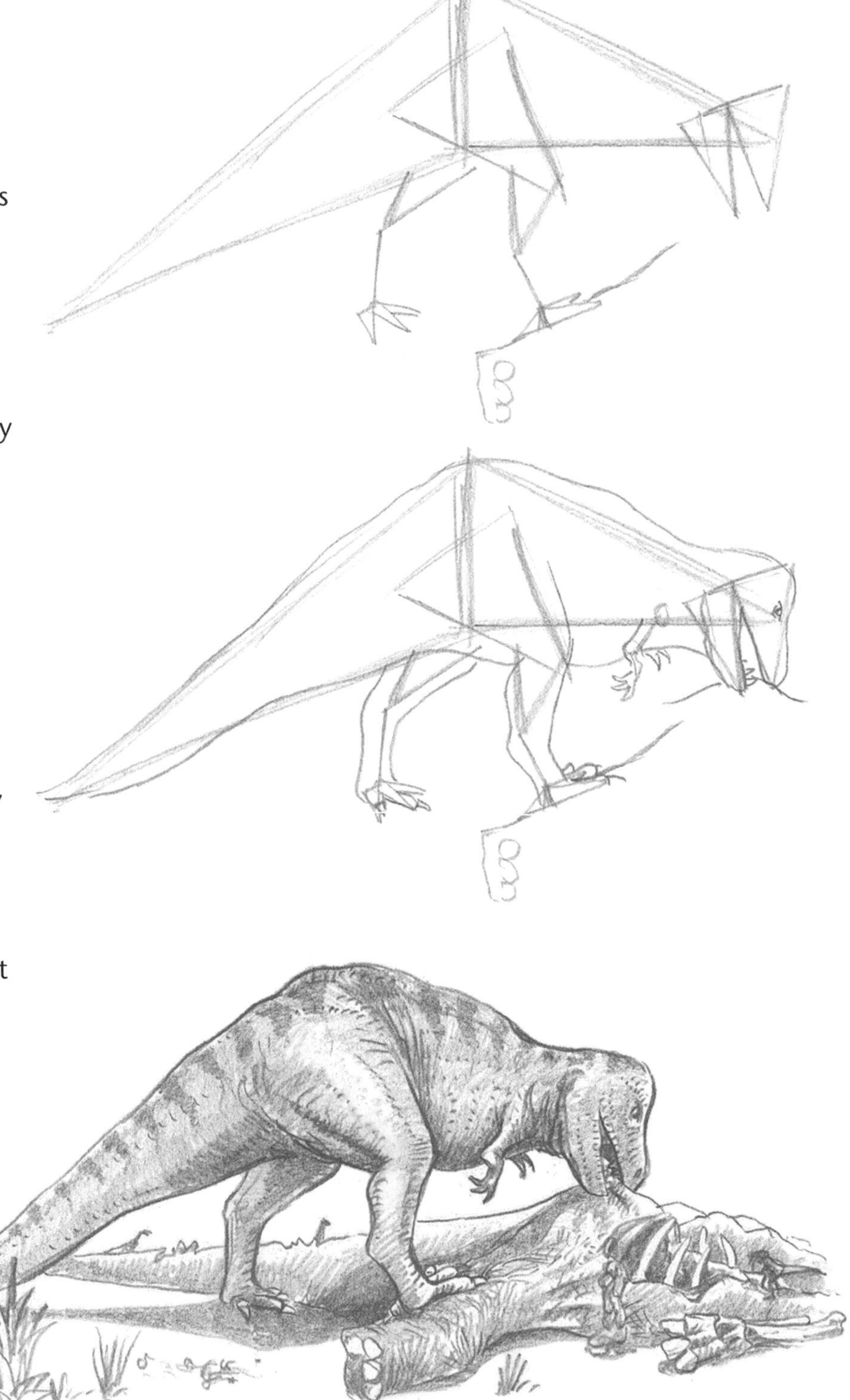

Always start out ***lightly***!

Velociraptor

VEL-OS-I-RAP-TOR

"Swift plunderer." Late Cretaceous; Mongolia, China, and Khazakhstan. 6 ft (1.8 m) long. Probably hunted in packs, attacking with claws and teeth. In 1971 a specimen was found that had died while attacking a Protoceratops.

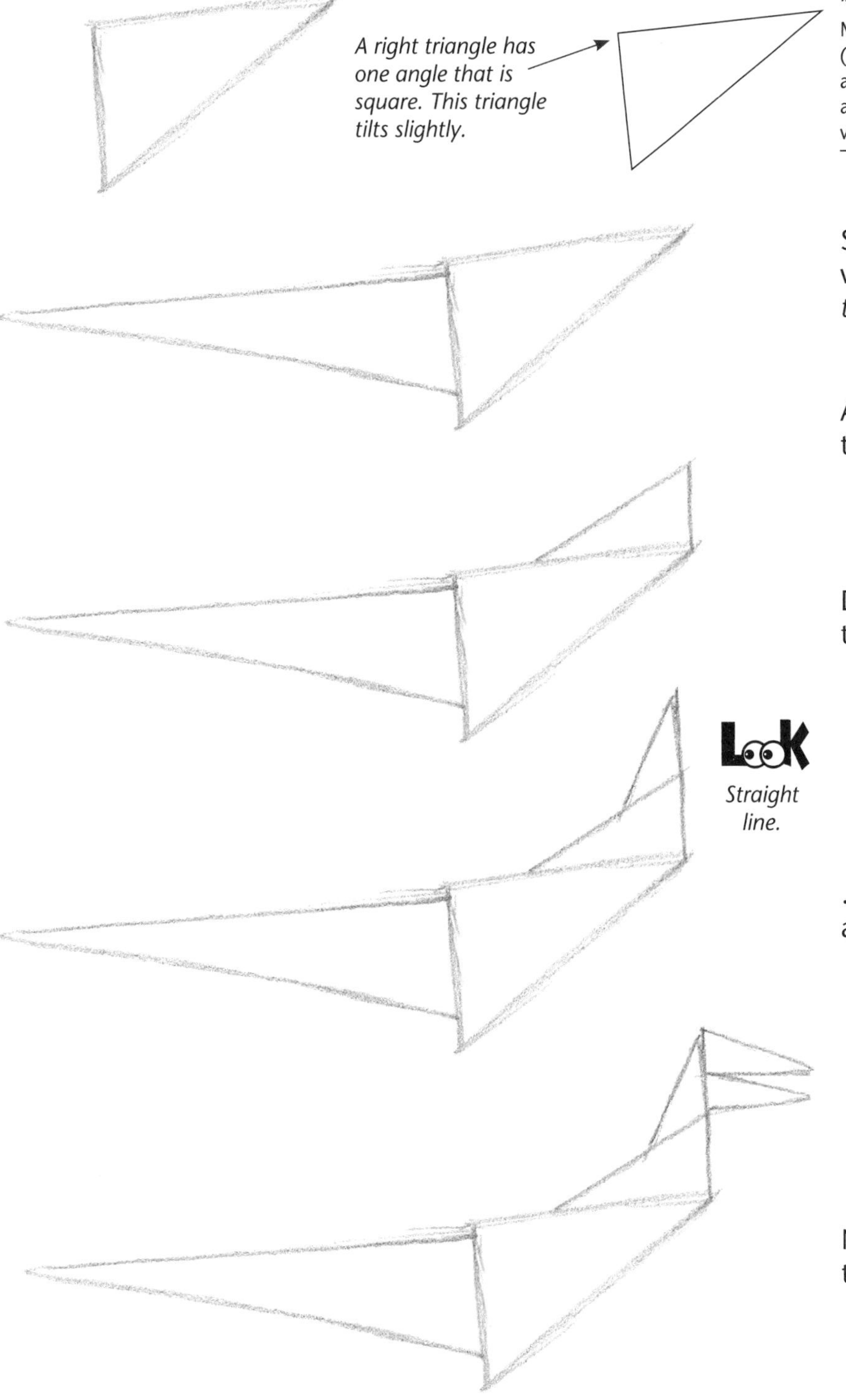

Start your raptor drawing with a slightly tilted *right triangle.*

Add a second, much longer triangle for the tail.

Draw a third triangle above the first triangle…

…and yet another triangle above it!

Now make two triangles for the jaws.

Origamisaurus?

Draw a big and a small triangle for the leg. Add a line for the lower leg, and toes.

Erase lines that you no longer need.

Add two arms, and the other leg, using rods and joints. Enhance the outline of the dinosaur by making the belly, neck and jaws bigger.

- Finish your drawing by adding texture, shading, and background.
- Look at your drawing in a mirror (or through the back of the paper) to spot areas you can improve.
- While your pencil is sharp, go over fine details and make lines cleaner. As it gets duller, add shading.

- Turn your drawing as you draw to avoid smudging it with your hand. Clean up any smudges with your eraser.

Always start out ***lightly***!

Pteranodon

TER-AN-O-DON

"Winged toothless." Late Cretaceous; Wyoming, USA. Wing span of 23 ft (7 m); greater than any known bird. Probably only weighed about 37 lbs (17 kg). Long, toothless jaw was counterbalanced by bony crest at top of head. Probably scooped fish out of the ocean, as pelicans do today – and probably had a pelican-like pouch as well.

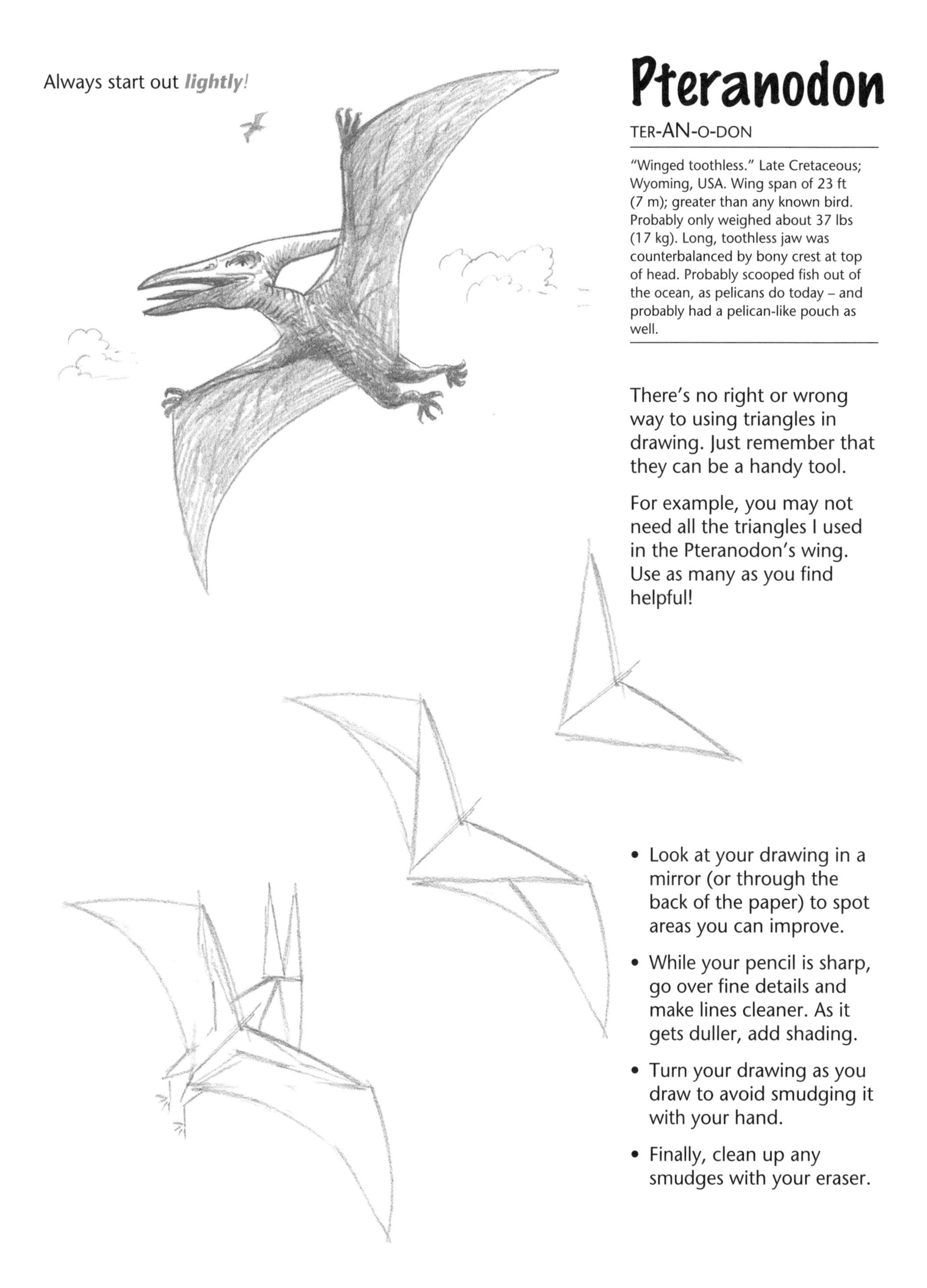

There's no right or wrong way to using triangles in drawing. Just remember that they can be a handy tool.

For example, you may not need all the triangles I used in the Pteranodon's wing. Use as many as you find helpful!

- Look at your drawing in a mirror (or through the back of the paper) to spot areas you can improve.
- While your pencil is sharp, go over fine details and make lines cleaner. As it gets duller, add shading.
- Turn your drawing as you draw to avoid smudging it with your hand.
- Finally, clean up any smudges with your eraser.

Basic forms

To draw solidsaurs, you'll find three forms most useful: cylinders, cones, and rounded forms based on ovals.

Shading makes your solid form look solid.

But for shading to work,it needs to follow the *contours* of the form. The middle drawing of each form shows *contour lines.* When you add shading, make the lines of the shading follow these lines.

Combined, the forms can make bodies, legs, and more....

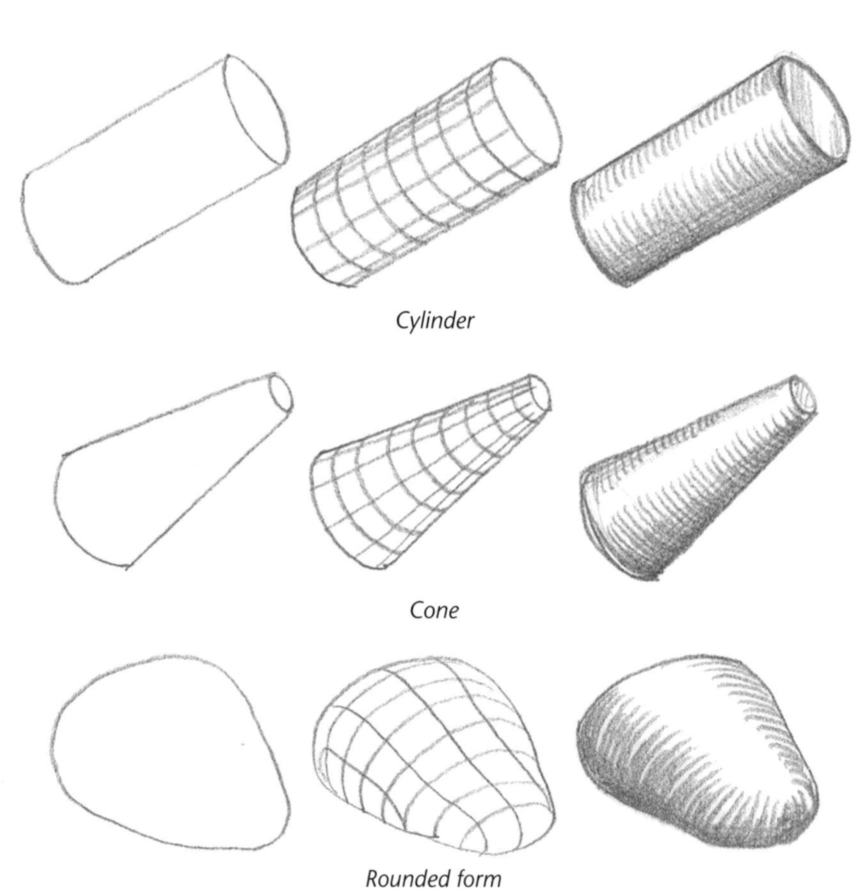

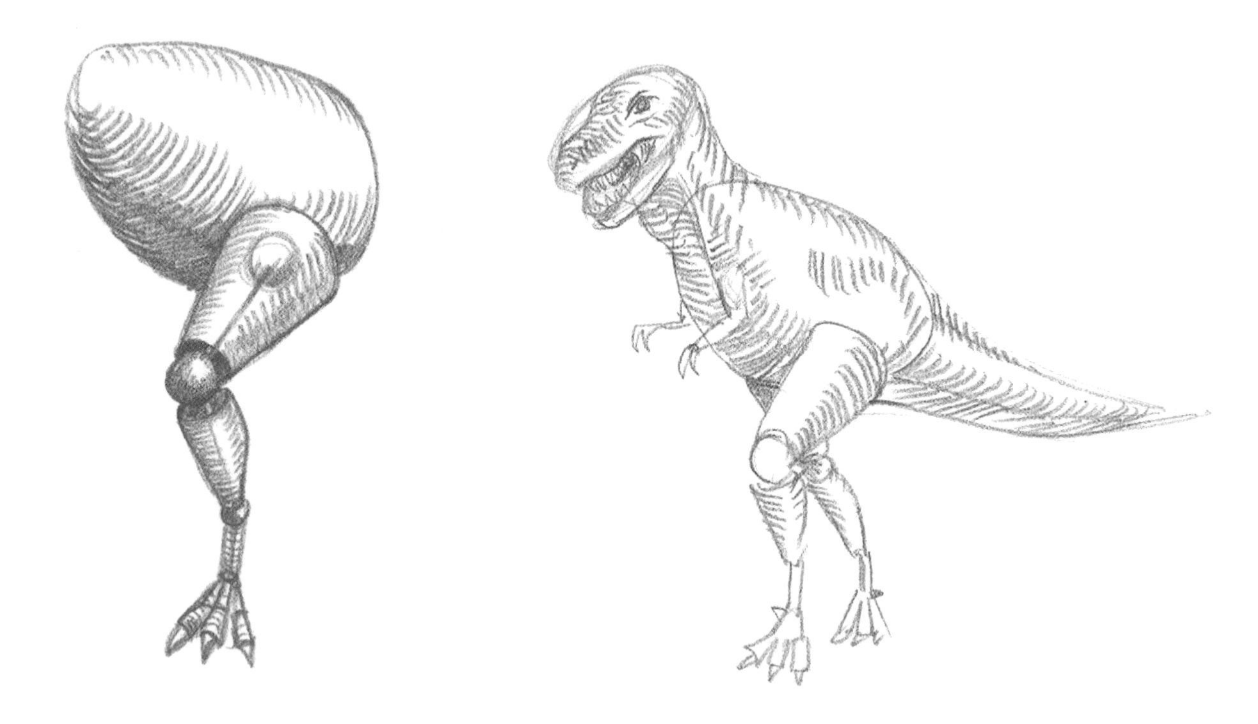

Always start out ***lightly***!

Using solid forms, you can choose whether to do serious, realistic drawings or make funny drawings and cartoon characters. In any case, understanding forms and contour lines will help make your drawings look more three-dimensional.

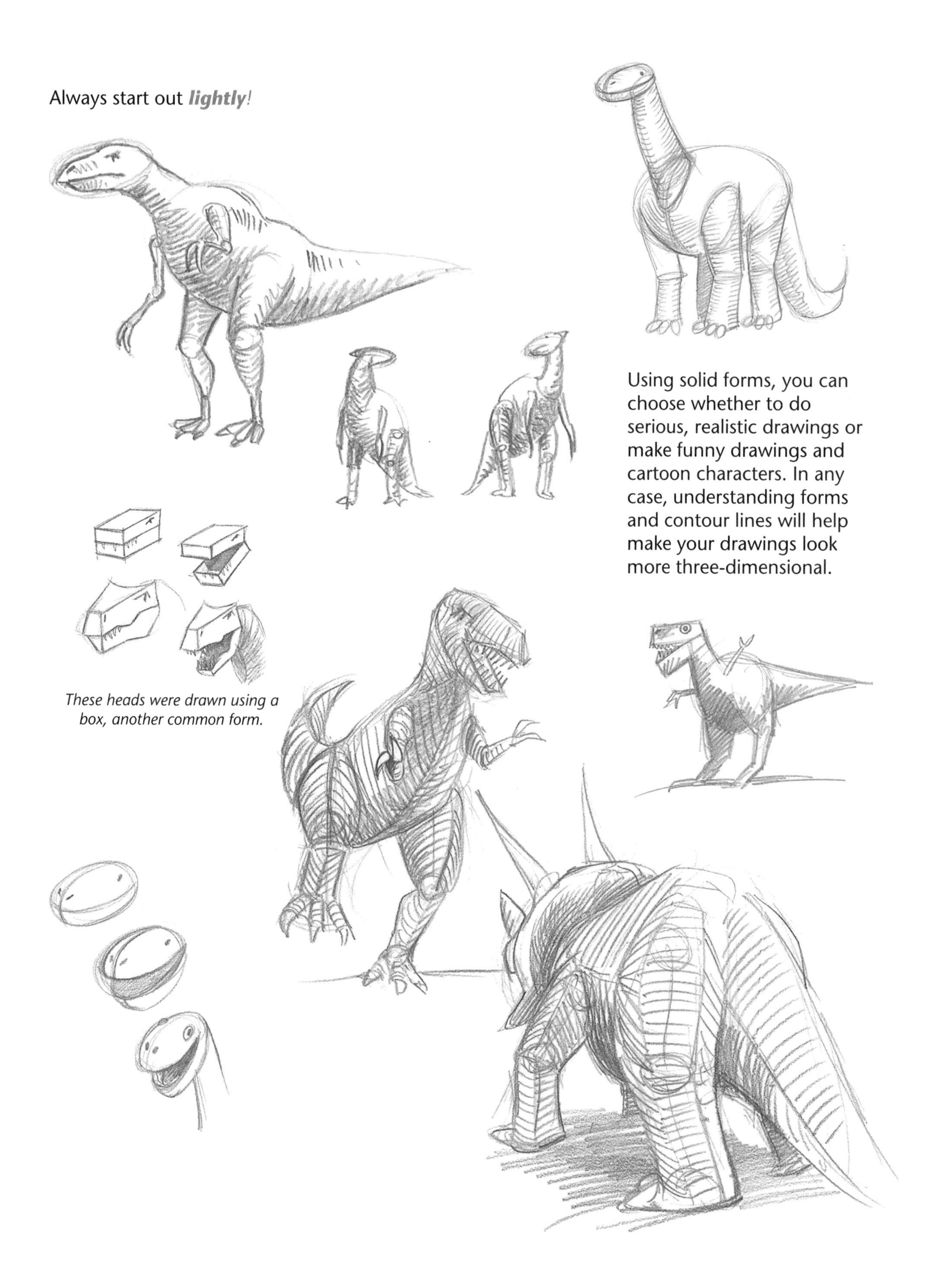

These heads were drawn using a box, another common form.

Scelidosaurus

SKEL-IDE-OH-SOR-US

"Limb lizard." Early Jurassic; southern England, Tibet. 13 ft (4 m) long. Probably a slow-moving dinosaur, it had very sturdy legs and was armored with bony knobs on its back. It's one of the few dinosaurs where fossils show an impression of the skin!

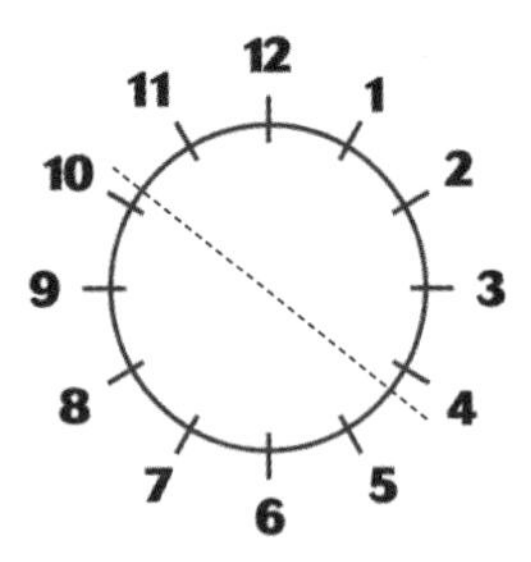

Use the clock face to compare angles of lines and ovals.

Draw a flat, tilted oval with contour lines showing the form.

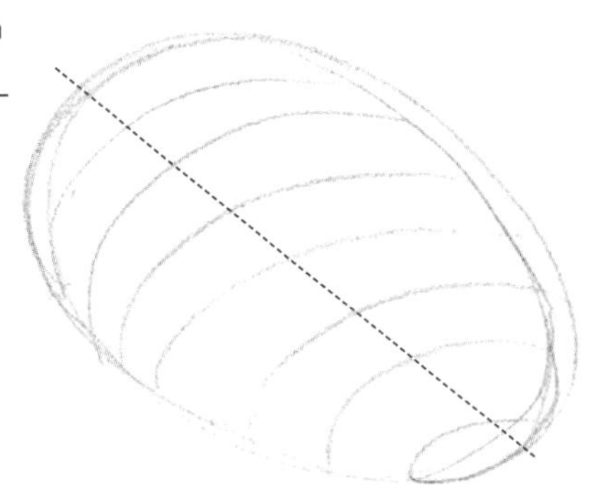

Add the neck and head. Use contour lines wrapping around the neck to create *foreshortening* (making it look like it's coming toward you). Add other lines where the rows of bumps will be on the back.

Using cylinders, draw the front leg.

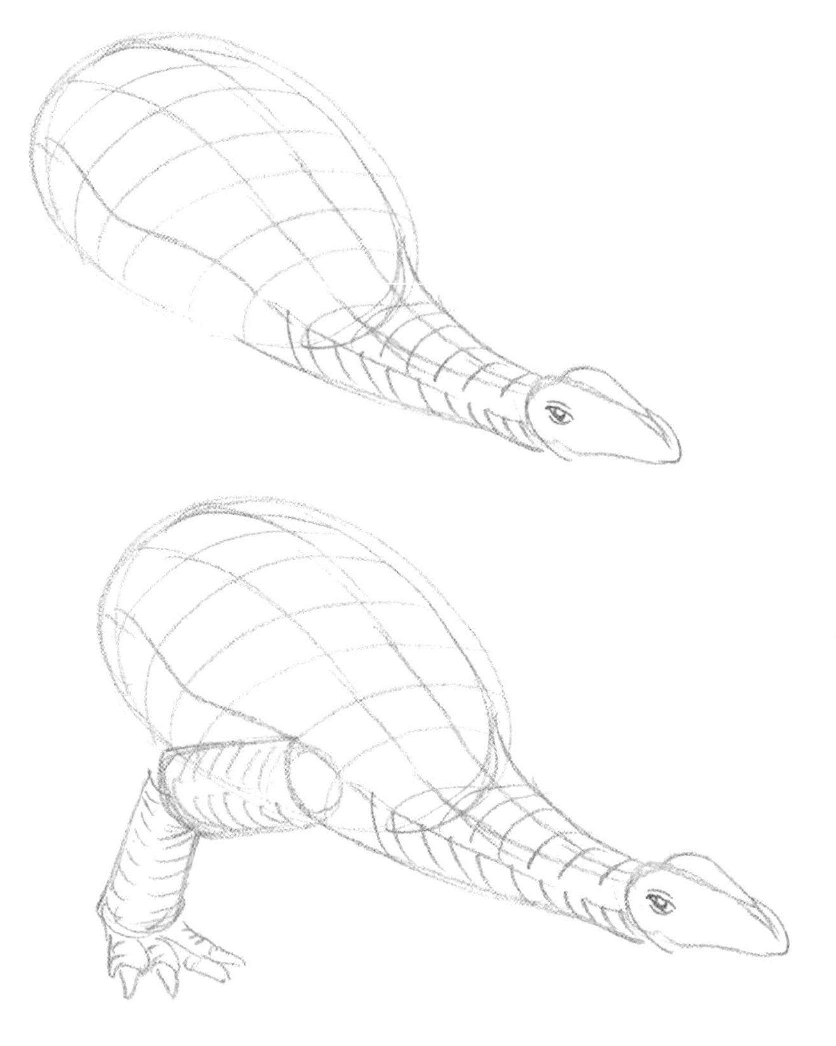

Always start out ***lightly***!

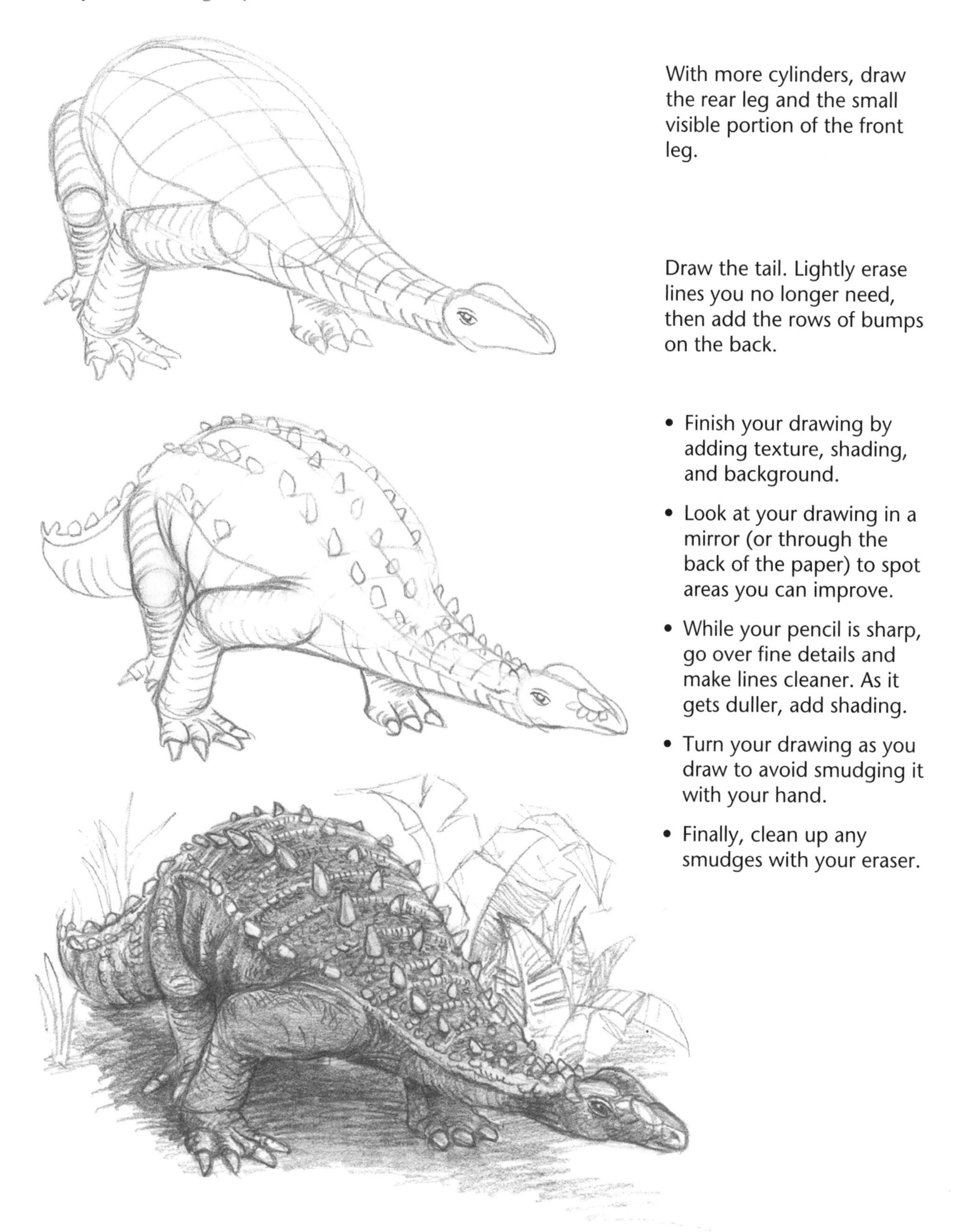

With more cylinders, draw the rear leg and the small visible portion of the front leg.

Draw the tail. Lightly erase lines you no longer need, then add the rows of bumps on the back.

- Finish your drawing by adding texture, shading, and background.
- Look at your drawing in a mirror (or through the back of the paper) to spot areas you can improve.
- While your pencil is sharp, go over fine details and make lines cleaner. As it gets duller, add shading.
- Turn your drawing as you draw to avoid smudging it with your hand.
- Finally, clean up any smudges with your eraser.

Finishing Touches

Before you add shading or texture, carefully remove lines that you don't want in the finished drawing.

It's OK if you erase some of the "good" lines. You'll go over them again to "sharpen" them.

Some paper erases well. Some paper doesn't. Don't be discouraged if erasing messes up your drawing, but do try to find a good "erasing" paper. Draw more lightly next time so you don't have as much to erase!

Erase lines you don't need in the final drawing: rods and joints, and where parts overlap.

A kneadable eraser starts out square, but you bend and twist it so you can erase small areas...a great help if you can find one.

Next, build tones (light and dark) by shading with a dull pencil. Don't just scribble with your pencil in every direction: follow the *contours* of the form.

A blending stump looks like a pencil made of paper. Use it or a rolled-up wad of paper to smooth shaded areas

With a blending stump or small rolled-up wad of paper, you can smudge the shading to make it very smooth.

While your pencil is sharp, add details and texture. Go over lines, making them sharper and stronger.

Add patterns to the skin, making them follow the *contours* of the body whenever possible.

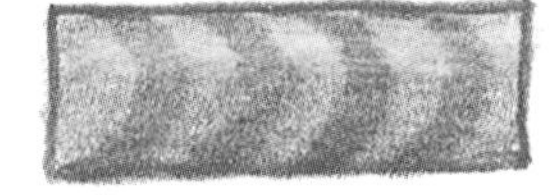

Follow contours when you shade. In the lower box, the stripes and shading show a curved contour, similar to the curve of an arm for leg. In contrast, the upper box looks flat.

Always start out ***lightly***!

Backgrounds

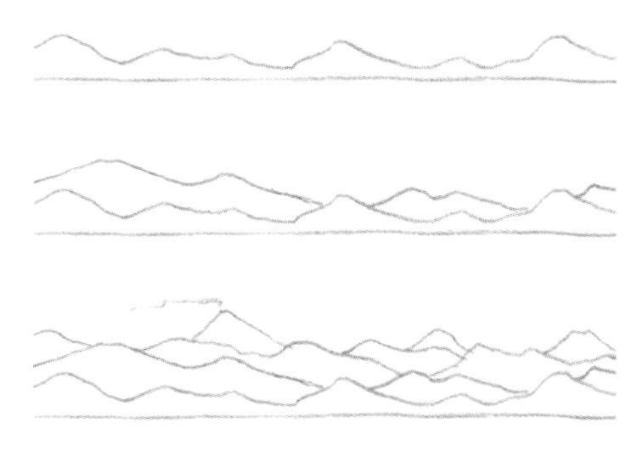

Adding background details can make your drawing much more fun to look at. For a quick background, draw a squiggly line of mountains. Add another, and another. Notice how the hills in front *overlap* those further away.

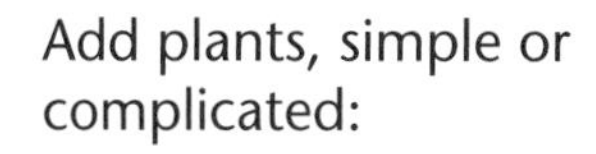

Add plants, simple or complicated:

A. *Simple pencil strokes suggest grass, and create a sense of scale for this small dinosaur.*

B. *Bushier plants make this dinosaur look larger.*

C. *Plants getting smaller create a sense of depth.*

D. *Broad, leafy plants as tall as the dinosaur add realism to the drawing.*

E. *Plants that hardly reach its knees make the dinosaur look bigger. But the volcano looks bigger still! Notice* overlapping.

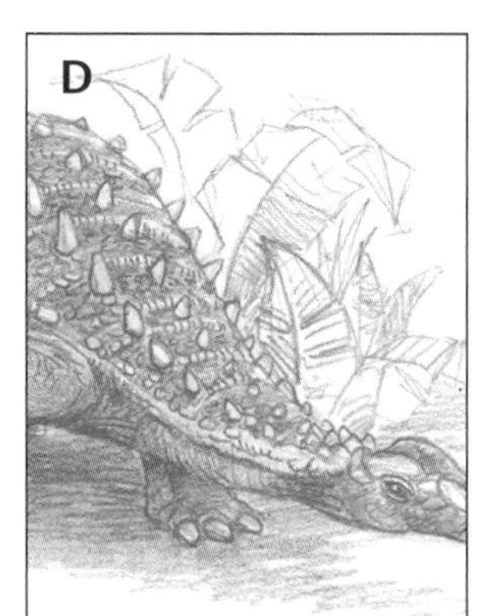

Use your imagination!

Some final thoughts

Remember

One of the great secrets of our world is that behind every success there's always plenty of practice. The people who do amazing feats of daring, skill, or ingenuity have been practicing, often for much longer than you'd imagine. They've probably failed more often than you can imagine, too, so don't waste time being discouraged. If your drawings don't look exactly the way you'd like them to (especially the first try), stop, look, and try again!

Save your drawings!

Whenever you do a drawing—or even a sketch—put your initials (or autograph!) and date on it. And save it. You don't have to save it until it turns yellow and crumbles to dust, but do keep your drawings, at least for several months. Sometimes, hiding in your portfolio, they will mysteriously improve! I've seen it happen often with my own drawings, especially the ones I *knew* were no good at all, but kept anyway.

If you don't have your own portfolio, here's a way to make one inexpensively (or you can buy one at an art supply store).

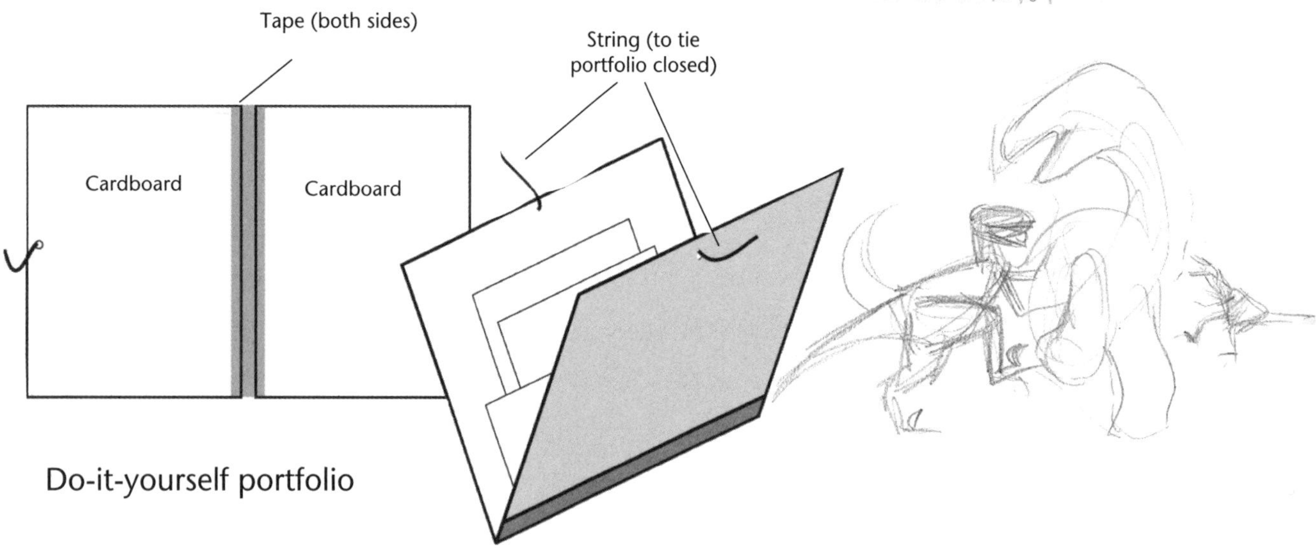

Do-it-yourself portfolio

Introduction

The rainforests, or jungles, of the world hold plenty of surprises for those who explore them. Let's do that with a pencil!

Draw Rainforest Animals shows you how to draw fascinating creatures, step by step. You may find some of them quite easy. Others present more challenges.

First

Read the instructions. LOOK carefully at the animal you wish to draw! See the shapes and pieces and how they fit together.

Then, lightly sketch the shapes in the right place.

When you sketch lightly, you can easily correct any mistakes before they ruin your drawing.

Second

Once you have the basic shapes and lines right,

- add more complicated parts,
- add shading,
- add detail, and
- erase lines you no longer need.

Third

Make your drawing jump off the page!

- add more shading,
- sharpen details,
- clean up with your eraser, and
- date and save your drawing in a portfolio.

Supplies

- **pencil** (2B or 3B will work well)
- **pencil sharpener**
- **eraser** (I like the kneadable type)
- **paper** (drawing paper erases best)
- **blending stump** if you want to do smooth shading (you can use your finger, too, but it's a bit messy)
- **place to draw** (good light, no distractions)
- **POSITIVE ATTITUDE!**

Always draw lightly at first!

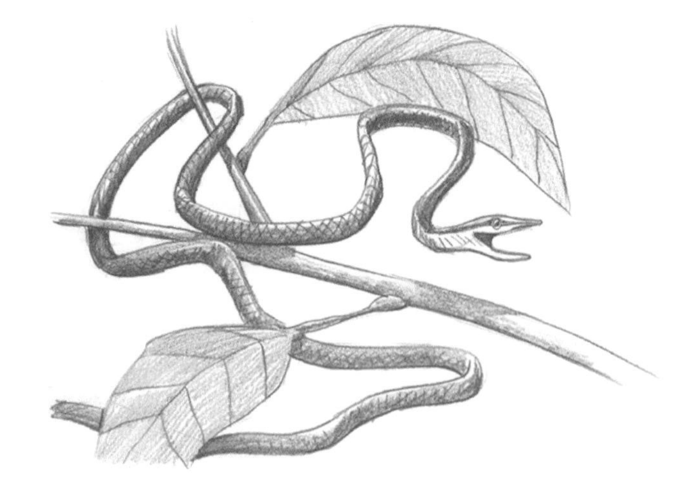

Just so you know...

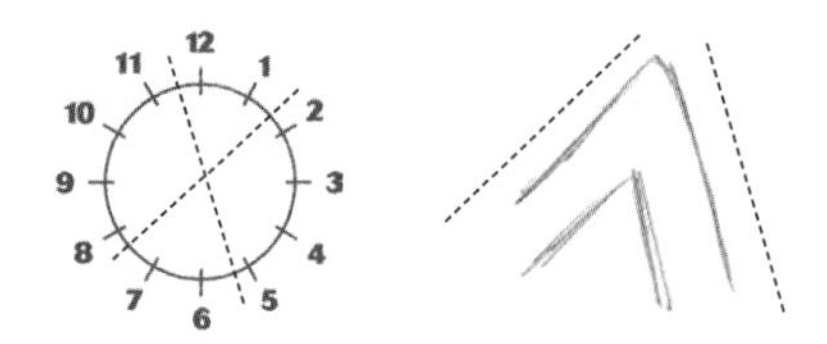

Clock faces appear from time to time. Use them as a reference to see the tilt of ovals, legs, and other angles in the drawing.

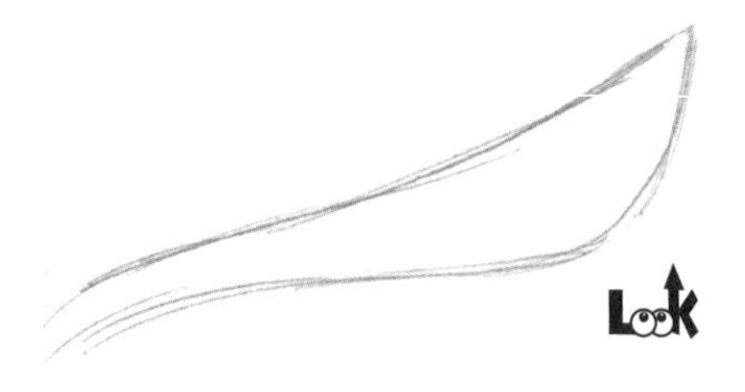

Look signs point out visual elements of the drawing – in this example, a curve turns almost vertical.

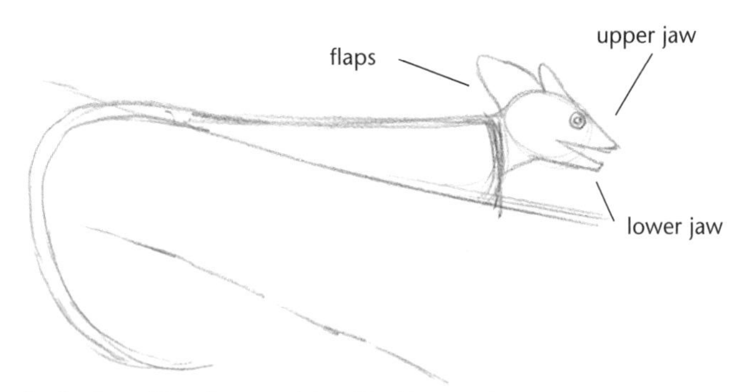

Labels will help you identify the parts of the animal mentioned in the text.

And now, let's

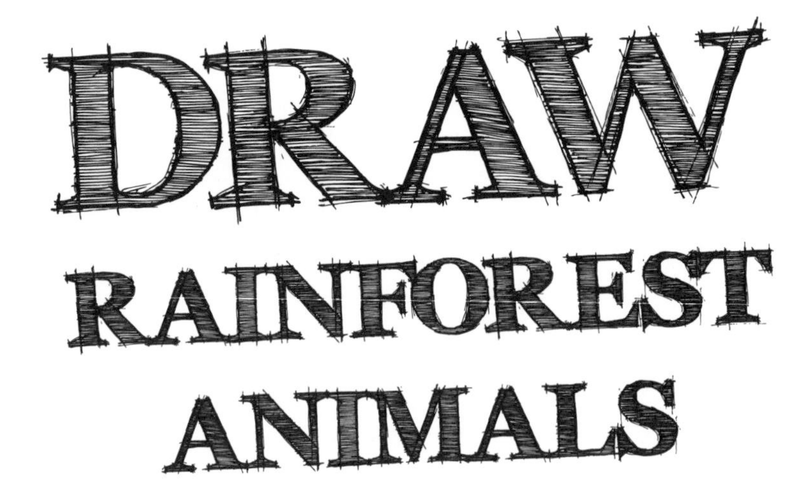

Chimpanzee

Pan troglodytes: Africa. Intelligent and expressive animals, chimpanzees spend most of their time on the ground, walking on all fours and occasionally standing erect. They are good climbers. They eat plant materials, plus insects and eggs – they even use tools like twigs to extract ants or termites!

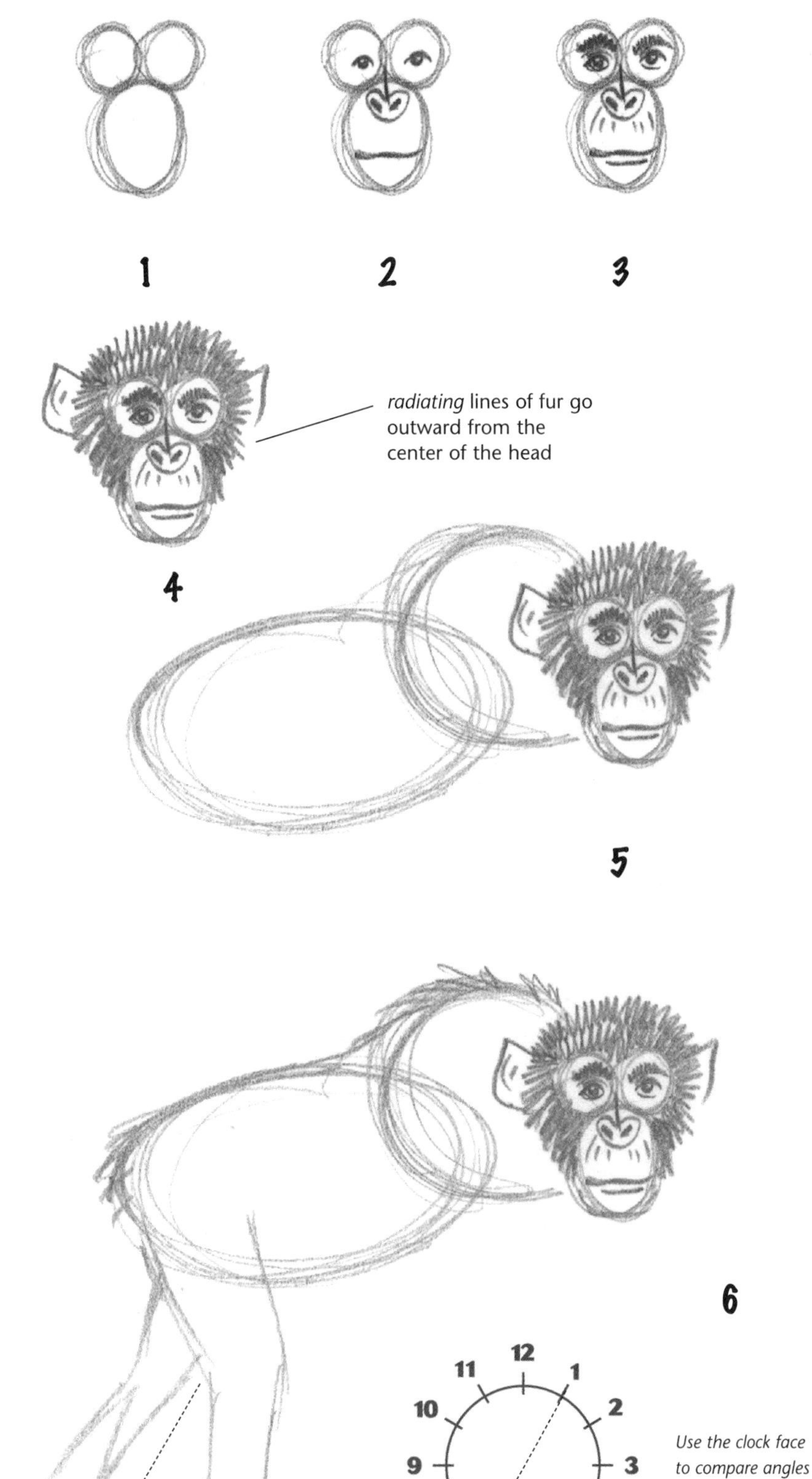

1. In this drawing, the face is important, so take time to get it right! Draw two light circles, with a tall oval touching the bottom of both.

2. Near the bottom of the lower oval, draw a line for the mouth. At the top of the oval, draw two nostrils with heart-shaped outline. Add curved lines for eyes.

3. Draw the lower lip. What other details do you see? Add them!

4. Add radiating lines to complete the head. Add ears.

5. Lightly draw two overlapping ovals for the body. Which is higher? Which is bigger? Which is flatter?

6. Look at the back legs. Which lines go straight up and down (vertical)? Where does each leg start? Which direction does it go? Now draw them – very lightly until you've got them just right.

7. Lightly draw the arms. (If it helps you, add a line for the ground.) Look carefully at the shape of the arms and hands.

   Make short pencil guide lines showing the direction of the fur.

8. Following those guide lines, add fur to the body. Look how the ovals disappear – no need to erase! Add a slight cast shadow on the ground.

Turn your drawing as you draw to avoid smudging it with your hand.

   Sit back, take a deep breath and really look at your drawing (perhaps in a mirror). Does it need darker fur? Sharper details on the face or hands? If so, do them now.

   Clean up any smudges with your eraser.

Psssst…if nobody's listening, make some chimp sounds….

Emerald Tree Boa

Boa caninus: South America
Size: 1.2 m (4 ft). Brilliant green snake with prehensile tail spends its life in trees, where it lies in wait for prey, often birds and bats. Fast, and a good swimmer.

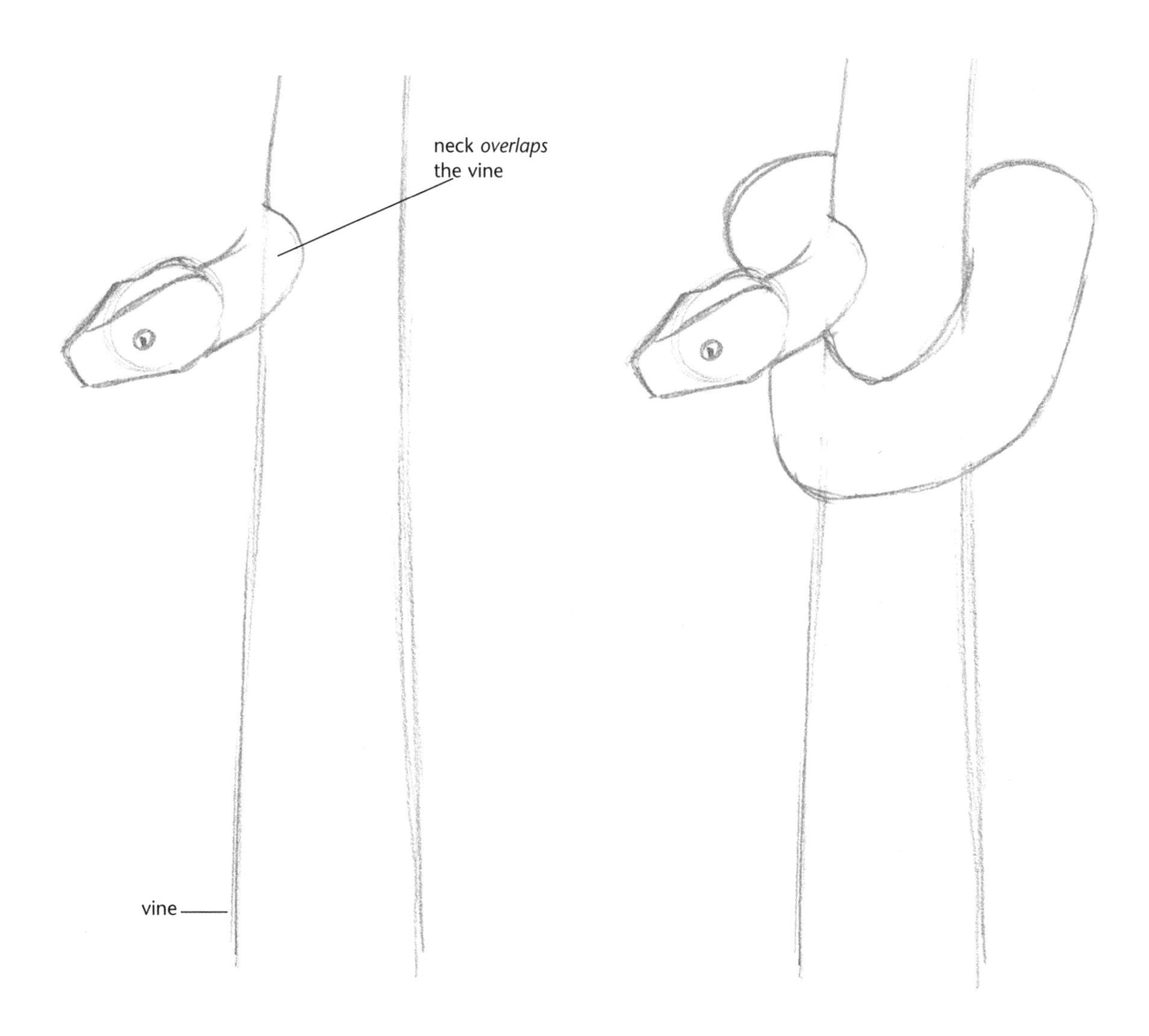

Be creative! Draw this snake in different positions. You don't have to follow my drawing exactly!

1. Start with two light *vertical* lines for the vine. Draw the head with eye, and the first section of the body, *overlapping* part of the vine.

   Make the front of the head blunt. Each eyebrow bulges slightly.

2. Add the next section of the body, forming a rough U shape.

Always draw lightly at first!

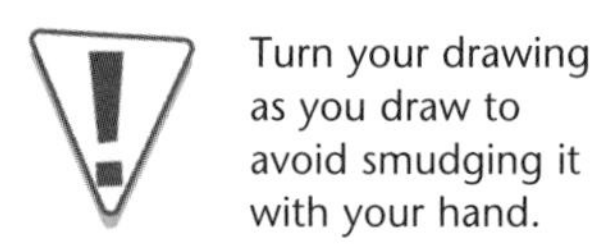

Turn your drawing as you draw to avoid smudging it with your hand.

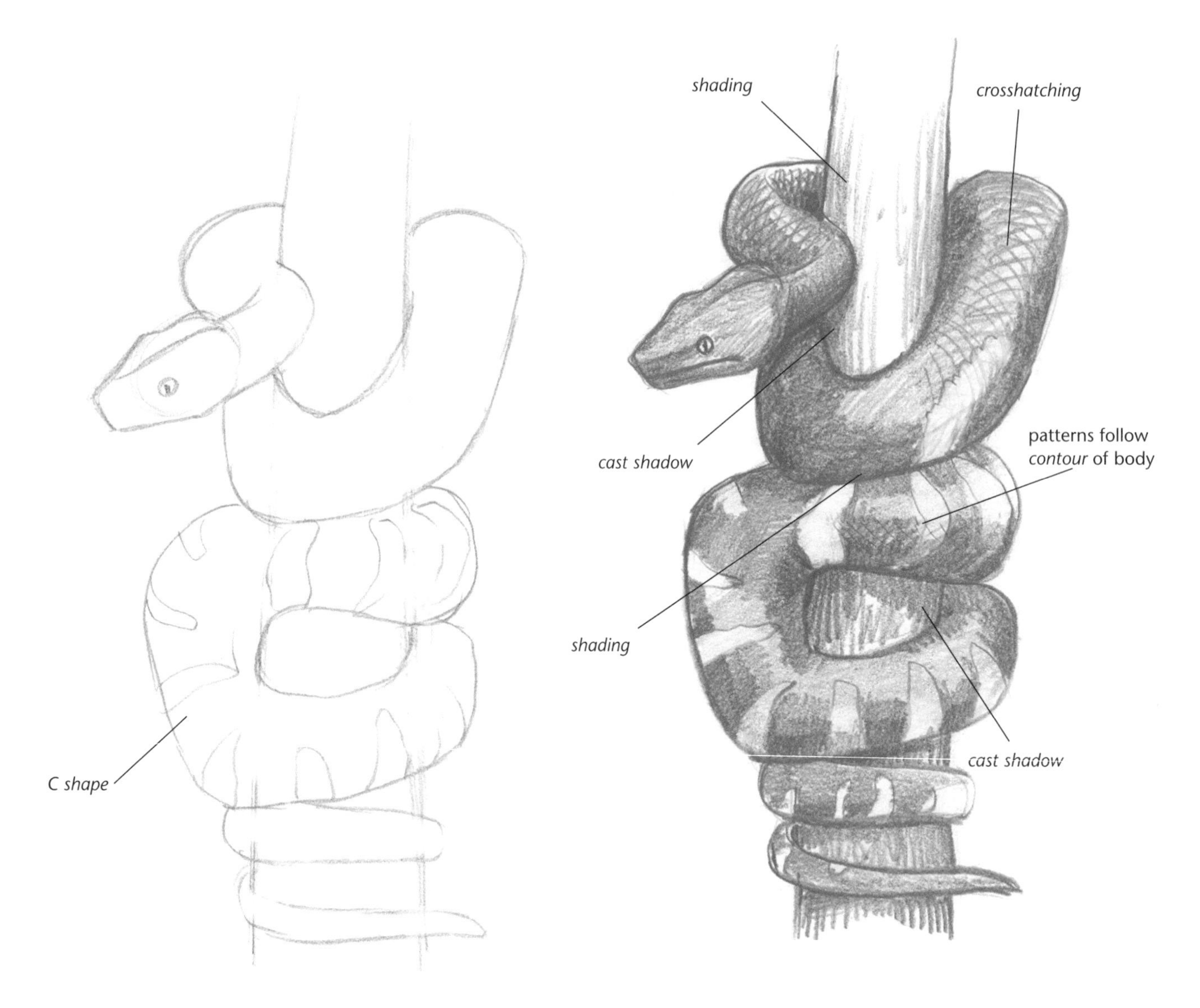

3. Below the U shape, make another section of the body, this time a fat C shape. Add a couple more sections, getting smaller and smaller....

   Notice that the snake doesn't wrap around the vine in one continuous spiral. The tail wraps all the way around, but the larger parts of the body reverse direction to form 'clamps' to hold to the vine.

4. Now try to make the snake and vine look round.

   Look carefully for:
   - the pattern of curving white spots,
   - crosshatching to suggest scales,
   - shading on the snake and the vine, and
   - cast shadows on the vine and snake.

   You're on your own! Keep shading until it looks like it's ready to jump off the page!

   Good looking boa!

Flying Squirrel

Anomalurus beecrofti (Beecroft's flying squirrel): West and central Africa. Size: 53-84 cm (20-33 inches) overall length. Lives in trees. Feeds mostly on berries, seeds and fruit. Glides up to 90 m (300 ft) from tree to tree.

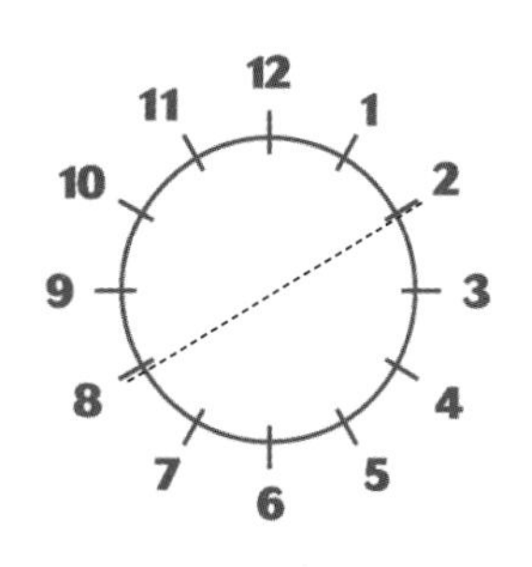

Use the clock face to compare angles of lines and ovals.

1. Draw a tilted oval, with two extended front legs. Make them bend slightly.

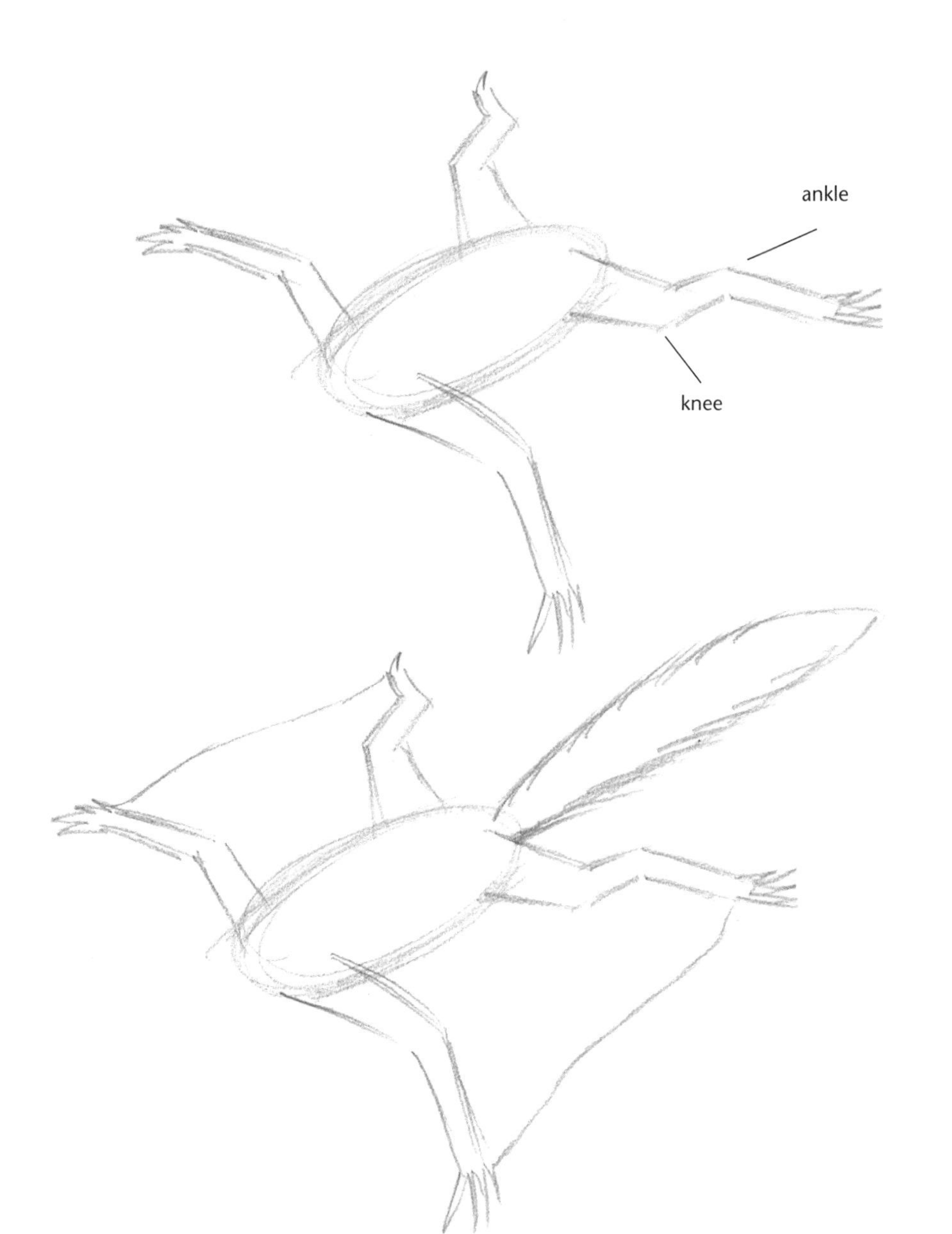

2. Add the rear legs, with two bends (knee and ankle).

3. Draw slightly curved lines to connect front and rear feet. Use short pencil strokes for the bushy tail.

Always draw lightly at first!

4. Draw an oval for the head, slightly pointed at the nose. Add the eye and ears.

5. Draw the fur, using short pencil strokes. Leave some areas white. Add detail to the eye. Draw whiskers. Sharpen details. Clean up any smudges with your eraser.

Idea: add some leaves behind the squirrel. Draw the branch the squirrel just launched from.

Frog 1 (Arrow Poison)

Dendrobates auratus: Central and South America. Size: 4 cm (1.5 inches). Bright red coloring warns predators that this frog is poisonous! Local tribesman know how to extract the poison, which they use on the tips of hunting arrows.

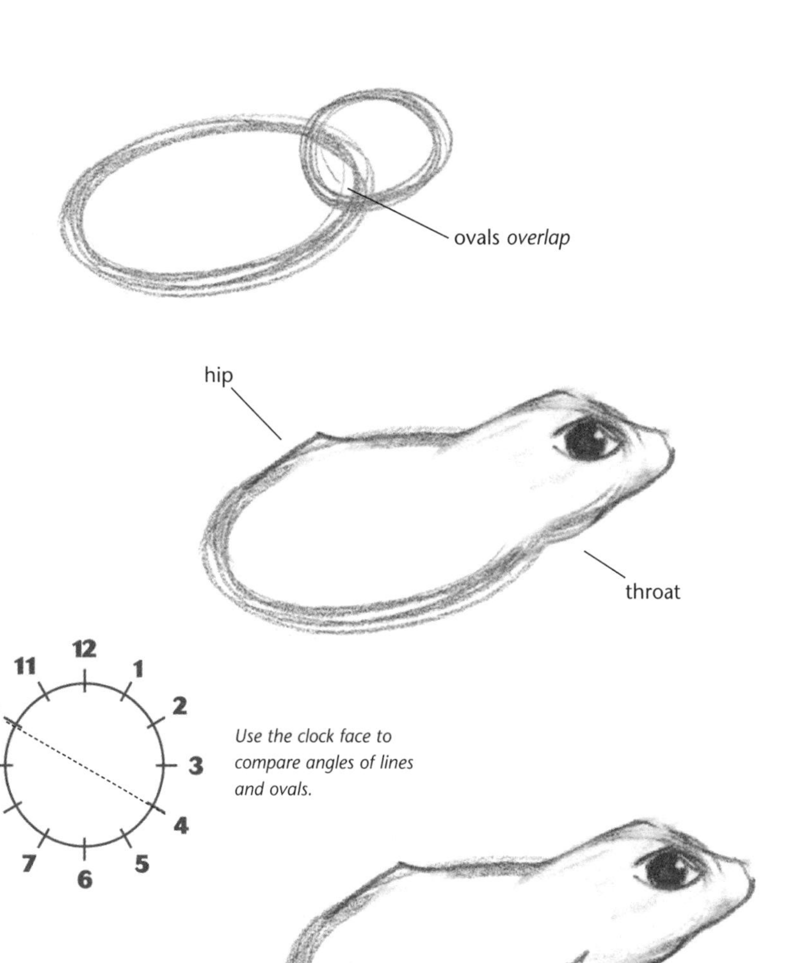

Use the clock face to compare angles of lines and ovals.

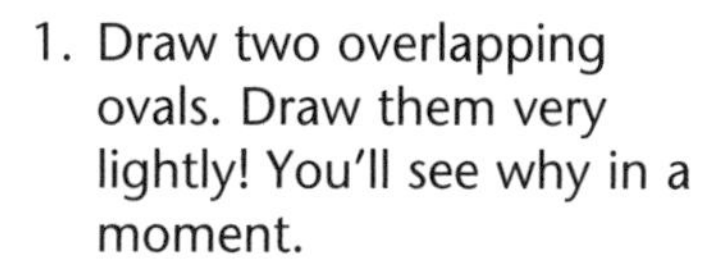

1. Draw two overlapping ovals. Draw them very lightly! You'll see why in a moment.

2. Add a bump for the hip, a bump at the top of the head, a bump for the nose, and one more for the throat. Erase the ovals where they overlap. Draw a circle for the eye – leave a small white spot when you darken it. Add the curving lines for the top and bottom of the eye.

3. Add the legs. Look where and how each leg attaches to the body, and the angles of each segment of the legs. Erase the oval where the leg overlaps it.

4. As your pencil gets dull, add shading. Leave part of the back very light to help make it look shiny. When you sharpen your pencil, go over details and outlines to make them sharper.

   Add the cast shadow under the frog. Clean up any smudges with your eraser.

   If you want to use color, make the frog bright orange with black spots.

cast shadow

Frog 2 (Flying)

Always draw lightly at first!

Rhacophorus nigropalmatus (Wallace's flying frog): Southeast Asia. This 10-cm (4-inch) long frog glides from tree to tree. The webs and skin flaps act like a parachute.

1. Draw a tall, narrow triangle for the body. Add two L-shaped arms to it.

2. Add bumps on the triangle for the nose and eyes. Draw four fingers to each arm. Connect the ends of the fingers to make the webs. Draw Z-shaped legs.

3. Add toes and webbing to the legs. Draw curves in the arms and legs.

4. Shade the dark, webbed parts of the feet. Add shading to the rest of the frog.

   Clean up any smudges with your eraser.

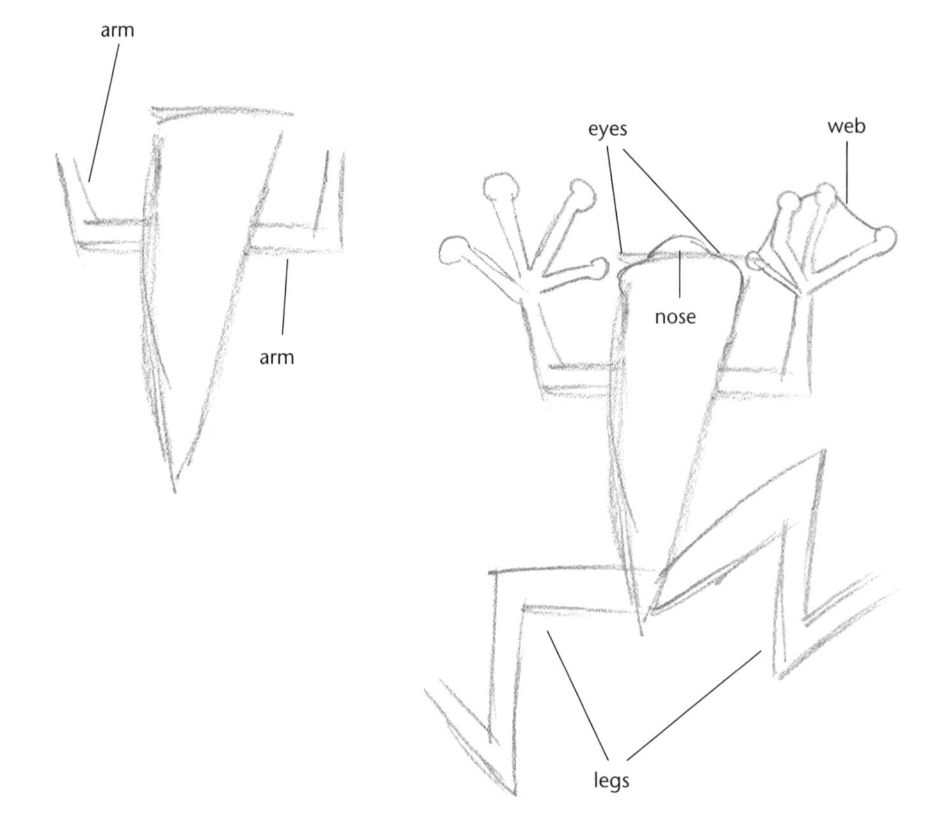

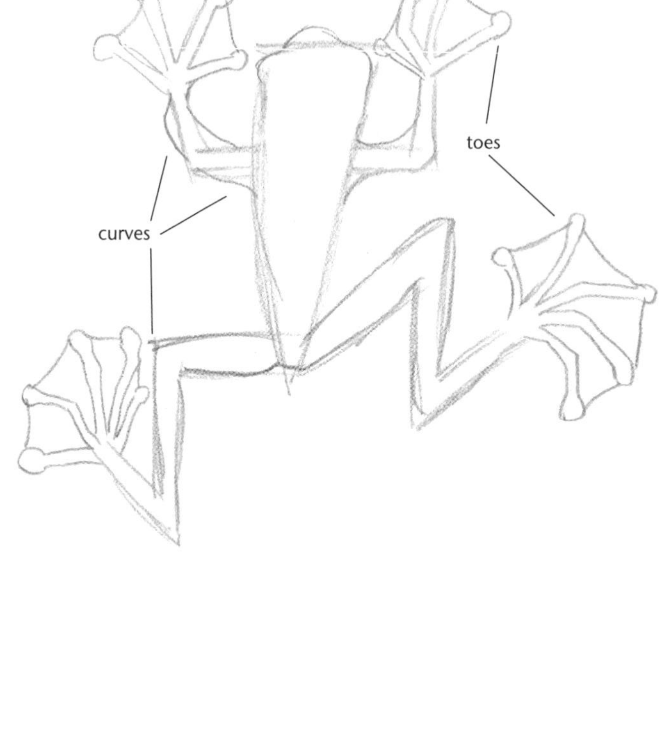

Idea: you're looking down on a frog gliding high above the ground. What would it see below it? Can you draw that?

Gorilla

Gorilla gorilla: Africa, in rain forests to fairly high elevations. Size: male height 1.7-1.8 m (5.5-6 ft); female height 1.4-1.5 m (4.5-5 ft). Largest of the primates, gorillas are gentle animals unless threatened. They eat mainly plants. They live in small groups. *Easy scientific name!*

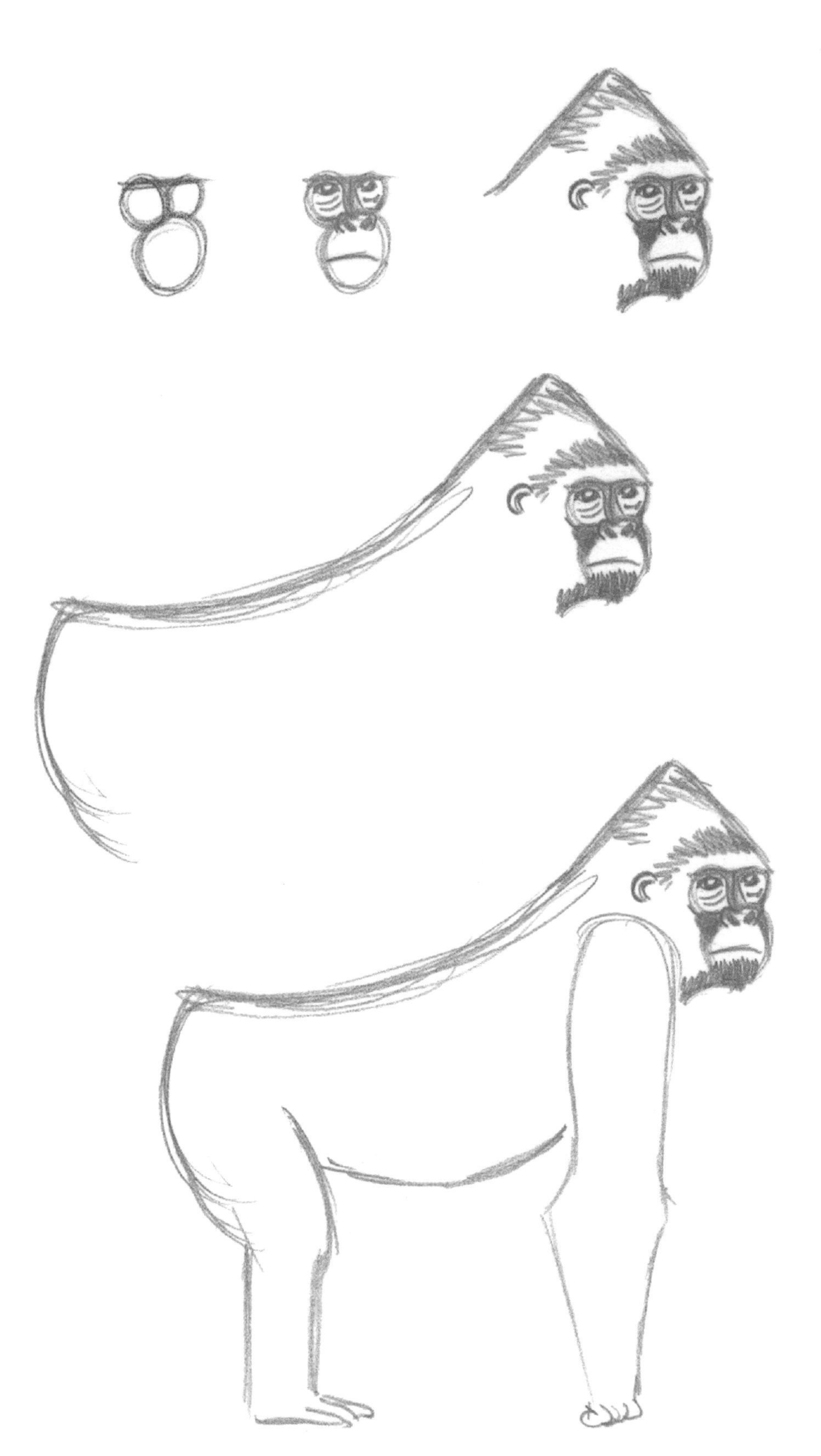

1. Draw two small circles on top of a larger oval. Make a line across them to help emphasize the strong brow of the gorilla.

2. Draw a line for the mouth. Add eyes, with lines under them. Draw slanting nostrils.

3. From the edge of the eyebrow, draw a line up to a point and back down – like a pyramid on the gorilla's head. This part of the head is almost as high as the face! Add the ear, and short pencil lines on the chin, face and forehead.

4. From the back of the head, make a long swooping line for the back, joined by another swooping line for the back of the leg.

5. Lightly draw the leg and arm, with toes and fingers. Notice the shape of the arm. Look how close the shoulder comes to the face.

Always draw lightly at first!

6. Add the other leg and arm. Before you add fur, make light *guide lines* to remind you which direction the shading needs to go.

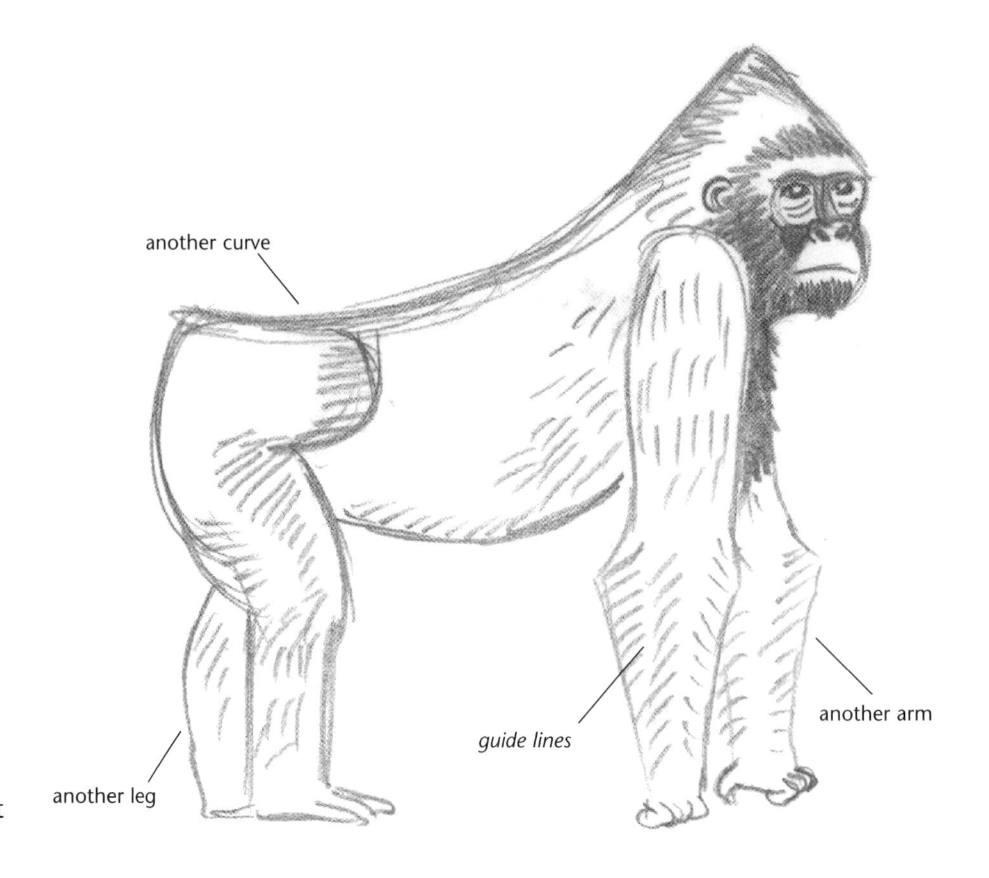

7. Cover the whole body with short pencil strokes. Be sure to follow the direction of your *guide lines*.

   Pay attention to areas that are lighter and darker. Go over lines that need to be darker or sharper, and refine details of the face if you need to.

   Add a cast shadow underneath.

Which areas are lightest?
Which areas are darkest?

Bright idea: if a gorilla charges you in the wild, *stand your ground.* If you run, you'll be in big trouble.

Iguana

Iguana iguana (common iguana): Central and South America. Size: 1-2 m (3.5-6.5 ft). Iguanas live in trees, but lay eggs in holes they dig in the ground. They feed on plants, but can defend themselves from other animals with sharp teeth and claws. They drop from trees into water to escape – they're great swimmers! *Easy scientific name!*

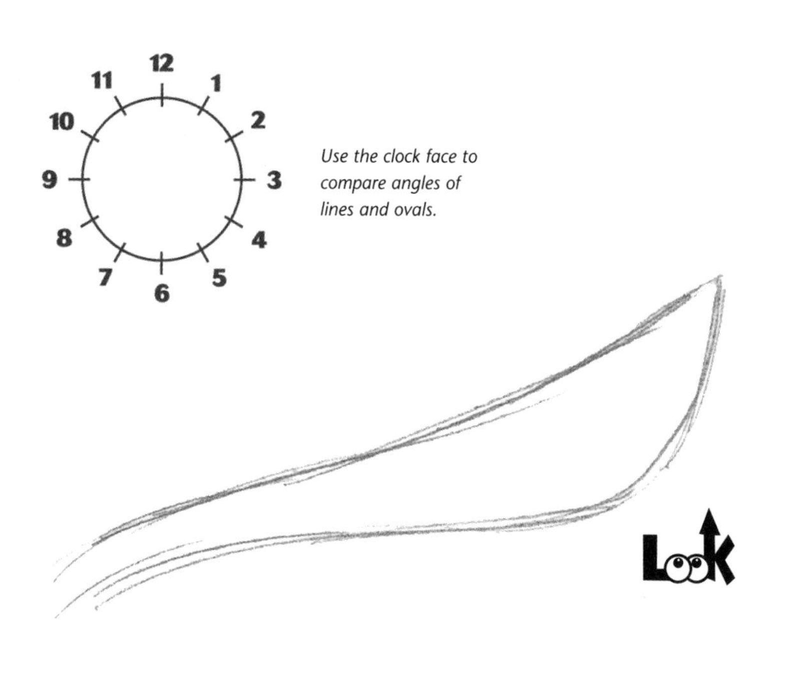

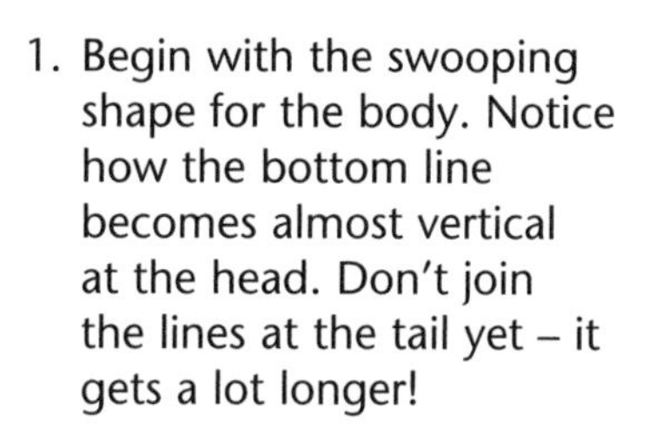

1. Begin with the swooping shape for the body. Notice how the bottom line becomes almost vertical at the head. Don't join the lines at the tail yet – it gets a lot longer!

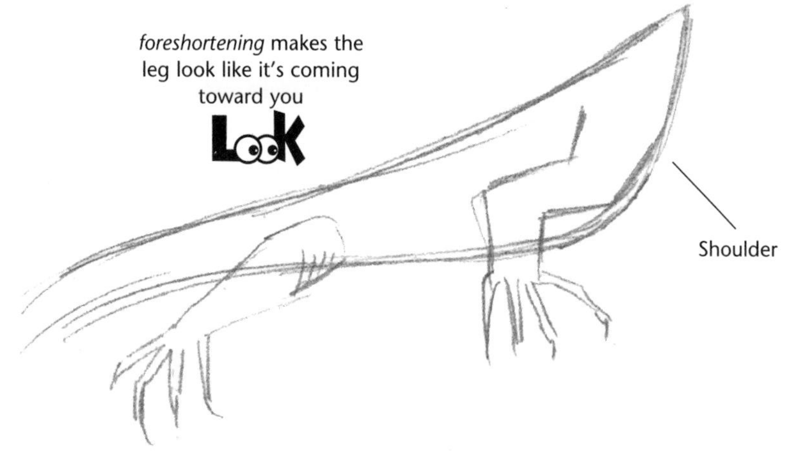

2. Look at the legs. The front leg starts at the shoulder, goes down, back, then down again. The back leg is foreshortened. This means that part of it (the part connecting to the body) comes straight toward you. Now draw the legs, and add toes and claws.

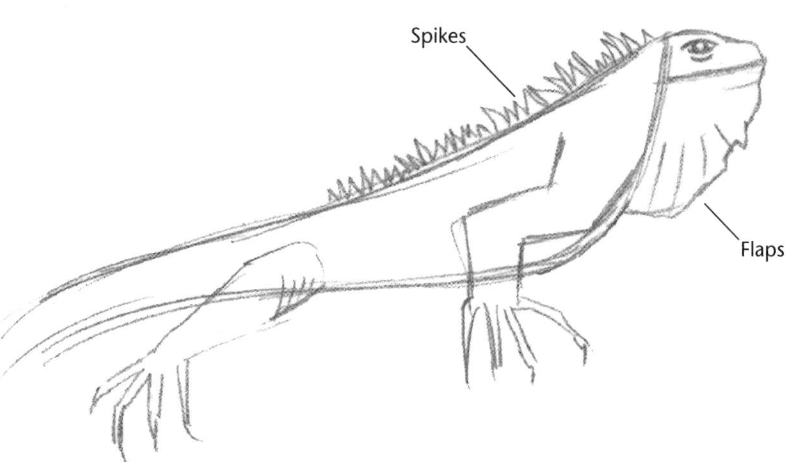

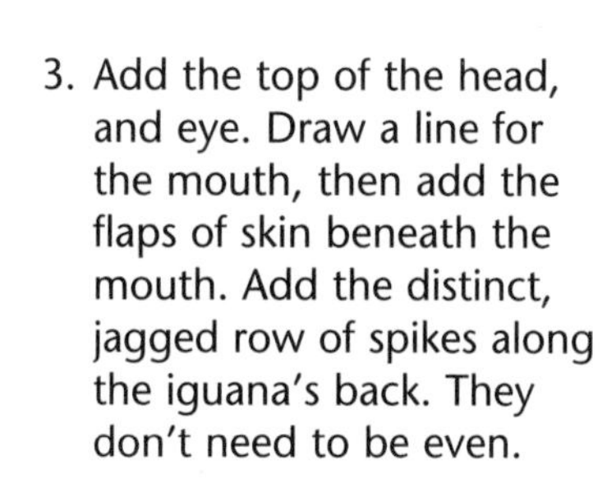

3. Add the top of the head, and eye. Draw a line for the mouth, then add the flaps of skin beneath the mouth. Add the distinct, jagged row of spikes along the iguana's back. They don't need to be even.

Always draw lightly at first!

4. Looking closely at my example (or at a photo, or better yet, a real iguana if you have one handy!), add the tail and details. Crosshatching suggests scales on the legs and head. Around the mouth add shapes you see in the example.

   Add a branch under the iguana. To make it more interesting, add a vine or two spiralling around it.

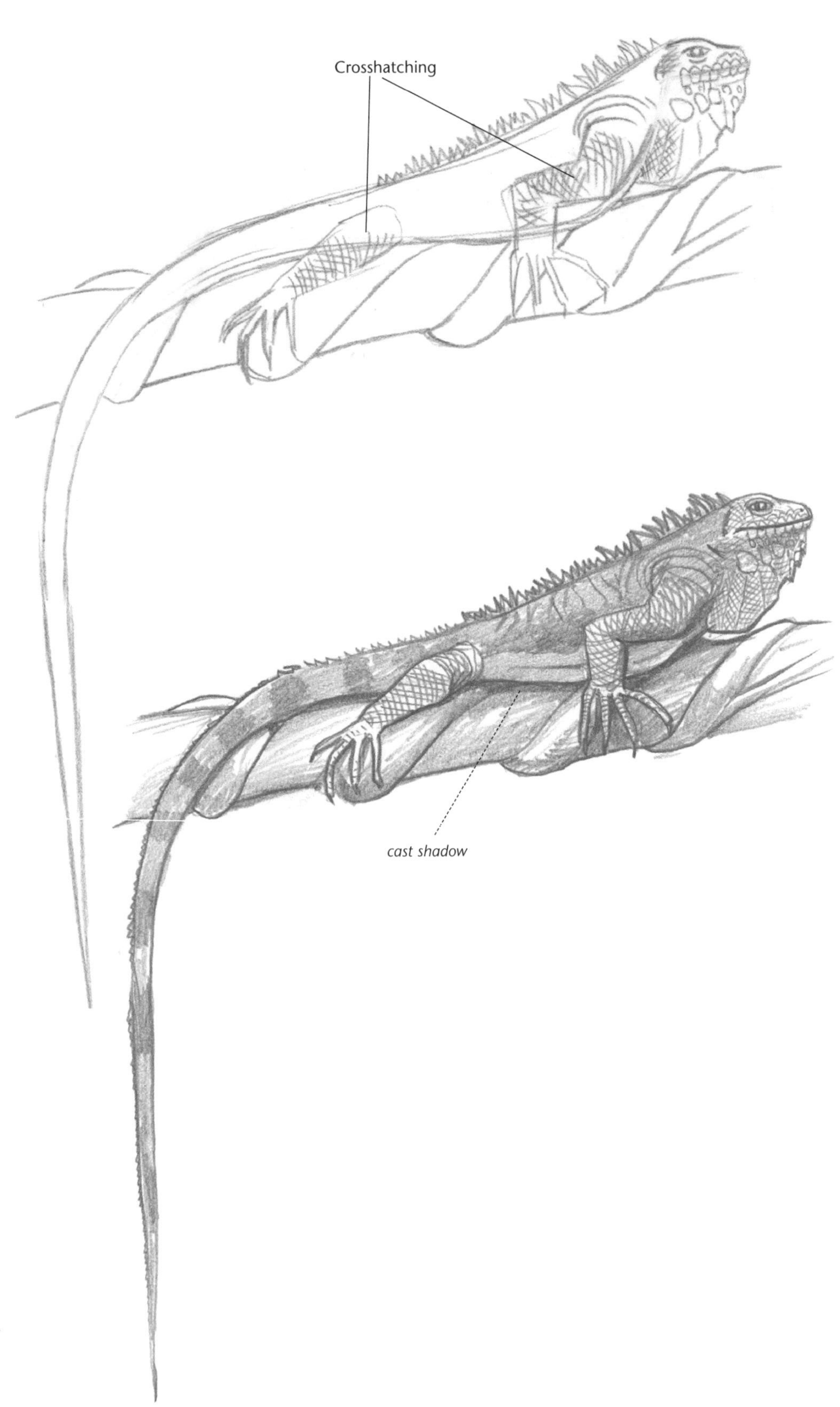

5. Now take your time as you turn your sketch into a finished drawing. Work slowly and carefully, paying close attention to details.

   Look at shading. Make the shading darkest where the branch is close to the iguana's body.

   Add the stripes on the tail!

   After shading, darken lines with a sharp pencil. Clean up any smudges with your eraser. Admire your creation!

Jaguar

Panthera onca: Central and South America. Size: 1.5-1.8 m (5-6 ft). Climbs trees to lie in wait for prey. Feeds on a variety of animals, even fish. Powerful animal with deep chest and strong limbs.

Head

1. Start by drawing two light, *overlapping* circles.

Mouth

2. Add the two sides of the mouth slanting downward, with the small vertical line in the centre.

The secret to drawing the jaguar – or other cats – is getting the face right. Rather than trying to draw this perfectly the first time, try it several times on scratch paper. Draw a little larger than you normally do. Pay attention to proportions.

3. Add a flat triangle for the nose.

4. Directly above the outside of the nose, draw two upside-down L shapes.

5. Make eyes by drawing curves down from the outside of the L shapes. Add ears.

When you have the face mastered, look ahead to steps 8-10. Leave enough room on your paper for the body!

6. Make a circle for the center of the eye – leave a small highlight in it.

7. Darken the rest of each eye. Add rows of dots on the muzzle and whiskers.

Always draw lightly at first!

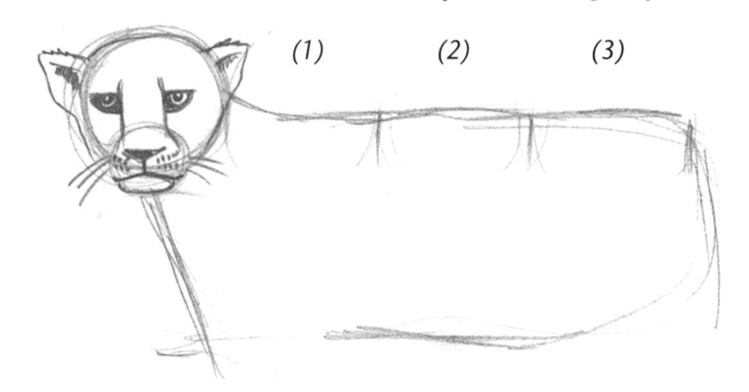

8. Measure three heads back for the length of the body. Make the back level with the bottom of the eyes, with a little curve at the neck. Make the front of the body slant slightly.

9. Add the legs and paws. *Draw lightly at first*. Look at your jaguar. Is everything the way you want it?

   If something looks wrong, try looking at your picture in a mirror, or hold it up to a light and look through the back.

10. Next add spots to the jaguar – dark patches, with one or more darker spots inside. These large spots become smaller spots and stripes on the legs and tail.

    Lightly lay out the pattern, then carefully add shading. It takes a while, but it's worth it!

While your pencil is sharp, go over fine details. As it gets duller, add shading.

Turn your drawing as you draw to avoid smudging it with your hand.

Clean up any smudges with your eraser.

Here, kitty…nice kitty…

Ruffed Lemur

Varecia variegata: Madagascar. Size: 120 cm (47 inches) including tail. This agile climber rarely comes to the ground. It eats fruit, leaves and bark, and is most active at dusk and the early part of the night.

1. Start with the eyes: small circles with a spot inside them, surrounded by wider, darker circles.

2. Draw the outline of the head, a rectangle above the eyes and a rounded triangle below the eyes.

3. Add the nose and mouth.

4. From the top sides of the head, lightly draw lines going out and up. Then draw the outline of the curving ruff, or collar, or beard, or whatever you want to call it.

   Draw lightly at first!

   Once you have the light outline in place, add radiating lines for the fur.

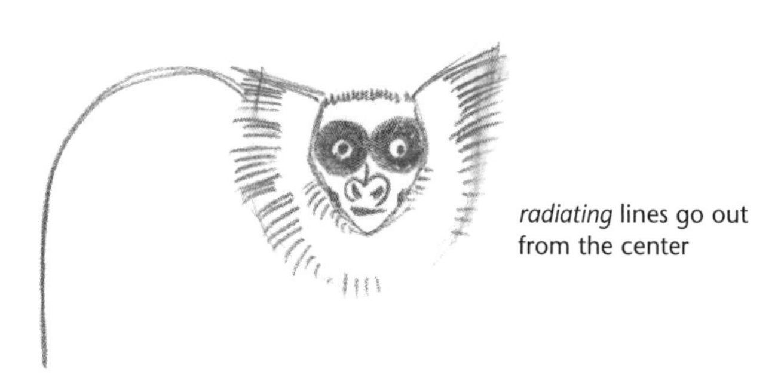

5. Draw a light curving line for the back. Continue adding lines for fur around the face.

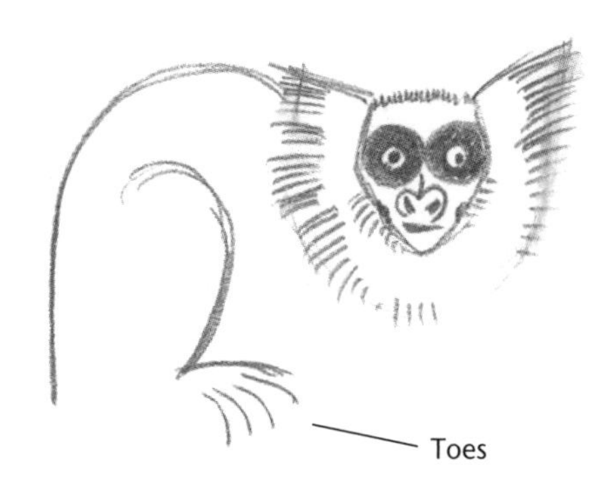

6. Draw the curve of the leg. *What number does this look like?* Add five radiating curved lines for the toes.

Always draw lightly at first!

7. Complete the rear foot. Draw the front arm and hand, with all five fingers. Draw the lines of the branch, adding a tiny bit of the thumb on the other hand.

8. Add a small upward curve for the lemur's belly, and the dark fur of the other arm. With short pencil strokes radiating from the shoulder, draw more fur. Add jagged lines along the back for texture, and a few fur lines on the face and body.

   What's missing?

9. A fat, long tail! Try drawing it using only short lines for the fur.

   While your pencil is sharp, go over fine details. As it gets duller, add shading.

Turn your drawing as you draw to avoid smudging it with your hand.

Clean up any smudges with your eraser.

Idea: add leaves and other branches in the background. Draw a dark background to make a night setting for this nocturnal animal.

Macaw

Ara macao (Scarlet macaw): Mexico to northern South America. Size: 85 cm (33.5 inches). Most familiar of South American parrots. Threatened by destruction of rain forest and people stealing baby birds to sell as pets. Don't buy them!

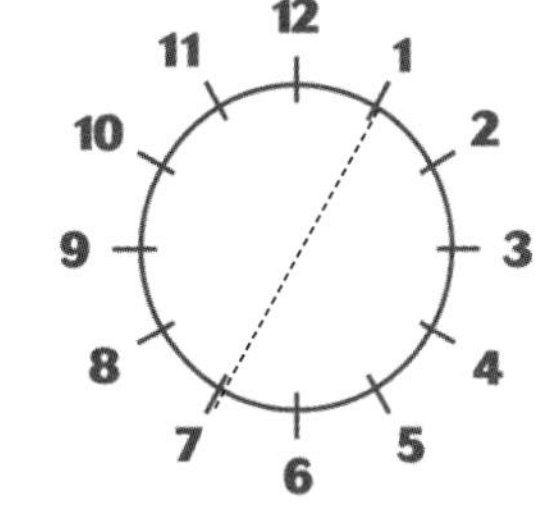

Use the clock face to compare angles of lines and ovals.

1. Lightly draw the top part of the beak, then the bottom.

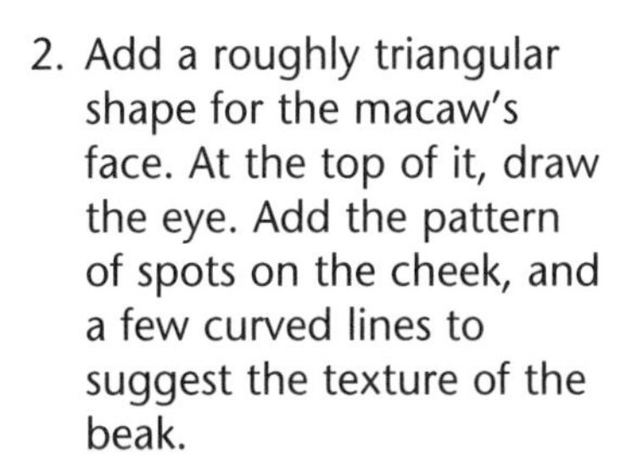

2. Add a roughly triangular shape for the macaw's face. At the top of it, draw the eye. Add the pattern of spots on the cheek, and a few curved lines to suggest the texture of the beak.

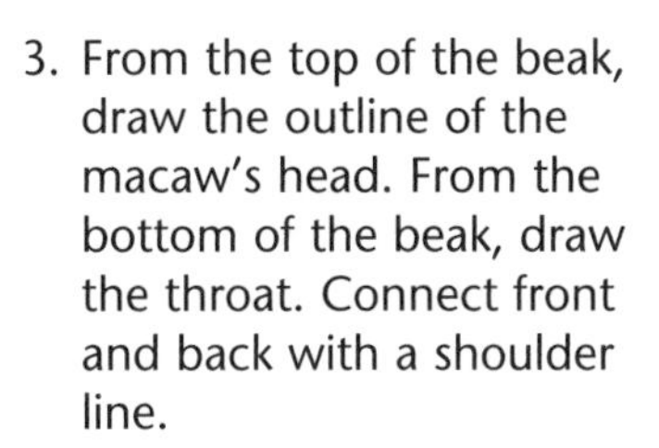

3. From the top of the beak, draw the outline of the macaw's head. From the bottom of the beak, draw the throat. Connect front and back with a shoulder line.

4. Lightly draw an oval for the bird's body. Draw two claws grasping a branch.

5. Sketch in the tail feathers. Notice that they stick out a bit, rather than pointing straight down.

Always draw lightly at first!

6. Add lines to these wing feathers, then draw the tail feathers, pointing downward underneath the wing feathers. Add three layers of feathers on the wing.

Layers

7. Carefully shade the feathers. While your pencil is sharp, go over fine details. As it gets duller, add shading.

Turn your drawing as you draw to avoid smudging it with your hand.

Look at your drawing in a mirror (or through the back of the paper) to spot any areas you can make better.

Clean up any smudges with your eraser.

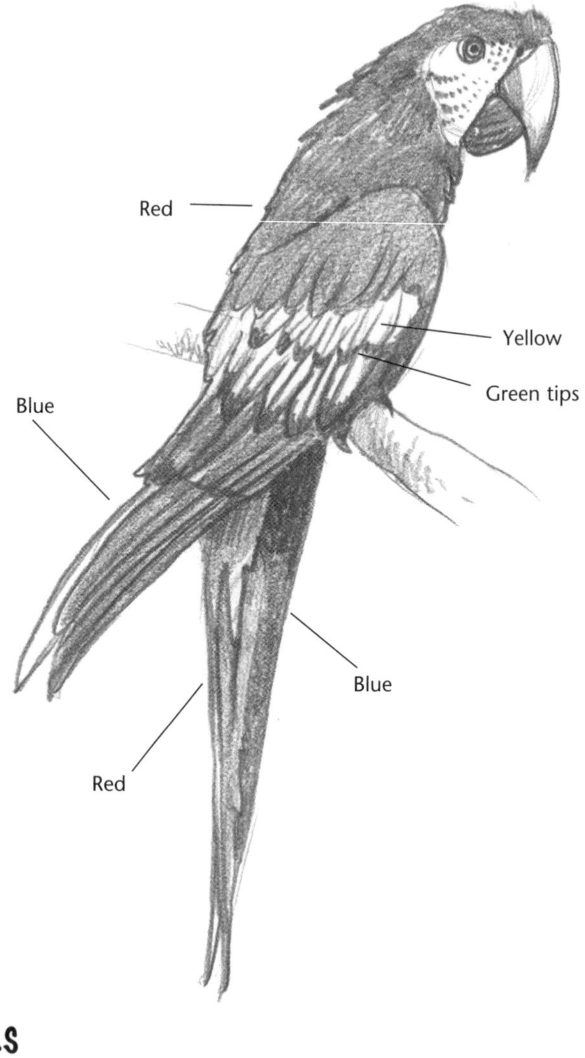

Red
Yellow
Green tips
Blue
Blue
Red

Idea: draw it in color!

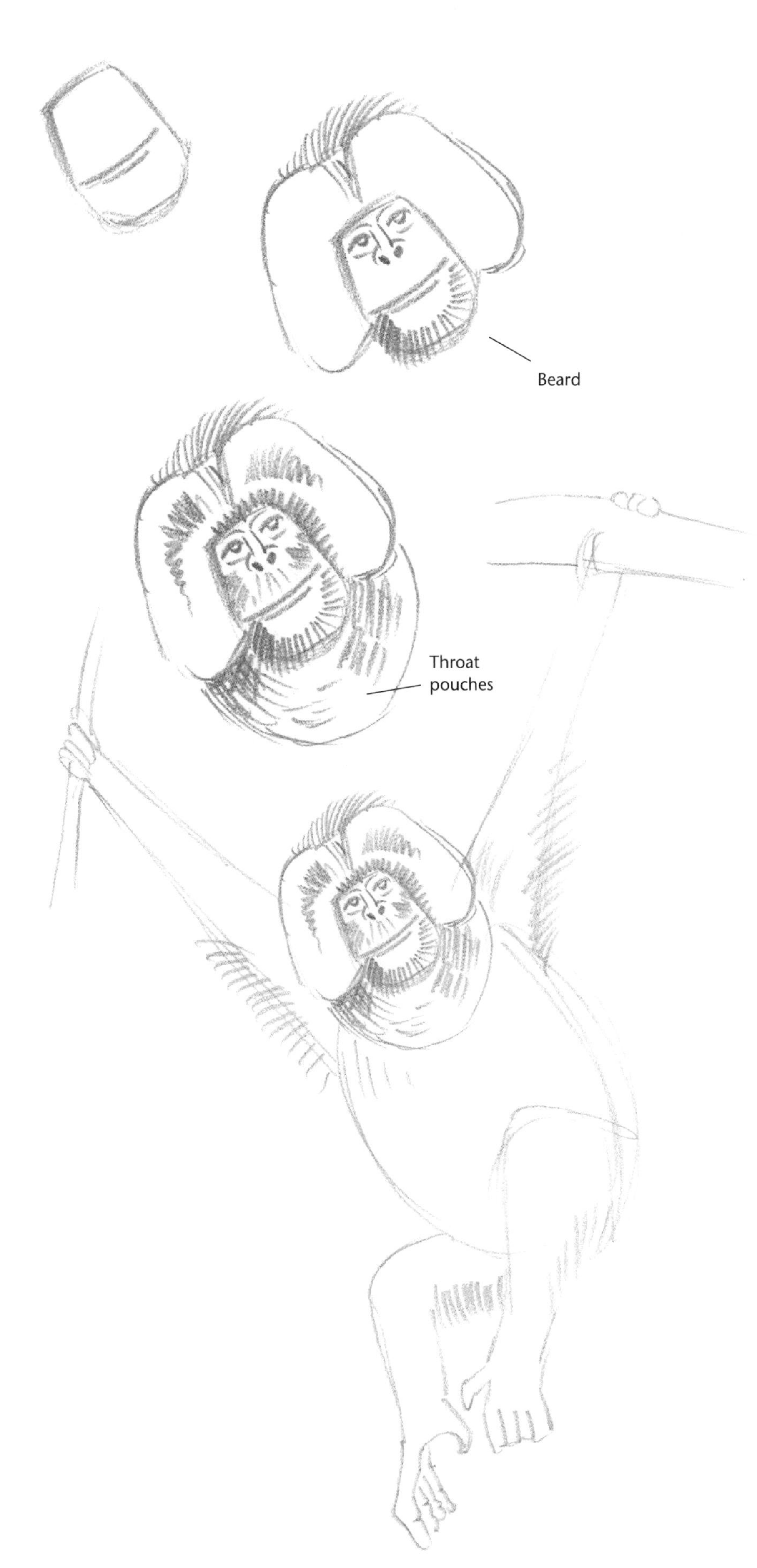

Orangutan

Pongo pygmaeus: Sumatra, Borneo. Size: 1.2-1.5 m (4-5 ft). The orangutan's arms are larger and stronger than its legs, and it is an agile climber. All adults have fatty throat pouches; only mature males have the distinctive cheek flaps surrounding the face. The shaggy fur is reddish-brown.

1. Draw the outline of the face, a tilted rectangle with a rounded bottom. Draw two lines near the middle of the rectangle for the mouth.

2. At the top of the rectangle, draw a series of curved lines to make the eyes. Draw two nostrils, and two lines to define the outside of the nose. Add radiating pencil strokes to make the 'beard.'

   Add hair at the top of the head. Lightly sketch the cheek flaps that surround the face. It may take you a try or two to get them just right.

3. Add the throat pouches, which look like a collar. Add shading to the face, cheek flaps and throat pouches.

4. Here's a big jump! *Draw lightly at first*, and redraw any parts that don't look right the first time. Draw an oval for the body. Add the legs, looking carefully at the position and the way the lines run. Add the outstretched arms, then draw the branch and vine for the orangutan to swing on.

5. Add another branch or two. Using short pencil strokes, draw the hair on the body. Pay close attention to the direction of the hair. Draw hair on arms and legs, pointing outward from the body. Add shading and texture to the branch and vine.

   Notice areas that are darker and areas that are lighter. Go over any lines that need darkening.

   While your pencil is sharp, go over fine details. As it gets duller, add shading.

Turn your drawing as you draw to avoid smudging it with your hand.

Clean up any smudges with your eraser.

Sloth

Bradypus tridactylus: Central and South America. Size: 56-67 cm (20-26 inches). Ve-ee-ee-ry slo-o-ow mo-oo-ving animal. Spends most of its life hanging upside down in trees. Eats leaves and tender buds.

1. Draw two lines for the tree branch. Make it interesting by adding curves. Below the branch, draw an oval for the sloth's body.

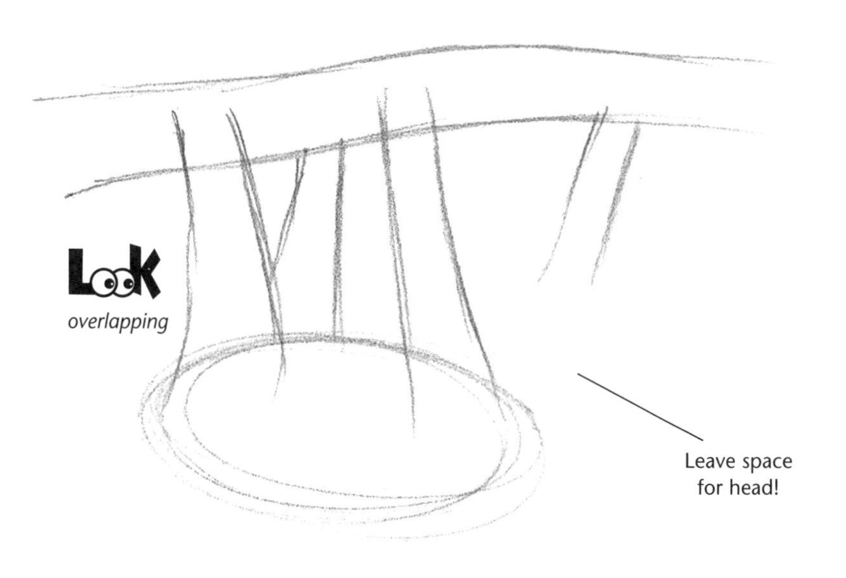

2. Draw straight lines upward for the legs, at angles. Notice how one leg *overlaps* part of the one behind it. Draw just part of one front leg, to save space for the head.

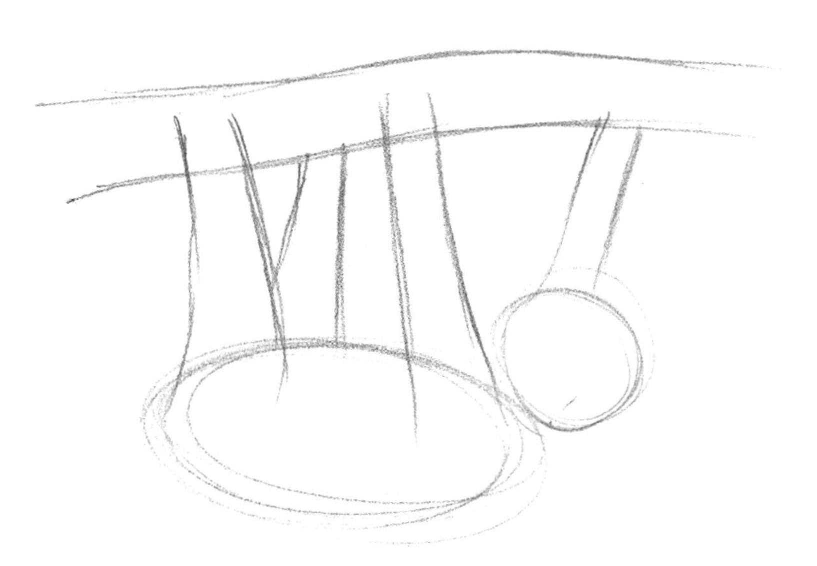

3. Lightly draw a circle for the head. Where is it in relation to the body?

Always draw lightly at first!

4. Add claws curving around the branch. Begin to add fur with short, downward strokes. The fur on a sloth grows this way because the sloth spends most of its life upside down!

5. Draw the face by starting with a small line for the mouth, at an angle, in the *center* of the circle. Add the nose, and the eyes just to the side of the nose. Draw dark fur areas extending from the eyes.

   Add short pencil strokes for the fur on the arms and legs, and on the back and neck.

6. Keep drawing short pencil lines to add fur to the rest of the body. Notice the areas that are darker, and the direction of the lines. Shade the tree branch. Fix any details you might have missed. Finally, clean up any smudges with your eraser.

Spider Monkey

Ateles paniscus (black spider monkey): Northern South America. Size: 1-1.4 m (39-55 inches). Tree dweller. Very agile, with a long reach and strong prehensile tail. Spider monkeys eat mostly fruit and nuts, and live in groups of 15-30.

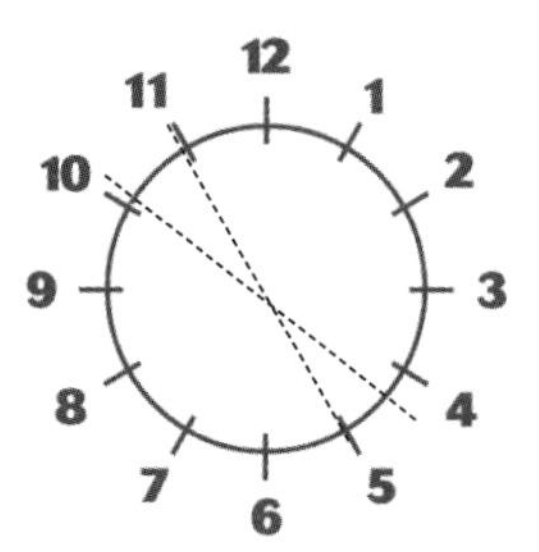

Use the clock face to compare angles of lines and ovals.

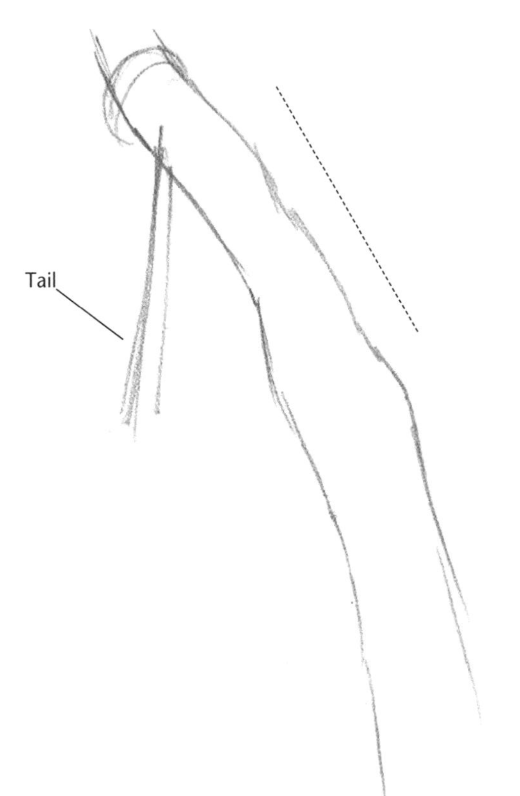

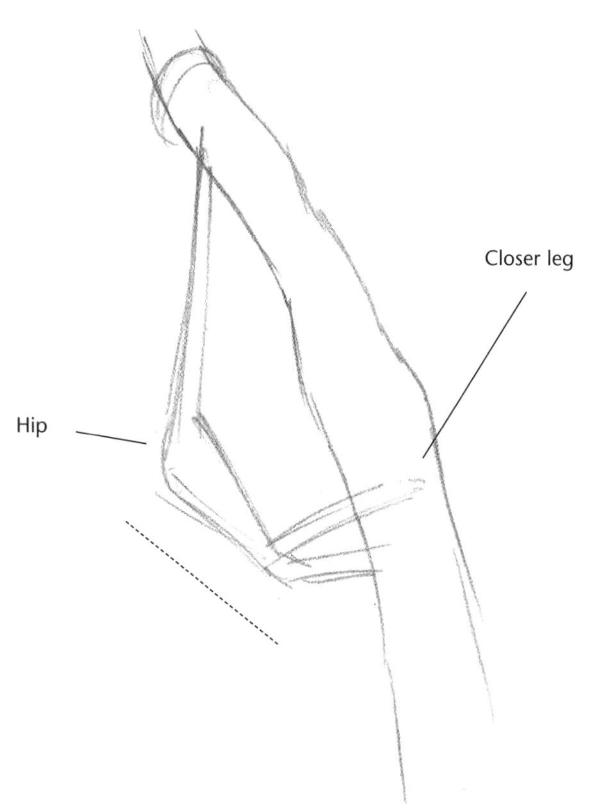

1. Draw the tree trunk, lightly. Make the lines interesting, not just straight!

   Draw two lines straight up for the tail. Then make the tail curling around the tree.

2. Add the hip and rear legs. The leg closer to you *overlaps* part of the one behind.

Always draw lightly at first!

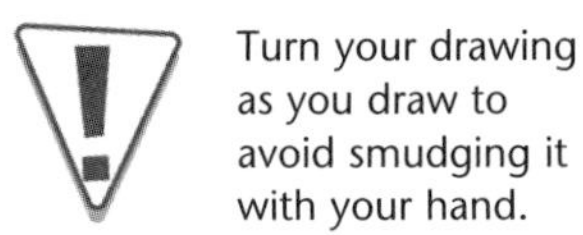

Turn your drawing as you draw to avoid smudging it with your hand.

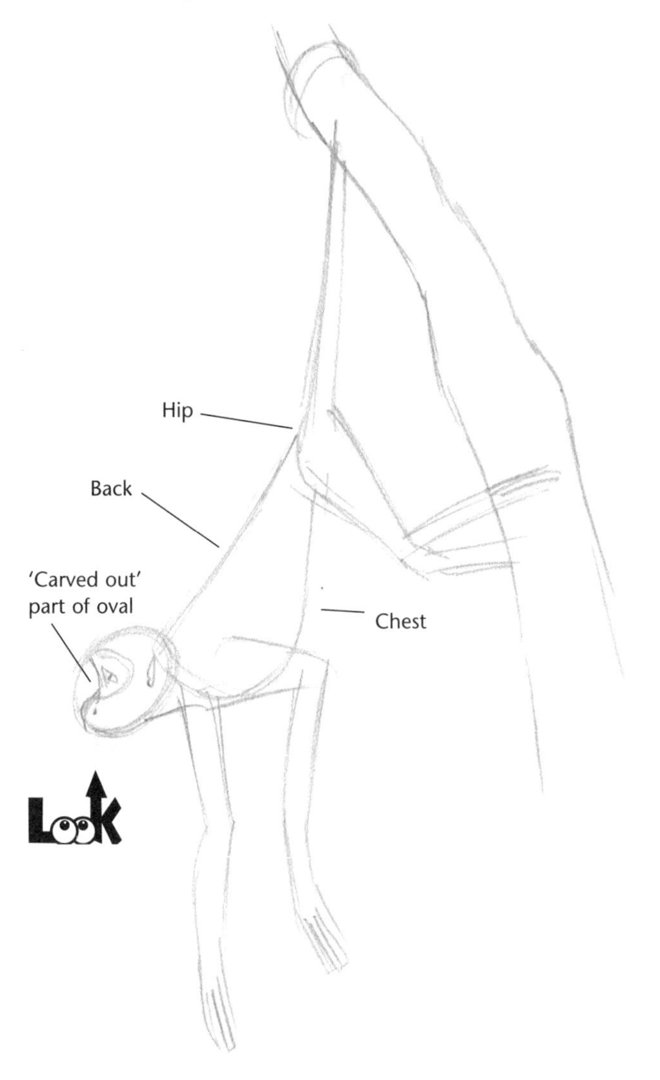

3. From the hip, draw a straight line for the back, and a swooping curve for the chest.

   Next, add long, spindly arms.

   Lightly draw an oval for the head, then 'carve out' part of it to make the space above the nose. Draw the ear, eye, and nose. Draw a line to connect the head with the body.

4. With many short pencil strokes, add the fur. Notice the direction of the fur on different parts of the body. Also, notice that it's darker in some places.

   Look for any lines that might need to be darkened. Add some shadows to the tree trunk. Clean up any smudges with your eraser.

Idea: this monkey looks like it's ready to reach for something, perhaps a vine or a branch...add vegetation to your drawing, including whatever the spider monkey is about to reach for.

Tapir

Tapirus terrestris (Brazilian tapir): South America. Size: 2 m (6.5 ft). Covered with short, bristly hair. Found near water (good swimmer). Feeds at night on leaves, buds, shoots, and small branches.

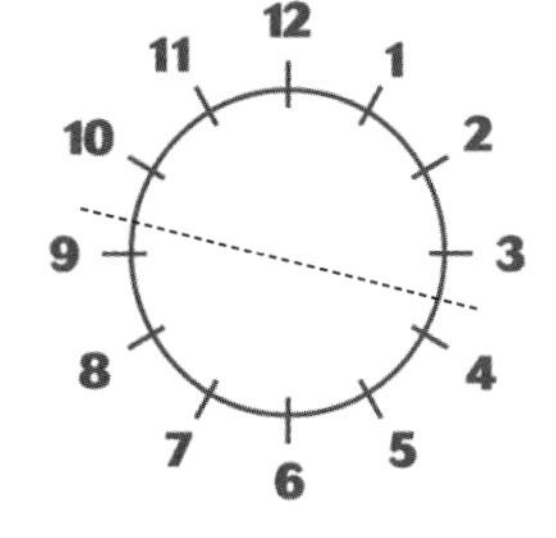

Use the clock face to compare angles of lines and ovals.

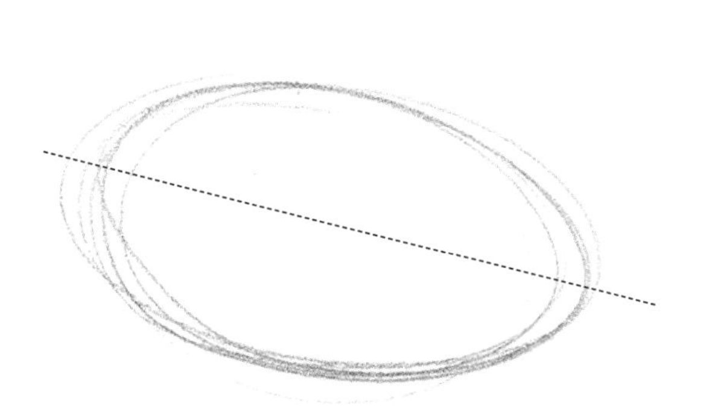

1. Drawing a tapir is quite easy. Start with a line for the ground, and above it, draw a slightly tilted oval.

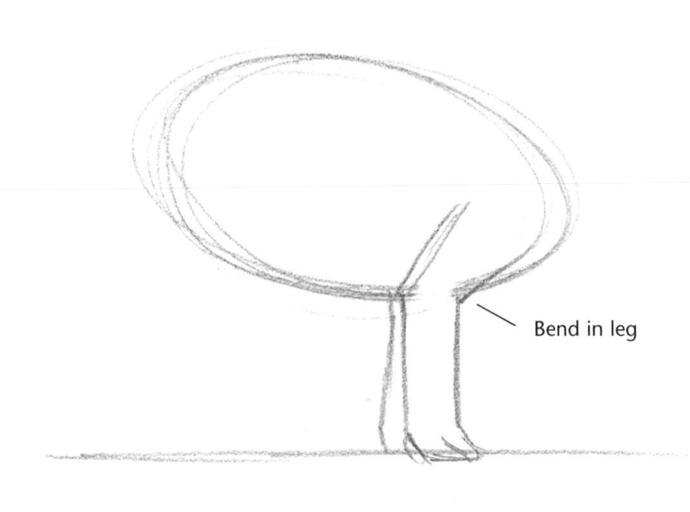

2. From the right side of the oval, draw the front leg with a bend in the middle, where it crosses the bottom of the oval. Erase the oval where the leg *overlaps* it. Draw the other front leg.

3. Draw the short tail, and the back legs. Notice how and where these legs bend – well below the oval.

4. Lightly draw another oval for the head. Connect it to the body with two lines for the neck.

5. In the middle of the oval, draw an almond shape for the eye. Extend the top of the head to make the nose. From the nose, draw the mouth and the neck. Carefully erase what's left of the head oval.

   Draw some leaves in the tapir's mouth. Add the short fur strokes above the eye. Draw the ears.

   What a pretty face!

6. To finish your drawing, make many short pencil lines for the fur. Notice which places are dark, and which are light. Darken outlines in shadow areas, such as underneath the body. Add bristly marks on the outline of the back.

   Add grass on the ground, and a bit of *cast shadow*, then clean up any smudges with your eraser and you're done!

Turn your drawing as you draw to avoid smudging it with your hand.

Idea: add bushes and trees in the background.

Toucan

Ramphastos toco (Toco toucan): South America, mainly Amazon basin. Size: 61 cm (24 inches). Toucans eat a variety of fruits and large insects. Strong claws help them hang onto tree branches. Toucans grab food with their beak, then toss their head backwards to get it into their mouth.

Use the clock face to compare angles of lines and ovals.

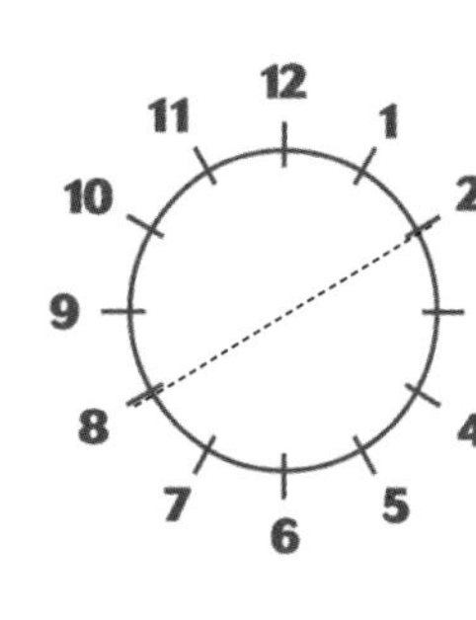

1. Draw the horizontal branch.

   Above it, at an angle, draw a tilted oval, not quite touching the branch.

   Add vertical lines for the legs, with claws wrapping around the branch.

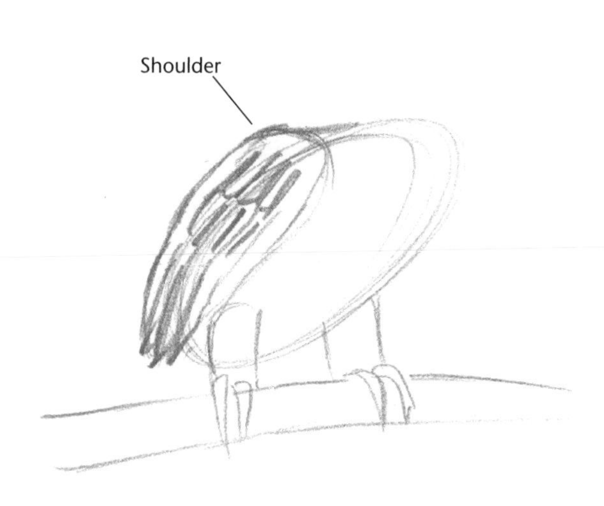

2. Add the wing, with a slight bulge at the shoulder.

   Draw lines on the wing to suggest feathers.

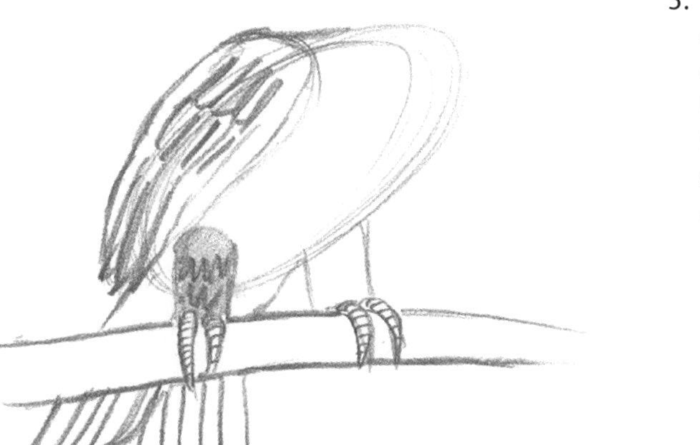

3. Extend the bottom of the oval for the tail. Draw the end of the tail behind and below the branch, with lines for feathers. Add small curved lines on the claws. Shade the leg.

Always draw lightly at first!

4. Draw a line from the shoulder for the top of the head. Make the front of the head vertical where the beak attaches. Draw the throat. Add the eye, and the triangle around it. Outline the white area on the front of the body.

5. Now draw the beak – but first, look carefully at its curves. Make the top part of the beak wider than the bottom. Add the dark spot at the tip. Draw the tongue.

6. Look at the final drawing. Shade the dark areas of the bird. Add the pattern to the beak. Darken lines that seem important. Add shading to the branch.

   While your pencil is sharp, go over fine details. As it gets duller, add shading.

Turn your drawing as you draw to avoid smudging it with your hand.

Look at your drawing in a mirror (or through the back of the paper) to spot any areas you can make better.

Clean up any smudges with your eraser.

Idea: draw a berry in the toucan's beak. Add color to your drawing…

Other ideas

When animals appear in the rainforest, chances are you won't see the whole animal because of the huge amount of vegetation all around them. To make your drawing more interesting, add foliage.

You'll find that it helps to draw the whole animal lightly, then draw the foreground elements, whether trees or leaves. Try not to cover up the most important parts of the drawing – for example, in the picture of the jaguar (left), I wouldn't want a leaf covering its face!

These two drawings are quick sketches – just a way of playing with ideas, to see what looks good and what doesn't. If I wanted to do a finished drawing of the howler monkey (left), I might do another sketch first, moving the leaves around to find a better arrangement.

The straight lines on the outside "crop" the drawing, to give a better idea how the finished drawing might appear.

Always draw lightly at first!

Try including some of these in your drawings:

1. Two of many leaf forms you can find in the rainforest.
2. *Epiphytes:* plants that live in the branches of trees high above the forest floor.
3. Buttressed roots that help tall trees stand securely in shallow soil.
4. Vines grow in abundance, and grow into one another over time. This could become a great design for a border for your drawing!

Introduction

The world of insects includes amazing diversity—and insects are *everywhere,* from frozen snow fields to inside other animals' bodies. Some feed on plants, some suck blood from mammals, and plenty of them eat other insects, spiders, and other creepy-crawlies.

So what is an insect?

Insects are those critters belonging to the class *Insecta,* in the phylum *Arthropoda* (arthropods). They live in all habitats. Arthropods have hard exoskeletons and jointed limbs–lobsters and crabs are arthropods, but they're not insects.

Insects have

- ***six legs***
- ***two antennae***
- ***three body parts***
- ***wings? Four, or two, or none at all.***

So think **6 legs**. And look for the other stuff as well.

OK, class dismissed!

You may now draw...

Tips

Find a **comfortable place to draw** – with decent light, so you can see what you're doing.

As you start to learn about insect anatomy, shapes and proportions, don't worry too much about materials.

Use a **pencil that's longer than your finger**. Also, think about using colored pencils.

Sharpen your pencil when it gets dull!

Get a **separate eraser**. My preference is a kneaded type, available in art supply and craft stores (the eraser on your pencil will disappear quickly).

For practice drawings, use **recycled paper** – for example, draw on the back of old photocopies or computer printouts.

*P.S. The **darkened images** on each page show you the actual size of what you're drawing.*

Ant

Order Hymenoptera
Family Formicidae

If you want to study insects, none are easier to find than ants! Their societies generally consist of wingless workers and winged reproducers. They live in underground nests or in dead wood. Most can 'bite' people if disturbed. Most ants scavenge, but some harvest seeds, cut leaves and farm fungus underground, or herd aphids to feed on their honeydew.

STUDY the final drawing *before you start!*

Do you see
- *three body parts?*
- *six legs?*
- *two antennae?*
- *wings?*
- *eyes?*

1. Draw the oval shape of the *head,* the peanut shape of the *thorax,* and the pointy oval shape of the *abdomen.*
2. Add the rear leg. *How many sections do you see?*
3. Draw the middle leg, and the front leg. Notice how the sections of the middle leg *overlap* to create depth.
4. Add *antennae, eye,* and *mouth.* Add the small visible bits of the other legs.
5. Add shading and texture. Draw a little tidbit and a cast shadow beneath the ant. Clean up any smudges with your eraser.

Great ant! To make your drawing more realistic, draw about a zillion of them, crawling all over the place....

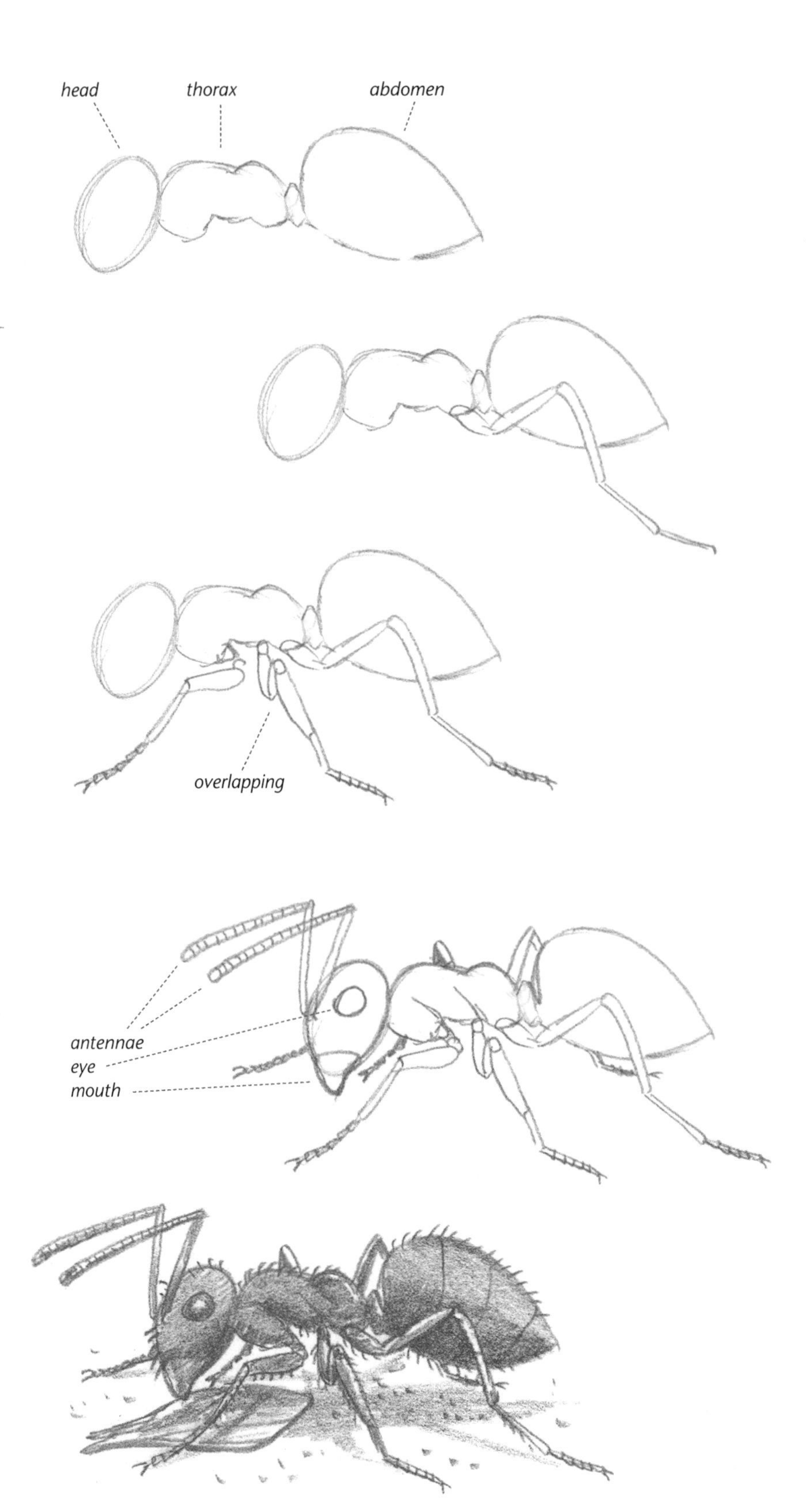

Aphid 

Order Homoptera
Family Aphididae

Ask any gardener about aphids! These little plant-suckers appear in large numbers on leaves and stems of plants, leaving them wilted and curled. They can also spread plant diseases. Aphids give birth to young during spring and summer, and lay eggs to last through the winter. Ants help the process by gathering the eggs, storing them during the winter, then transporting the aphids from one food plant to another during the spring. Why? Because aphids also secrete something called honeydew, which the ants eat.

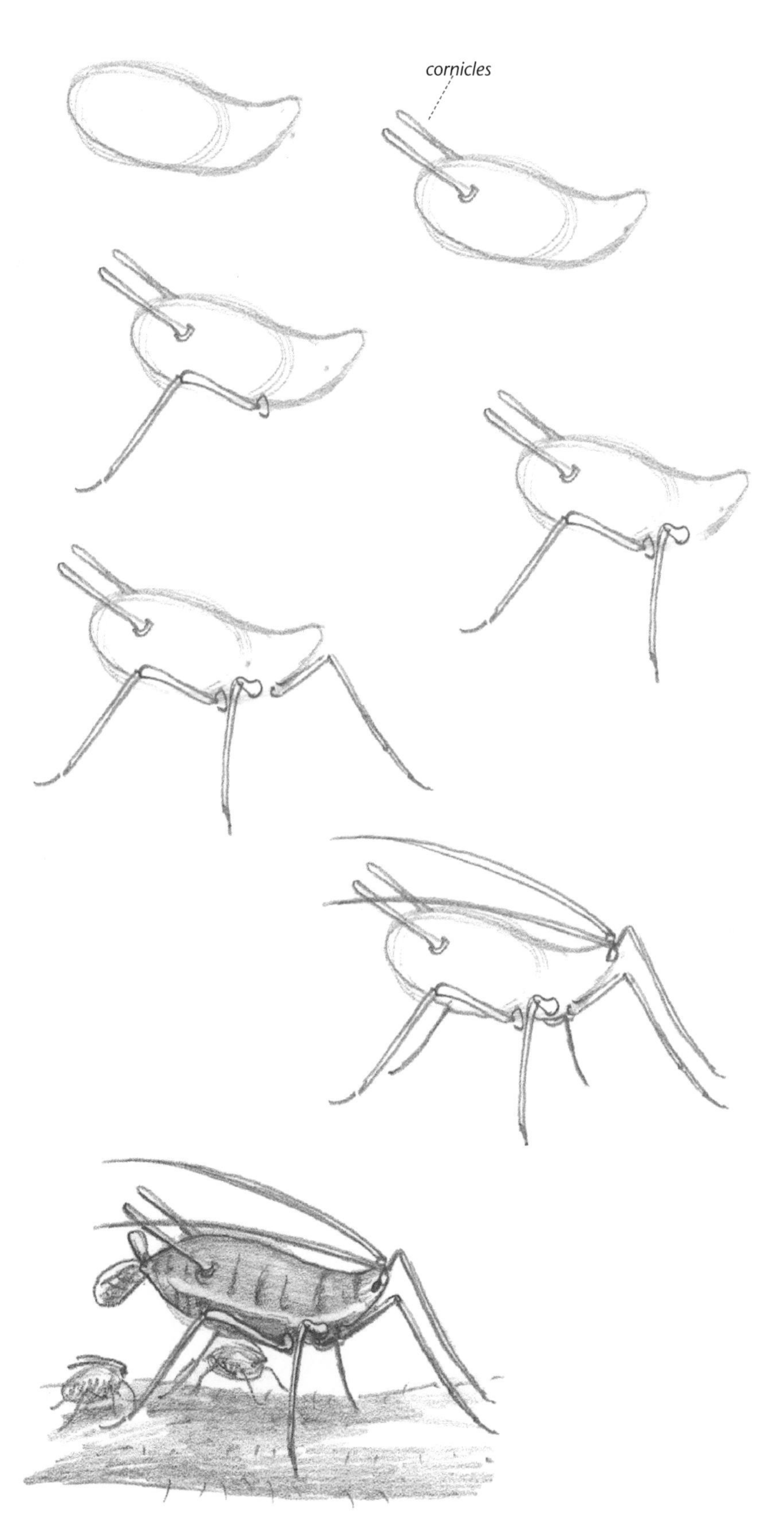

STUDY the final drawing *before you start!*

Do you see
- *distinct body parts?*
- *six legs?*
- *two antennae?*
- *wings?*
- *eyes?*

1. Draw the body, almost pear-shaped.
2. Add the distinctive *cornicles* at the rear end of the aphid.
3. Draw the rear leg,...
4. ...the middle leg,...
5. ...and the front leg.
6. Add the antennae and eye.
7. Finish your drawing by shading and going over fine lines with a sharp pencil. Add a little plant stem and shadows.

Now add a little flap in the back and more baby aphids popping out, eager to devour your house plants....

Bumble Bee

Order Hymenoptera
Family Apidae

Bumblebees usually live in cooler areas, where their thick hair protects them from the cold. Usually they build nests underground. Their very long proboscises can reach into the deepest flowers, and some depend almost completely on bumblebees for fertilization. When the English brought clover to New Zealand, for example, it didn't grow well until they imported bumblebees. The English biologist Charles Darwin made the suggestion.

STUDY the final drawing *before you start!*

Do you see
- *three body parts?*
- *six legs?*
- *two antennae?*
- *wings (how many)?*
- *eyes?*

Does the insect look
- *shiny? smooth? fuzzy?*
- *hard? soft?*

1. Draw the circle of the *thorax,* leaving white spaces on either side where the wings attach. Add the flattened oval of the *abdomen,* with lines showing segments.
2. Add head, eyes, and antennae.
3. Carefully outline one *fore wing* and *hind wing.*
4. Repeat on the other side, and add veins to the wings.
5. Now draw the six legs.
6. Add shading, shadow, and texture. Notice which parts of the body are darker, and which are lighter.

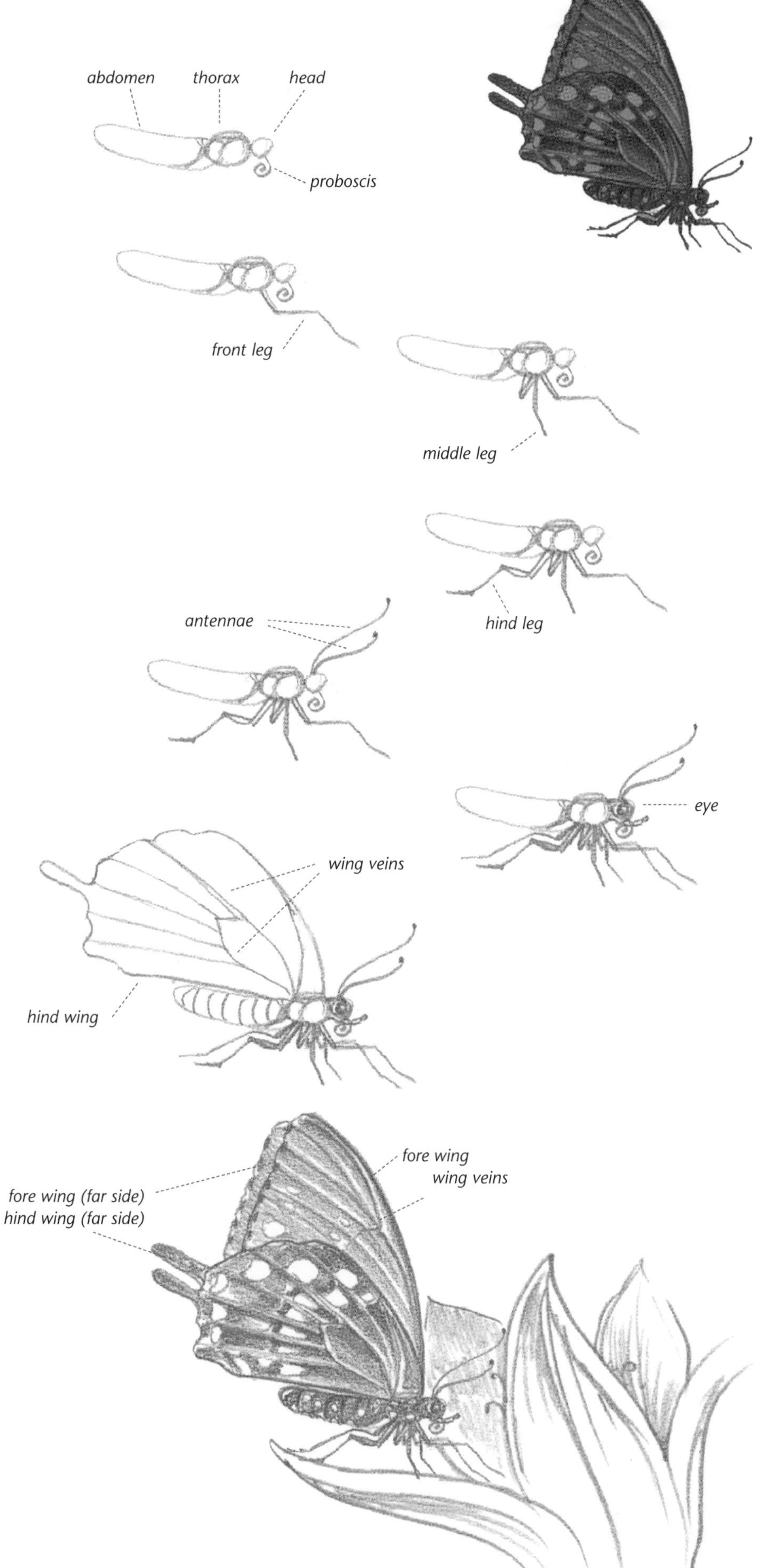

Butterfly

Order Lepidoptera
Family Papilionidae

Swallowtail butterflies are easily recognized by the long tails on the hind wings. Their wings have patterns of black, yellow, or white, and can have blue or red spots. Papillon, *a word taken from this family of butterflies, means butterfly in French. (The German word, on the other hand, is* Schmetterling. *Go figure.)*

STUDY the final drawing
before you start!

Do you see
- *three body parts?*
- *six legs?*
- *two antennae?*
- *wings (how many)?*
- *eyes?*

Does the insect look
- *shiny? smooth? fuzzy?*
- *hard? soft?*

1. Draw the *thorax, head* and *proboscis.*
2. Add the *front leg…*
3. *…middle leg…*
4. …and *hind leg.*
5. Draw the two *antennae.*
6. Add the *eye.*
7. Carefully outline the *hind wing* and its *veins.* Add lines for abdominal segments.
8. Draw the *fore wing.* Add the small visible portion of the fore wing and hind wing on the far side of the insect. Add shading. Go over lines with a sharpened pencil.

Caterpillar 

Order Lepidoptera

Caterpillars are young butterflies or moths. They may have horns, spines, and bristles; they show distinct colors and patterns. All caterpillars have three pairs of legs in the thorax, and up to five pairs of abdominal "prolegs."

STUDY the final drawing *before you start!*

Do you see
- *three body parts?*
- *six legs?*
- *two antennae?*
- *wings?*
- *eyes?*

Does the insect look
- *shiny? smooth? fuzzy?*
- *hard? soft?*

1. Draw two tall, rounded rectangles with tiny projections for *legs.*
2. Add a triangle shape and another leg, and small bump with a dot for the head. Draw a little horn on top.
3. Draw two more rounded rectangles of the *abdomen.*
4. Add another, with a little bump for a *proleg...*
5. ...and another...
6. ...and two more...
7. ...then three plain segments and a last segment with another proleg.
8. Now add pattern and shading, leaving a light area on each segment to make the caterpillar look shiny. And give it a little something to munch on!

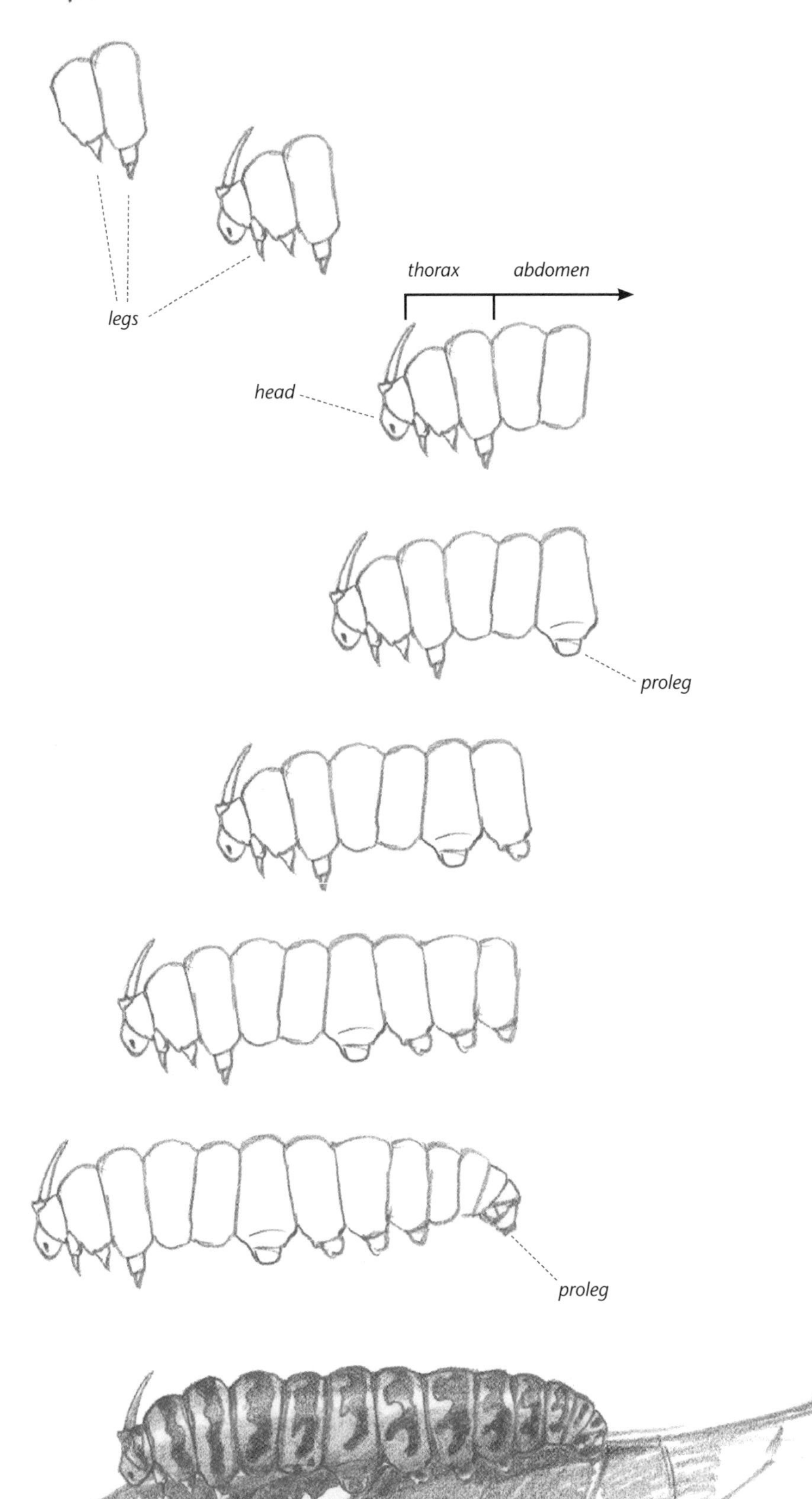

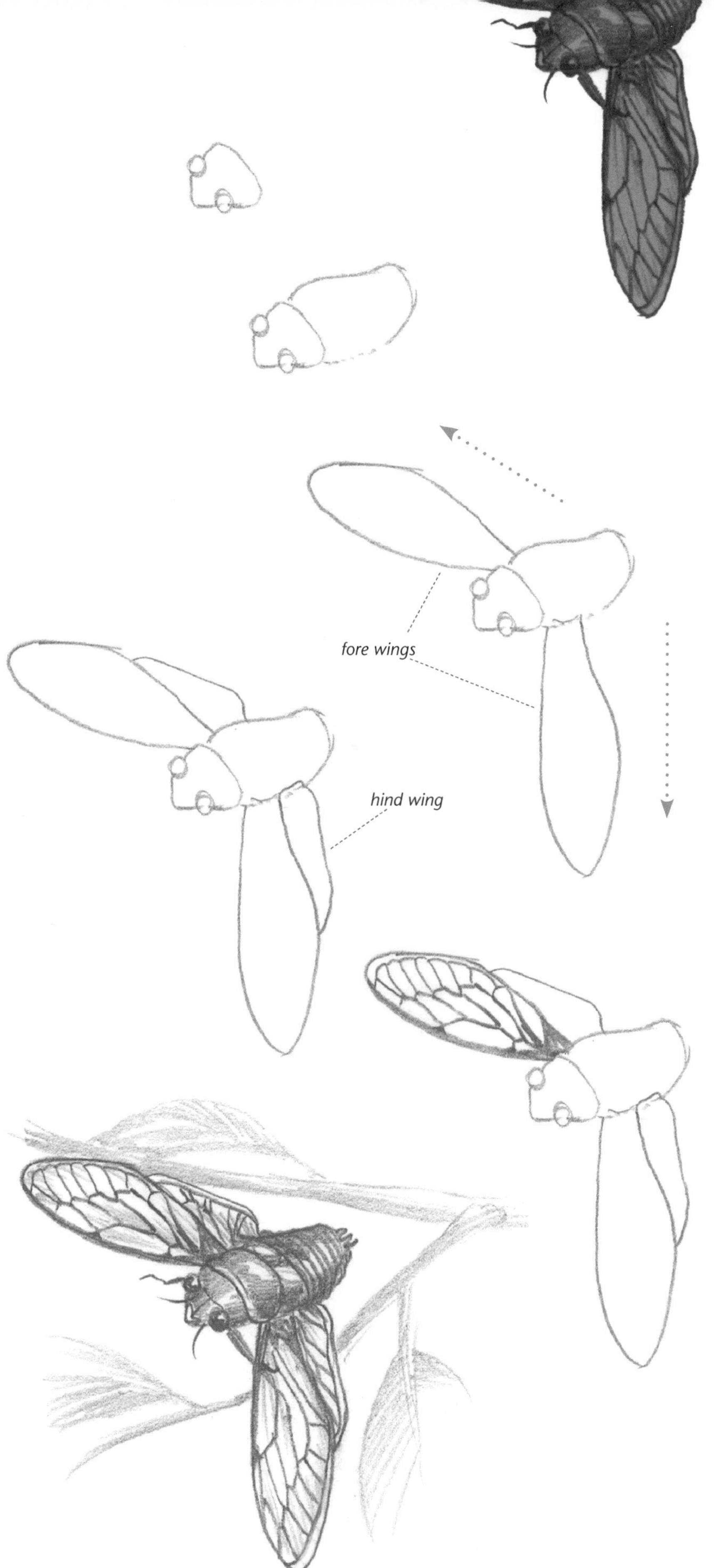

Cicada

Order Homoptera
Family Cicadidae

Cicadas live in trees and make loud, pulsating buzzing sounds. They lay eggs on twigs, which usually die and fall to the ground. The nymph cicadas then feast on roots before crawling up a tree. Certain cicadas repeat this cycle only once every 13 or 17 years.

STUDY the final drawing *before you start!*

Do you see
- *three body parts?*
- *six legs?*
- *two antennae?*
- *wings (how many)?*
- *eyes?*

Does the insect look
- *shiny? smooth? fuzzy?*
- *hard? soft?*

1. Draw a rounded triangle with a little circle on the bottom and one side.
2. Add the peanut shape of the body on the other side of the triangle.
3. Outline the *fore wings.* Notice how one points down on the page, while the other points up at an angle.
4. Add the *hind wings.*
5. Carefully outline the veins in one wing. Take your time! Look carefully!
6. Complete your drawing by carefully adding veins to the other wings. Draw legs and segments of the body. Then add shading, and go over any fuzzy lines with a sharp pencil to make them look cleaner.

Cockroach

Order Blattodea
Family Blattidae

Cockroaches do not transmit human disease, but...they infest buildings, contaminate food, and have an unpleasant smell. They are active and fast runners at night; during the day they hide in cracks. They almost never fly, though they are among the oldest winged insects (350 million years). Some have become almost immune to pesticides after numerous attempts to eradicate them. And don't bother trying to starve them to death: some have lived for months on little more than dust!

STUDY the final drawing *before you start!*

Do you see
- *three body parts?*
- *six legs?*
- *two antennae?*
- *wings (how many)?*
- *eyes?*

Does the insect look
- *shiny? smooth? fuzzy?*
- *hard? soft?*

1. Draw a small flat oval for the *head* and a half-circle for the *pronotum.*
2. Add the long shape of the *wings.*
3. Draw details on the head, and add the visible bits of front legs.
4. Carefully add the remaining two pairs of legs.
5. Add antennae, bristly hairs on the legs, and shading.

For added realism, draw your cockroach nibbling on a chocolate chip cookie!

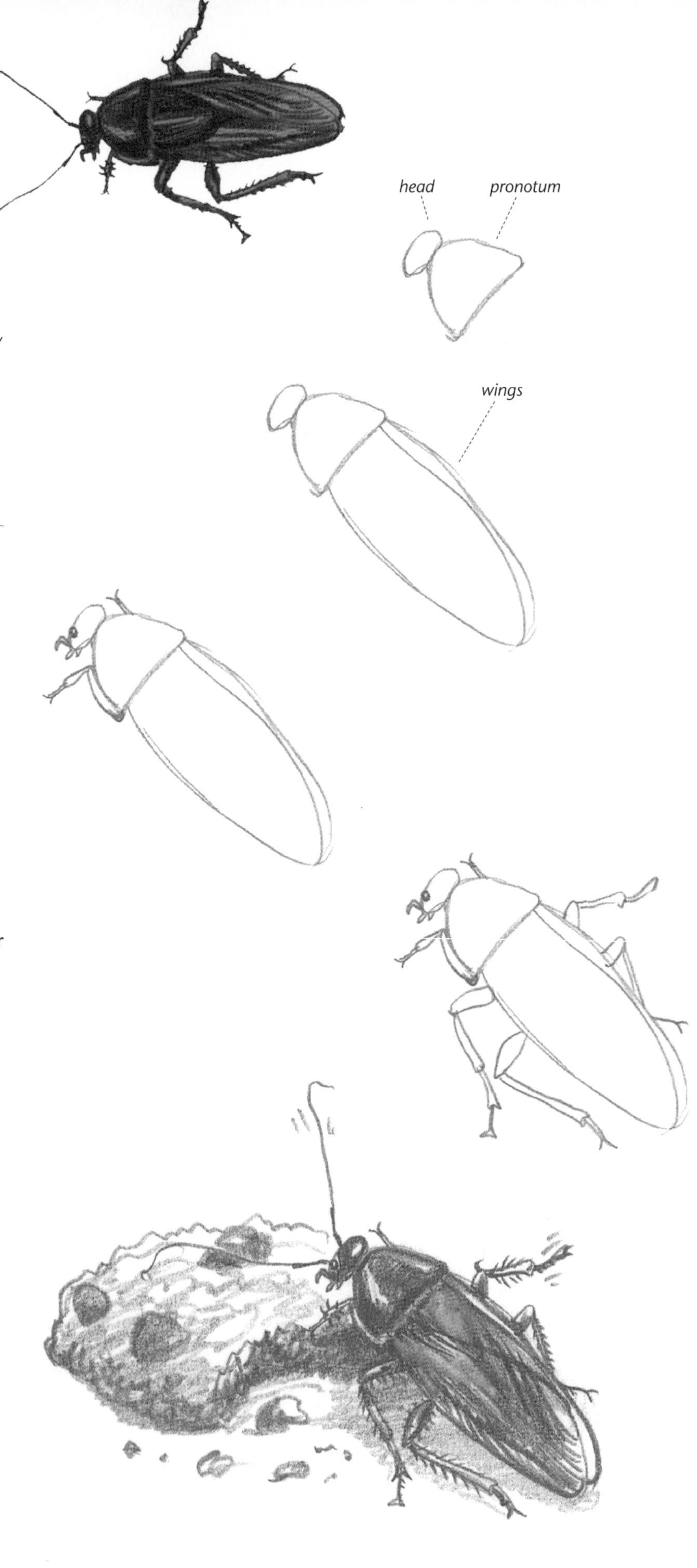

Deer Fly

Order Diptera
Family Tabanidae

This pest looks like a jet airplane when it lands after circling above its prey – and it feels like one too when it bites! As with horse flies and mosquitoes, only female deer flies feed on blood; the males drink plant juices. The larva feed on small aquatic insects. Some deer flies transmit bacteria that can cause tularemia in rabbits and hares...and occasionally people.

STUDY the final drawing *before you start!*

Do you see
- *three body parts?*
- *six legs?*
- *two antennae?*
- *wings (how many)?*
- *eyes?*

Does the insect look
- *shiny? smooth? fuzzy?*
- *hard? soft?*

1. Starting with the *head* and two eyes, then add rounded rectangles of the *thorax* and *abdomen.*
2. Draw the wings, extending beyond the abdomen.
3. Add six legs, and antennae.
4. Look closely! Draw the markings on the back and the veins on the wings. Add markings on thorax and abdomen, and shade the eyes, leaving highlights.
5. Add shading to head, thorax, and abdomen. Shade the wings to make them look translucent: you can see shapes through them, but they're not completely clear.

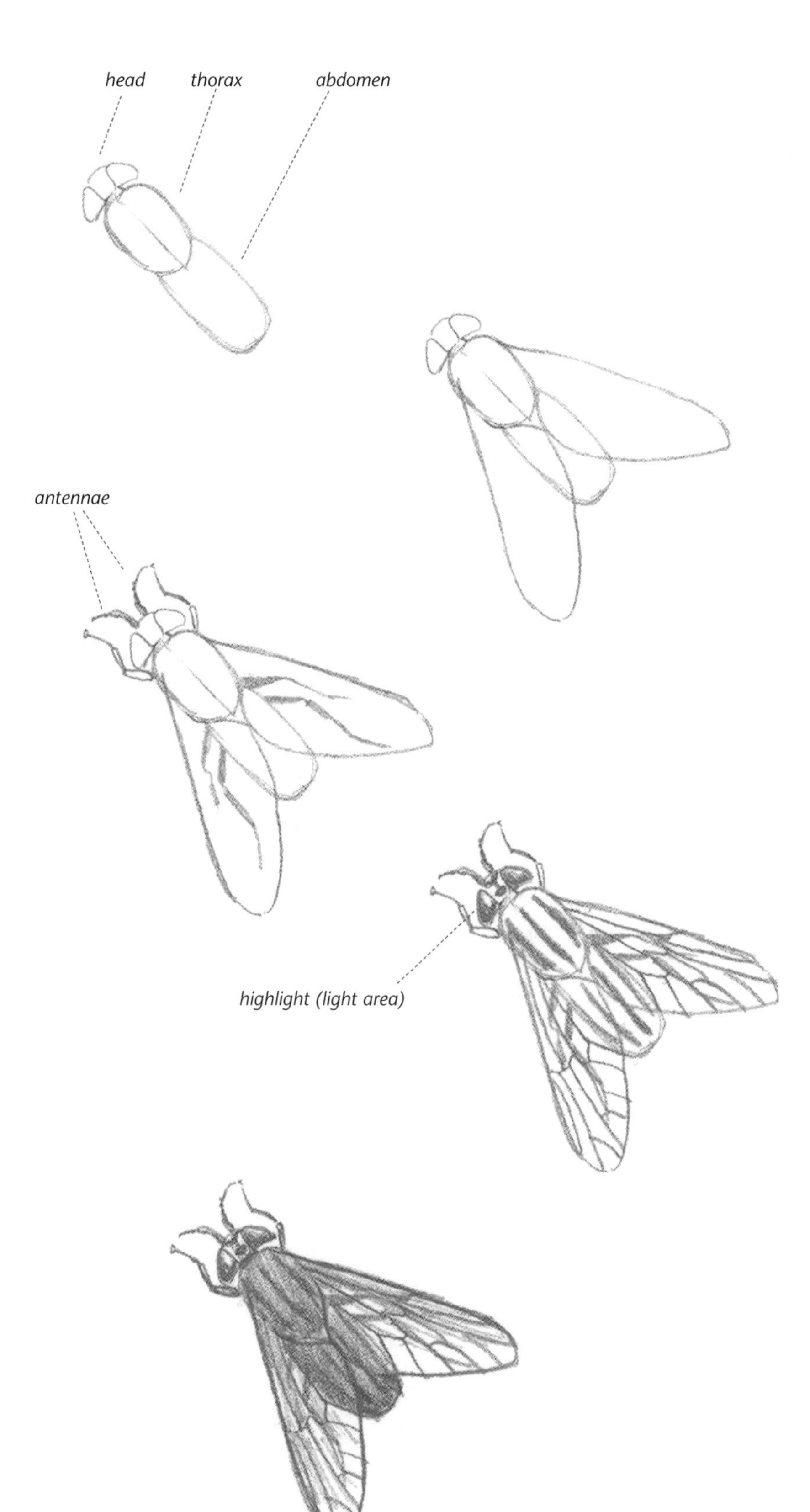

Dragonfly

Order Odonata
Suborder Anisoptera

Dragonfly nymphs live in ponds and streams, so you often see adult dragonflies around water, though they can range several miles. Often brightly colored, dragonflies fly well and often, catching mosquitoes and midges in flight. They're fast! No wonder they have such big eyes!

STUDY the final drawing *before you start!*

Do you see
- *three body parts?*
- *six legs?*
- *two antennae?*
- *wings (how many)?*
- *eyes?*

Does the insect look
- *shiny? smooth? fuzzy?*
- *hard? soft?*

1. Start with two small circles for the *head* and *thorax,* and draw the long rectangle of the *abdomen.*
2. Draw one *hind wing.*
3. Add the *fore wing.*
4. Draw wings on the other side as well.
5. Add details on head, front legs, veins in wings, and lines on the abdomen.
6. Complete your drawing by adding more shading and about a zillion cells on each wing. Look closely at the example, and take your time drawing them!

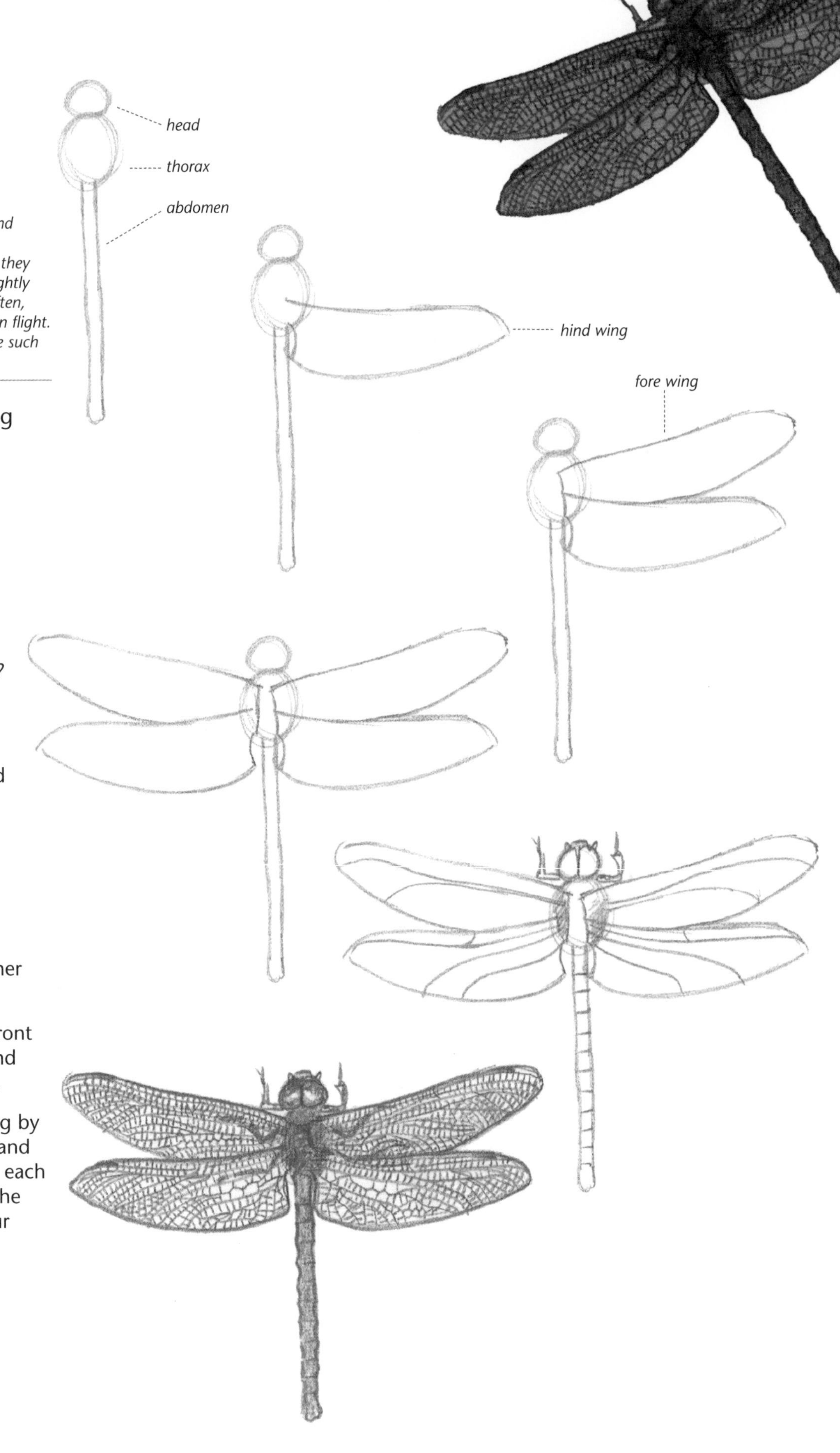

Dazzling dragonfly!

Earwig

Order Dermaptera
Family Forficulidae

Their strange name comes from an old superstition that these insects got into people's ears (they don't…I don't think). They live and lay their eggs in plant debris, scavenging or feeding on plants at night. They use their pincerlike cerci in defense, and can pinch painfully. They also squirt a foul-smelling liquid if handled.

STUDY the final drawing *before you start!*

Do you see
- *three body parts?*
- *six legs?*
- *two antennae?*
- *wings (how many)?*
- *eyes?*

Does the insect look
- *shiny? smooth? fuzzy?*
- *hard? soft?*

1. Start by drawing the *head* and *thorax.*
2. Add the long *abdomen* with curving lines…
3. …and add the nasty-looking *cerci* at the end.
4. Draw the rear legs…
5. …the middle legs…
6. …and then the front legs and segmented antennae.
7. Add shading, leaving light areas on the back to make the form look round.

I can understand the "ear" part, but where do you suppose the "wig" comes from?

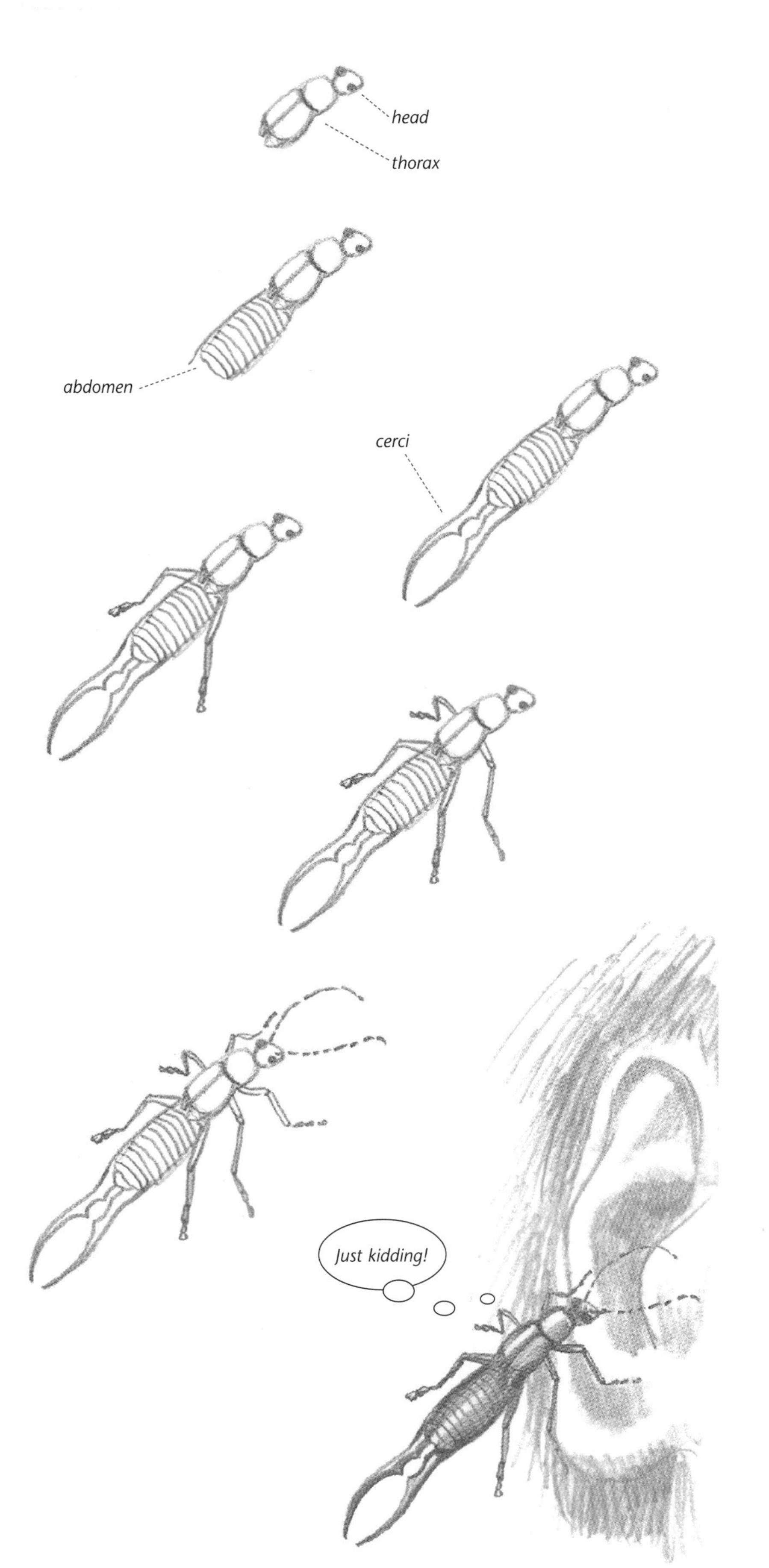

Firefly (Lightning Bug)

Order Coleoptera
Family Lampyridae

During spring and early summer, these beetles use their luminous abdominal sections to attract other fireflies for mating. Although other insects can glow, fireflies are unique in being able to flash, and the rhythms are distinct for each species. Active at night, they live under bark or in moist places under debris.

STUDY the final drawing *before you start!*

Do you see
- *three body parts?*
- *six legs?*
- *two antennae?*
- *wings (how many)?*
- *eyes?*

Does the insect look
- *shiny? smooth? fuzzy?*
- *hard? soft?*

1. Start by drawing the *pronotum* and *elytron* (one of two hard fore wings).
2. Draw the triangular head (almost completely covered by the *pronotum)* and the front leg.
3. Add the middle leg…
4. …and the rear leg.
5. Draw the body, and shade most of it dark. Leave the end of the abdomen light: this is the part that flashes. Make the eye dark, leaving a little reflective white spot.
6. Draw antennae, and the other three legs.
7. Carefully shade your drawing, leaving a light area at the top of the shiny protective shell. Draw a little branch for it to sit on.

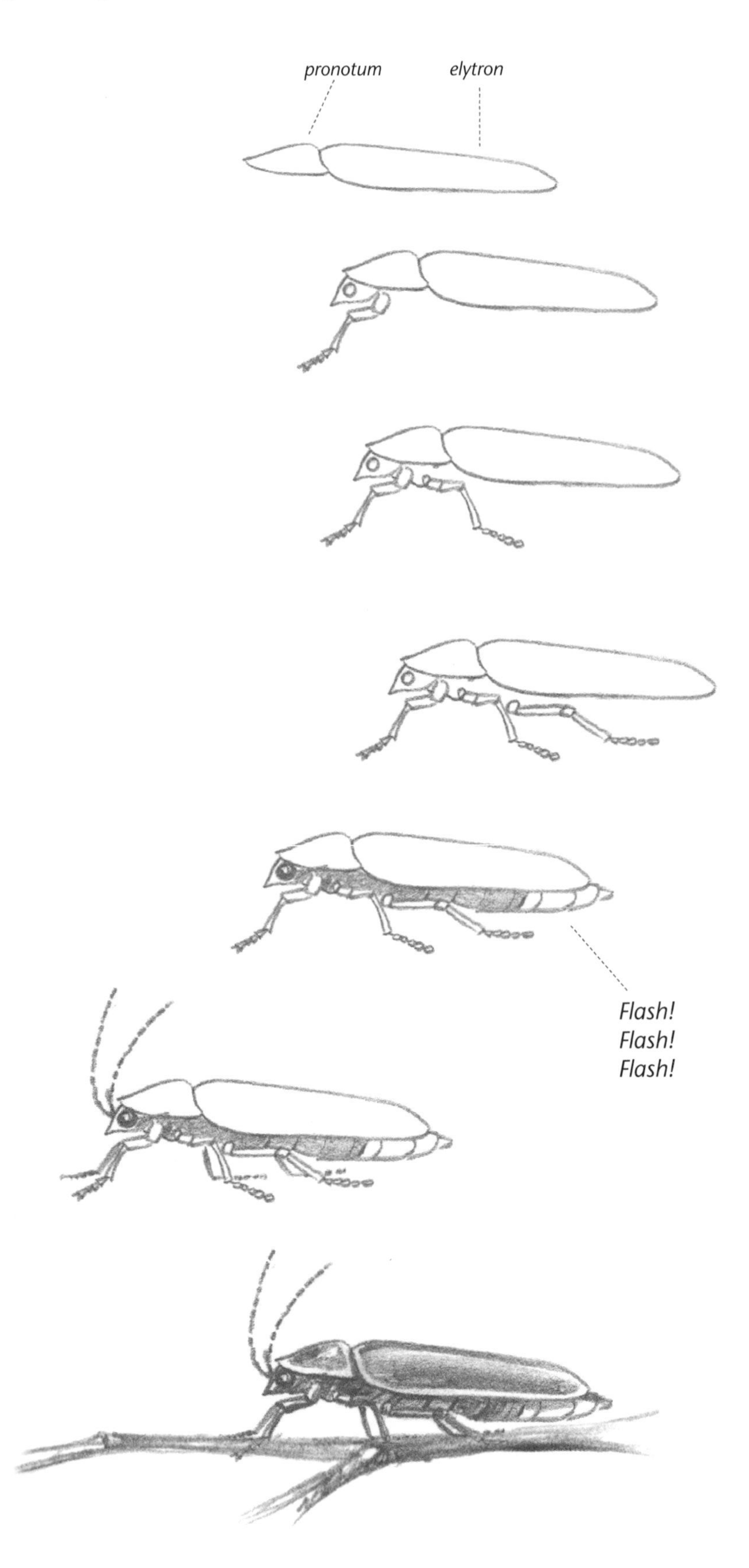

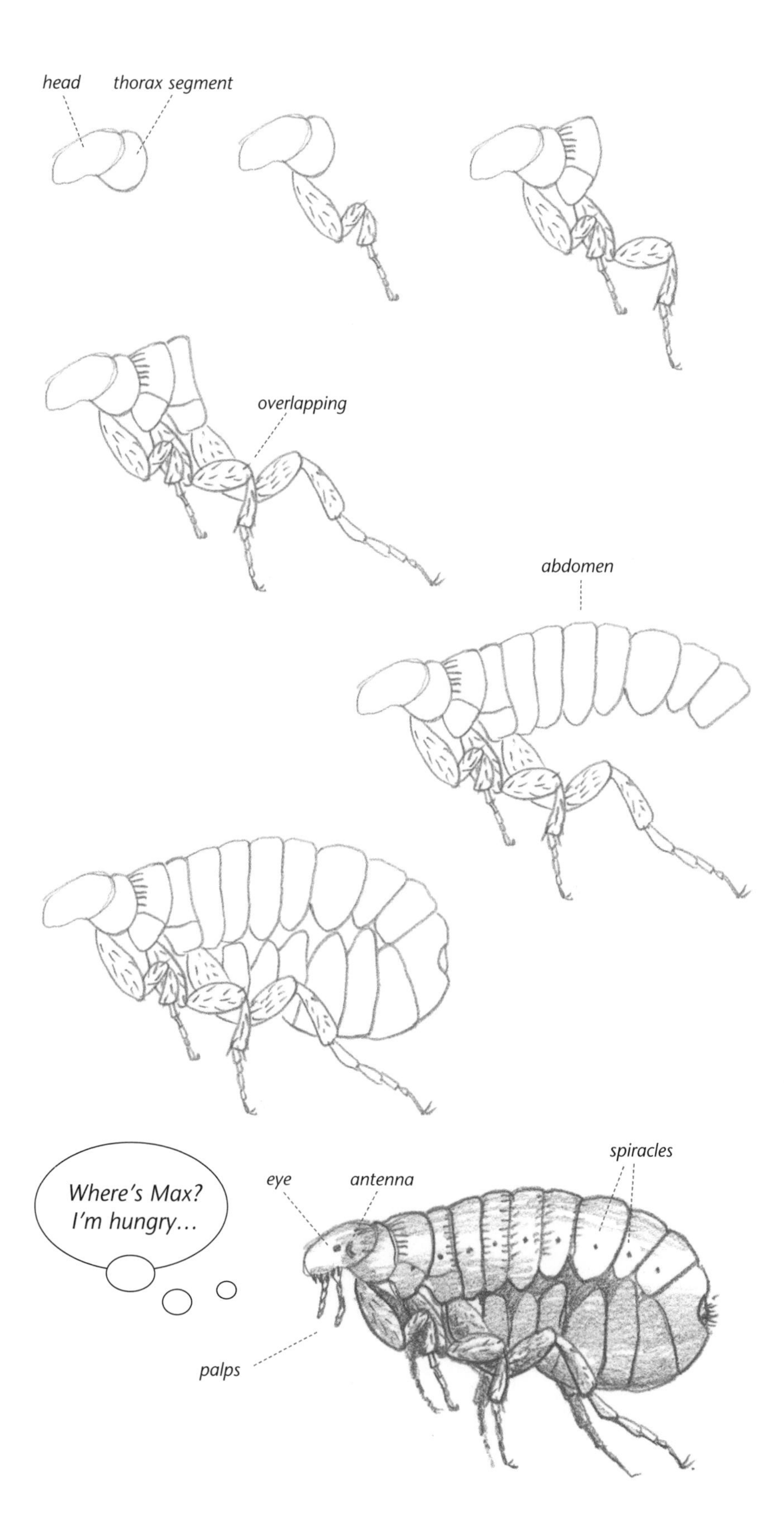

Flea

Order Siphonaptera
Family Pulicidae

Fleas are annoying parasites that live off the blood of their host; they lay eggs on their host or in its nest. Fleas help pets get tapeworm and can spread disease such as bubonic plague.

STUDY the final drawing *before you start!*

Do you see
- *three body parts?*
- *six legs?*
- *two antennae?*
- *wings?*
- *eye?*

1. Draw the head and first *thorax segment.*
2. Draw the front leg, attached to the first thorax segment. Count the sections of the leg, and look carefully at which direction each goes.
3. Draw the second thorax segment and middle leg, *behind* the front leg.
4. Draw the third thorax segment and powerful rear leg, *behind* the middle leg.
5. Add the top part of the abdomen…
6. …and the bottom.
7. Add *eye, antenna, palps,* three more legs, and shading. Don't forget the breathing *spiracles!*

Ladybug Beetle 

Order Coleoptera
Family Coccinellidae

Labybugs, also called Ladybirds, are welcome in the garden because they feed on aphids. They also eat scale insects and mites which otherwise damage plants

STUDY the final drawing *before you start!*

Do you see
- *distinct body parts?*
- *six legs?*
- *antenna?*
- *wing?*

Does the insect look
- *shiny? smooth? fuzzy?*
- *hard? soft?*

1. Draw the *fore wing* and the shape that looks like the head, but is actually the *pronotum,* which covers the head.
2. Add the front, middle, and rear leg.
3. Make a line for the edge of the stem, and draw the other three legs.
4. Add spots on the front wing and *pronotum.* Draw the *antenna (one of two; the other you can't see),* and the *beak.* Add shading and a *cast shadow.*
5. And now *(YES!!)* make the ladybug sucking the life out of an aphid.

Guten appetit, ladybug!

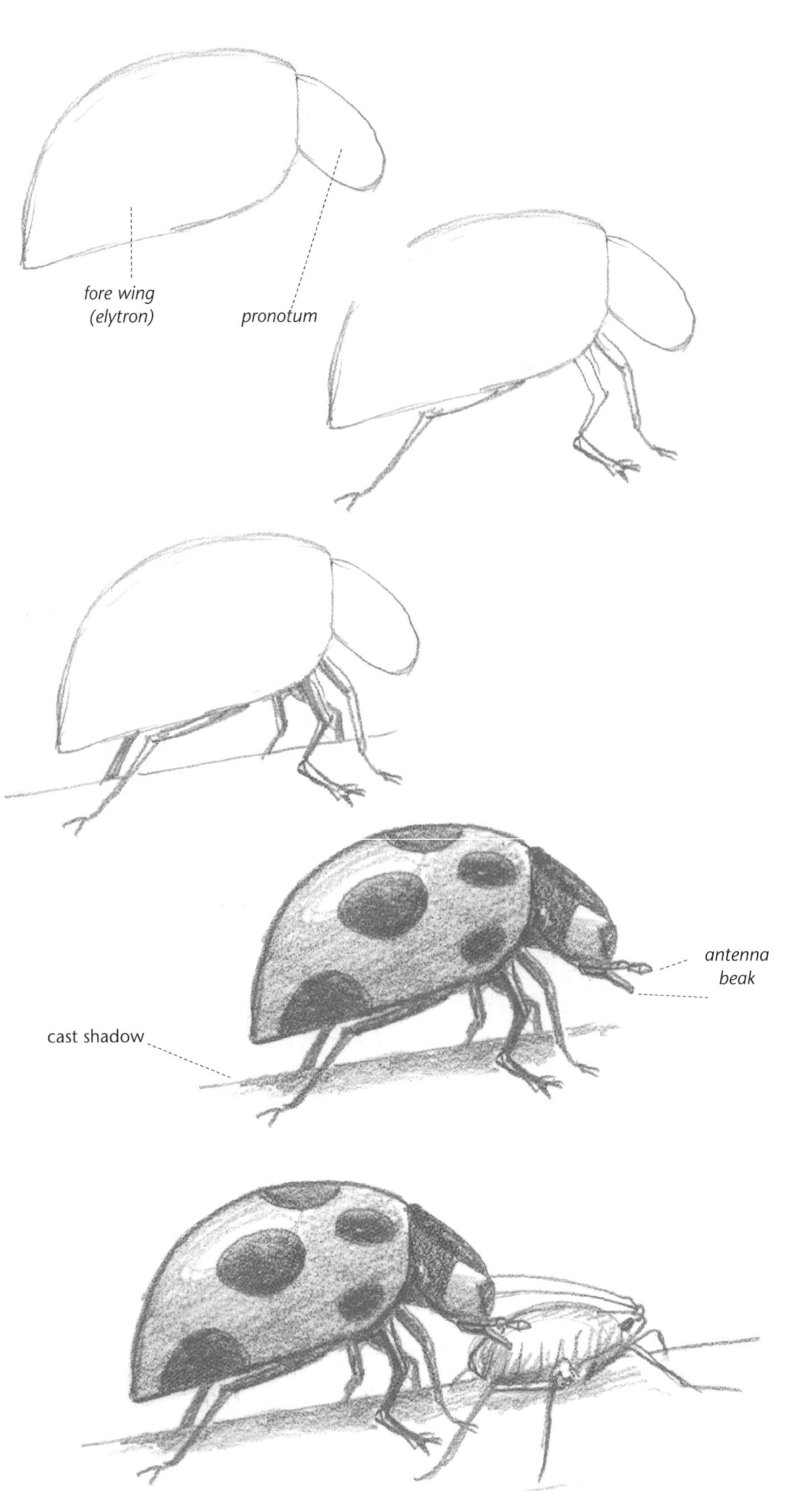

Leaf Insect

Order Phasmatodea
Family Phylliidae (leaf insects)

A few insects imitate plants so well that they won't move during the day, even if you pick them up! They can also drop legs if necessary, then grow them back the next time they molt. The ability to mimic plant structure is called phytomimesis *(thought you'd want to know).*

STUDY the final drawing *before you start!*

Do you see
- *three body parts?*
- *six legs?*
- *two antennae?*
- *wings (how many)?*
- *eyes?*

Does the insect look
- *shiny? smooth? fuzzy?*
- *hard? soft?*

1. Starting with a center line, draw the pear-shaped wings.
2. Add the *thorax* and *head.*
3. From the first segment of the thorax, draw two skinny front legs, then add the leaf shape to them.
4. Draw the middle legs connecting to the second thorax segment, and the rear legs sticking out from under the wings. Add the outline of the *abdomen.*
5. Add lines and shading to make it look like a leaf! Take your time, and look closely at the example for ideas.

   Add camouflage! Draw sticks and leaves, so that someone looking at your drawing won't even know there's an insect there....

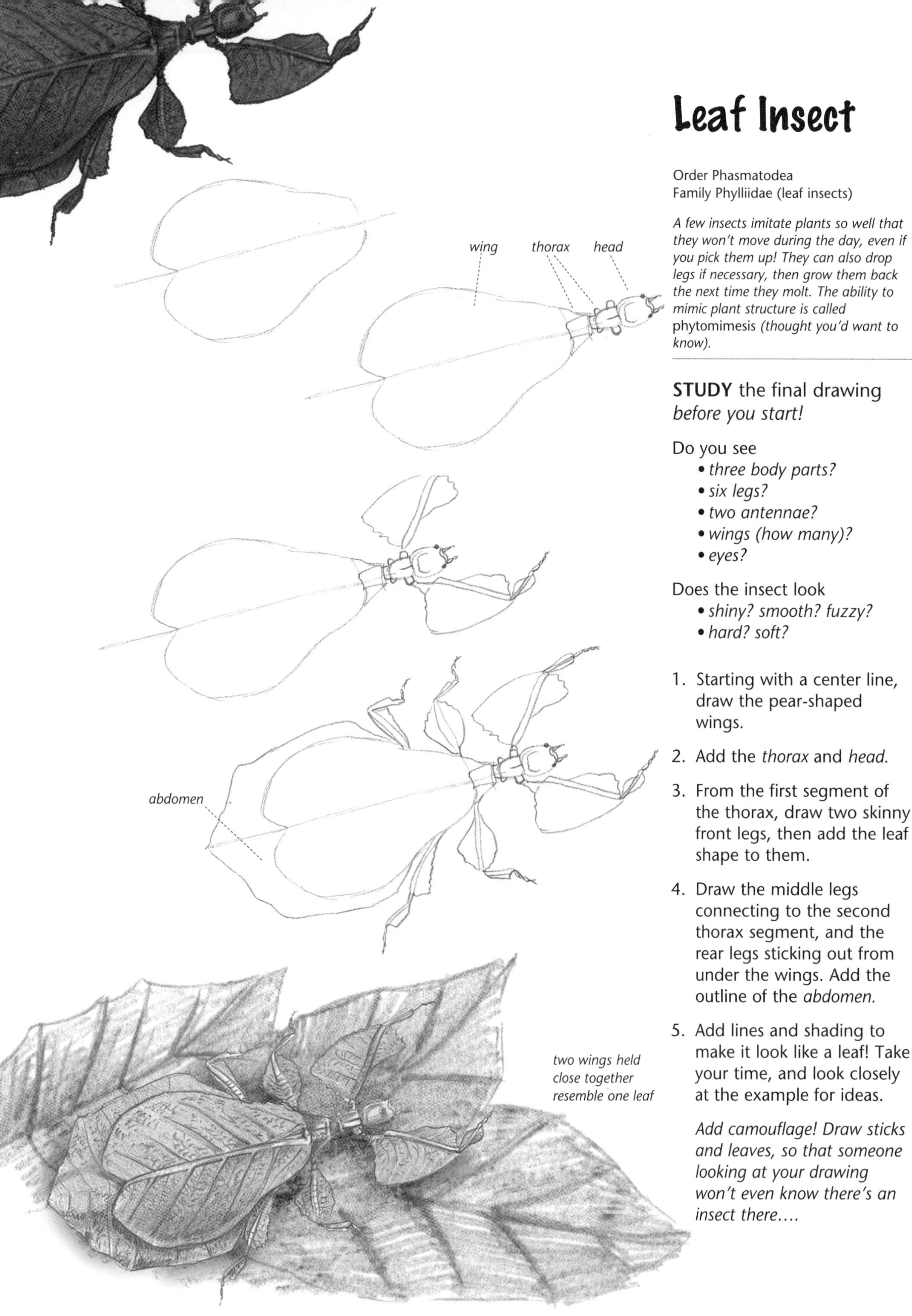

Locust

Order Orthoptera
Suborder Caelifera

Certain grasshoppers are called locusts, from the Latin word for grasshopper. Only nine of 5,000 species of the suborder Caelifera make mass migrations, but when they do, they eat all vegetation in their path. There's the Old Testament plague of locusts descending on Egypt; in modern times trains have been delayed during locust migrations because the tracks were "slimy" from dead insects. Grasshopper Glacier in Montana is full of dead locusts. In the US in the 1870s, a single swarm was estimated to contain 124 billion insects.

STUDY the final drawing *before you start!*

Do you see
- *three body parts?*
- *wings (how many)?*
- *six legs?*

1. Start with two small circles and a longer, rectangular shape for the *head, thorax,* and *abdomen.*
2. Draw the two front legs stretched out either side. Add details to the head, and antennae.
3. Add the second, short pair of legs pointing backwards, and the much longer rear legs. Draw short curved lines for the abdominal segments.
4. Carefully outline the wings.
5. Now add about a zillion little veins and cells. Take your time–it's worth it! Add shading and texture to the body.

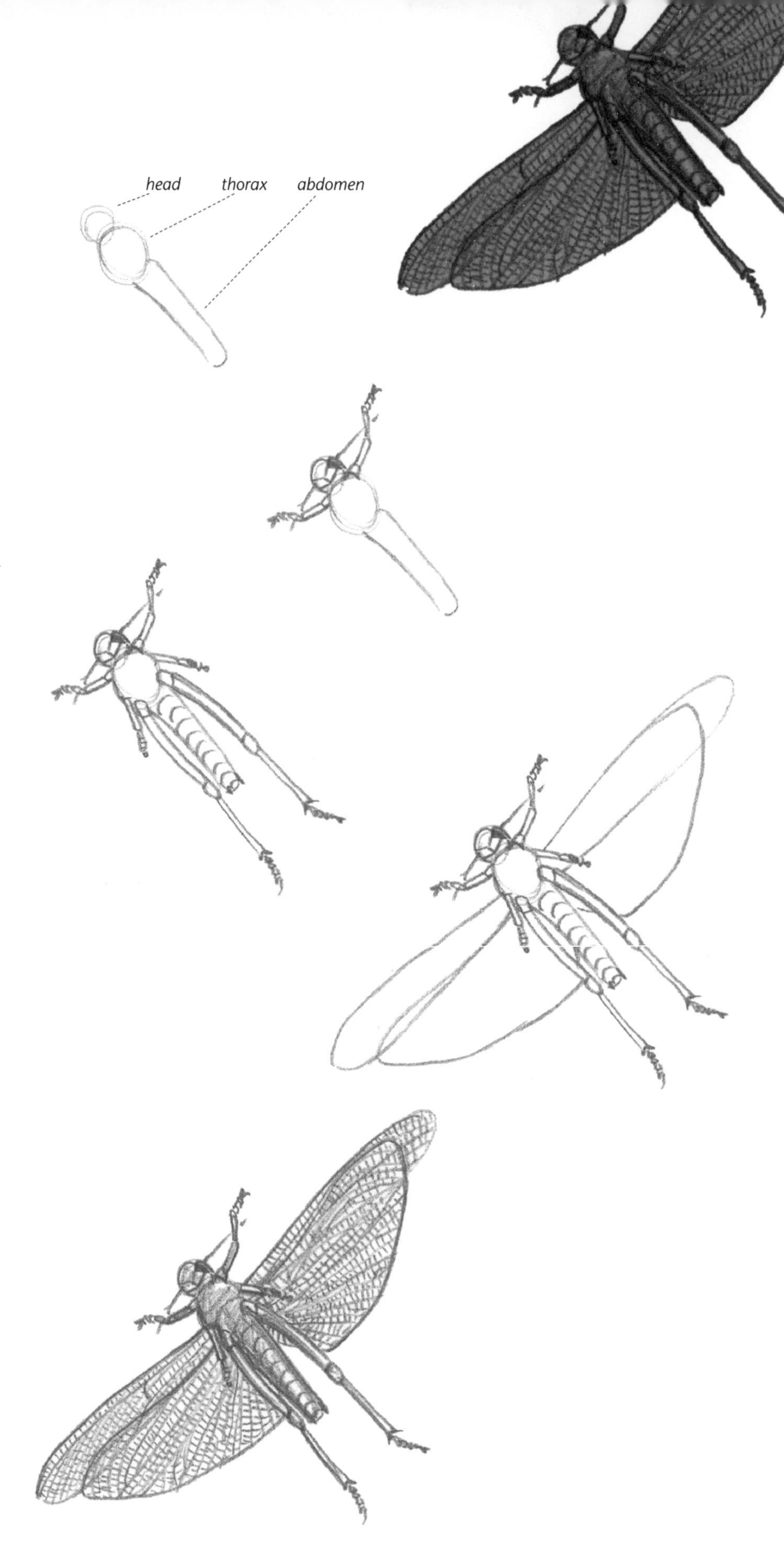

Luna Moth

Order Lepidoptera
Family Saturniidae (giant silkworm moths)

This beautiful pale green moth is only found in North America, and is considered endangered. Many have been killed by pesticides and pollutants.

STUDY the final drawing *before you start!*

Do you see
- *three body parts?*
- *six legs?*
- *two antennae?*
- *wings (how many)?*
- *eyes?*

Does the insect look
- *shiny? smooth? fuzzy?*
- *hard? soft?*

1. Draw a cocoon-shaped oval for the body, and add two feathery antennae.
2. Carefully (and lightly) draw one fore wing.
3. Carefully (and lightly) add the other fore wing.
4. Draw the hind wings, with their long tails. Go slowly; turn your paper if it helps you draw the curves.
5. Add wing veins, spots, shading and texture. (If you have colored pencils, shade it a light green color. The large *costal vein* is maroon.)

Mosquito

Order Diptera
Family Culicidae

You can tell this is a female mosquito because it has only a few hairs on the antennae (on males, they're more feathery), and lacks the male's two additional beak-like palps. Only the females bite. Mosquitoes can convey diseases such as malaria, generally only in tropical areas.

STUDY the final drawing *before you start!*

Do you see
- *three body parts?*
- *six legs?*
- *two antennae?*
- *wings (how many)?*
- *eyes?*

1. First, make some high-pitched, whining noises to get in the mood.... Now draw the *head, thorax,* and *abdomen.*
2. Add the middle leg...
3. ...the front leg...
4. ...and the hind legs, curving up into the air.
5. Draw the eye and *antennae,* and the *beak,* or *proboscis,* ready to do business. Add texture to the thorax.
6. Add the wing, covering part of the abdomen, and the lines for abdominal segments. Draw the other hind leg.
7. Add the other two legs, and shading, a bit of cast shadow and a few human hairs.

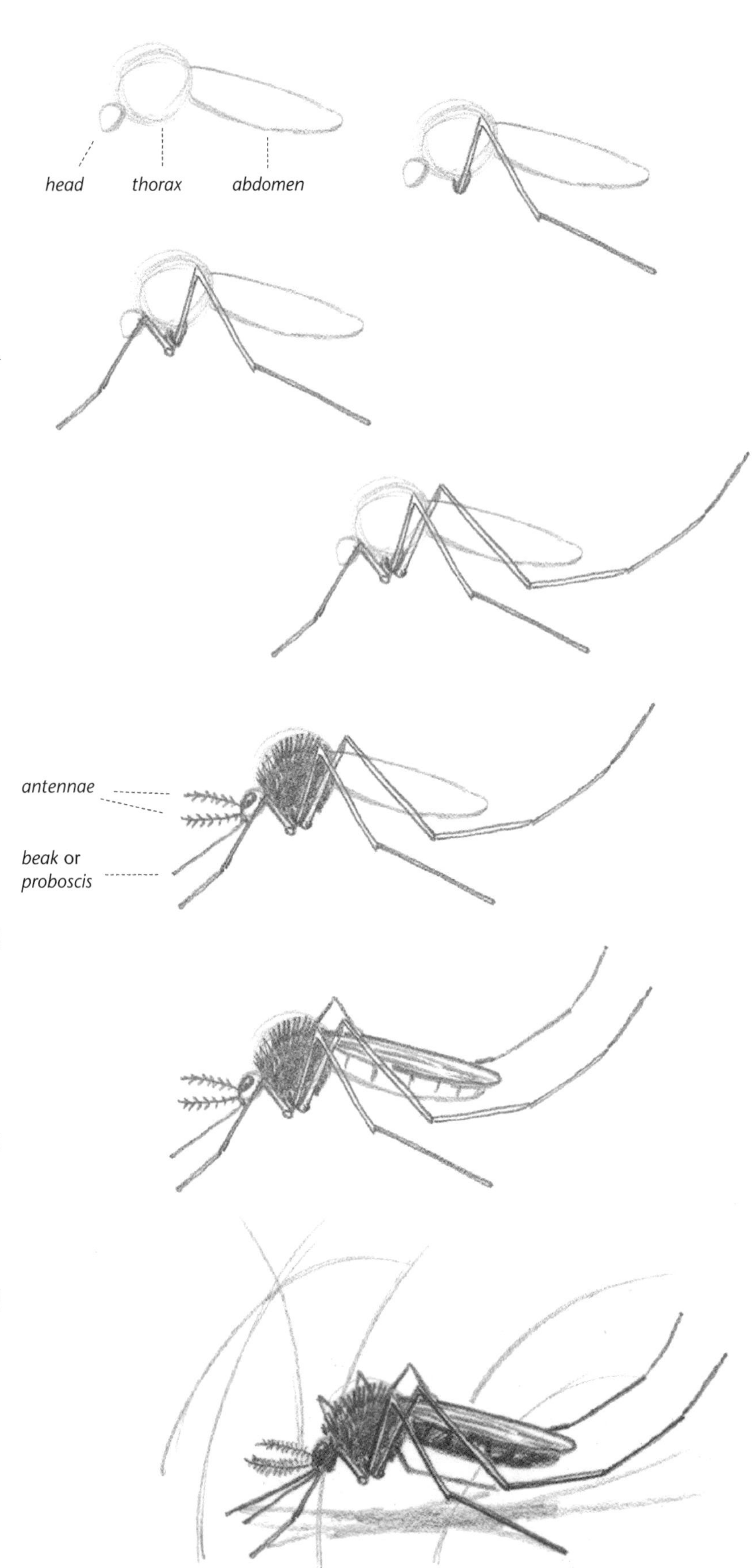

Praying Mantis

Order Mantodea
Family Mantidae

The praying mantis waits in ambush, suddenly moving its spiny fore legs to catch prey. With its strong mouthparts, it can cut through the heads of tough insects like wasps. Its flexible neck means the mantis can turn its head to look at you–a rather eerie feeling! Mantises are cannibalistic; the female often devours the male while mating.

STUDY the final drawing *before you start!*

Do you see
- *three body parts?*
- *six legs?*
- *two antennae?*
- *wings?*
- *eyes?*

Does the insect look
- *shiny? smooth? fuzzy?*
- *hard? soft?*

1. Draw the long *abdomen* and *wing.*
2. Add the *thorax* at a slight angle, then *eyes,* head, and mouthparts.
3. Draw the segments of the front leg, raised and ready to snare prey.
4. Add antennae and the other front leg.
5. Draw the two rear legs. Look carefully at the way each bends.
6. Now add the other two rear legs. Add shading, texture, and details.

And ask yourself, *"What is that insect thinking when it looks at me like that?"*

Scarab Beetle

Order Coleoptera
Family Scarabaeidae

This is one of about 20,000 kinds of scarab beetle! Some have fabulous metallic colors; others dramatic horns. All have distinctive, clubbed antennae. Ancient Egyptians put scarabs in much of their artwork, and their sun god had a beetle head, since they believed the sun was pushed through the sky the same way a dung beetle rolls a ball of dung along the ground.

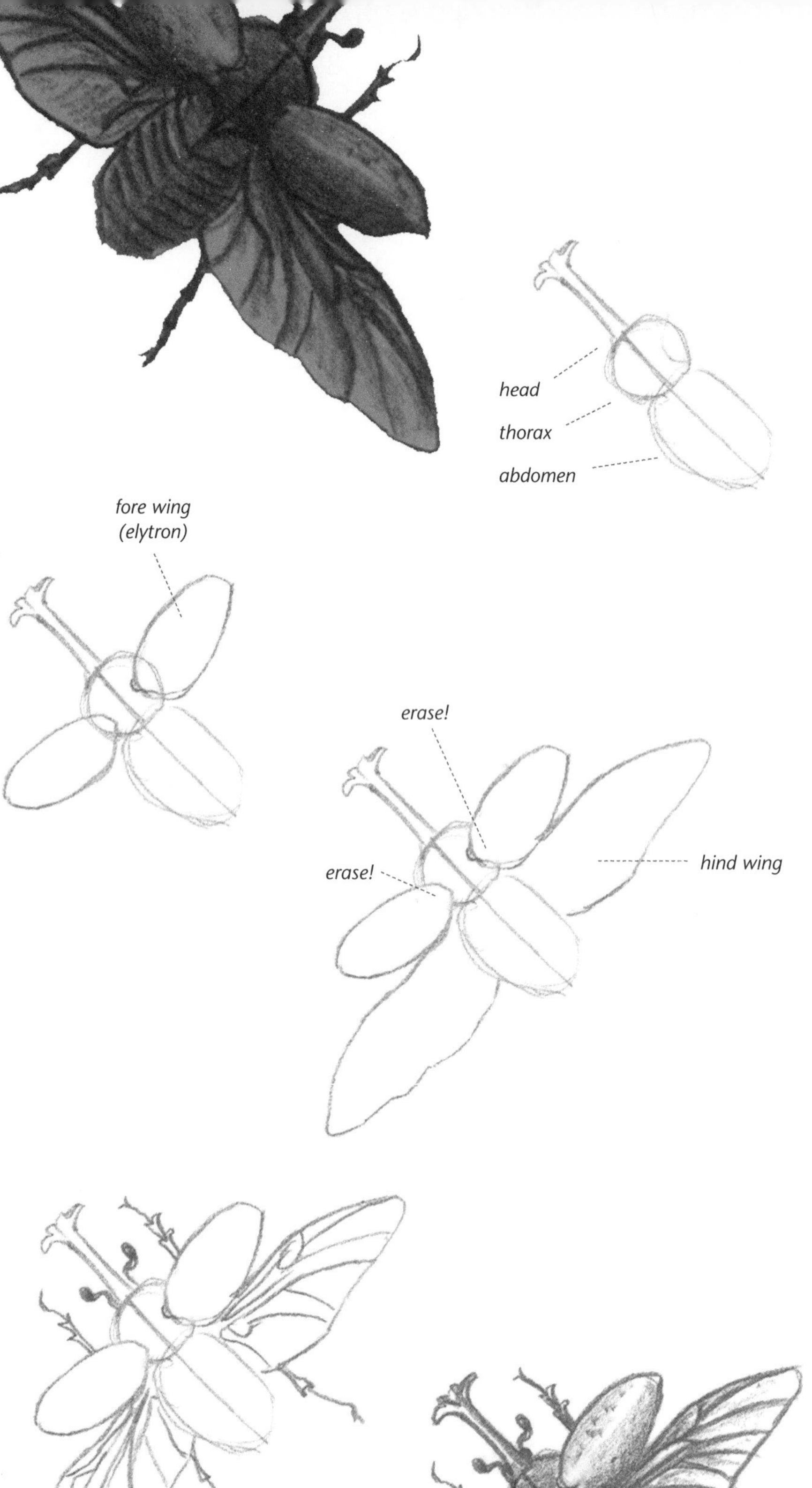

STUDY the final drawing *before you start!*

Do you see
- *three body parts?*
- *six legs?*
- *two antennae?*
- *wings (how many)?*
- *eyes?*

Which parts look
- *shiny? smooth? fuzzy?*
- *hard? soft?*

1. Draw the *head* (with long horn), *thorax,* and *abdomen.*
2. Add the protective *fore wings (elytra).*
3. Erase the thorax outline where the front wings overlap it. Draw the *hind wings* (used for flying).
4. Carefully draw the veins in the wings, the front legs and hind legs, and the club-like antennae.
5. Add shading and details...

...cool beetle!

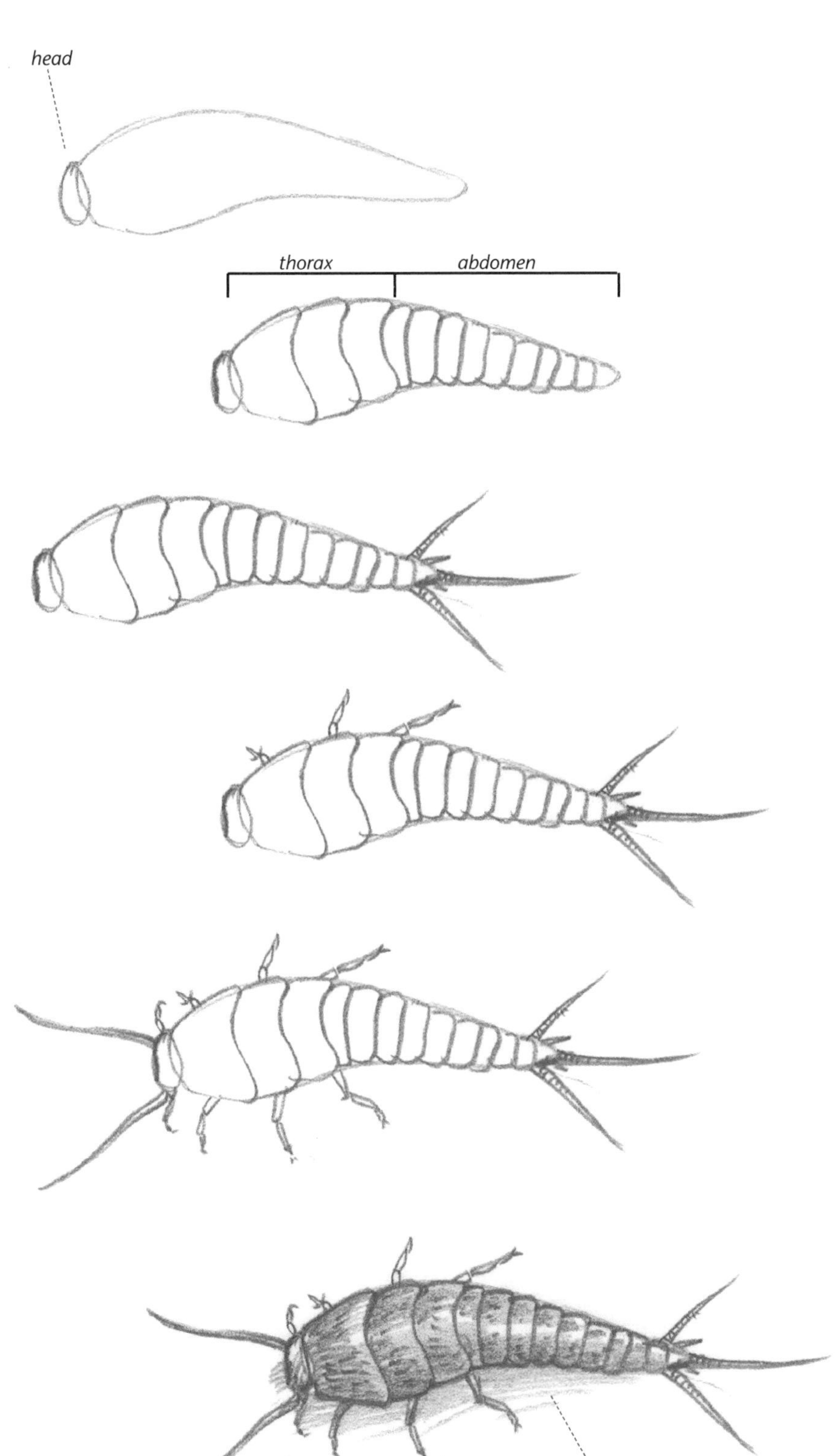

Silverfish

Order Thysanura (common bristletails)
Family Lepismatidae

The scaly covering of the silverfish makes it difficult for ants and spiders to grab it. It lives in warm, dry or damp places such as closets, and can be a pest: it eats starchy stuff, including flour, starch in clothing, and book bindings. It can survive without food for months.

STUDY the final drawing *before you start!*

Do you see
- *three body parts?*
- *six legs?*
- *two antennae?*
- *wings (how many)?*
- *eyes?*

Does the insect look
- *shiny? smooth? fuzzy?*
- *hard? soft?*

1. Start by lightly drawing the long, slightly curved, pointed oval of the body, and a much smaller oval for the *head.*
2. Draw the segments of the *thorax* and *abdomen.*
3. Add the distinctive, three-part bristly tail.
4. Make three little legs on one side.
5. Add three legs on the other side. Draw antennae and the small mouth parts *(maxillary palps).*
6. Add texture and shading, and a slight *cast shadow.*

Scintillating silverfish!

Stink Bug 

Order Hemiptera (true bugs)
Family Pentatomidae

Stink bugs release foul-smelling fluid when disturbed. Some stink bugs eat caterpillars and larvae, while others live off plant sap.

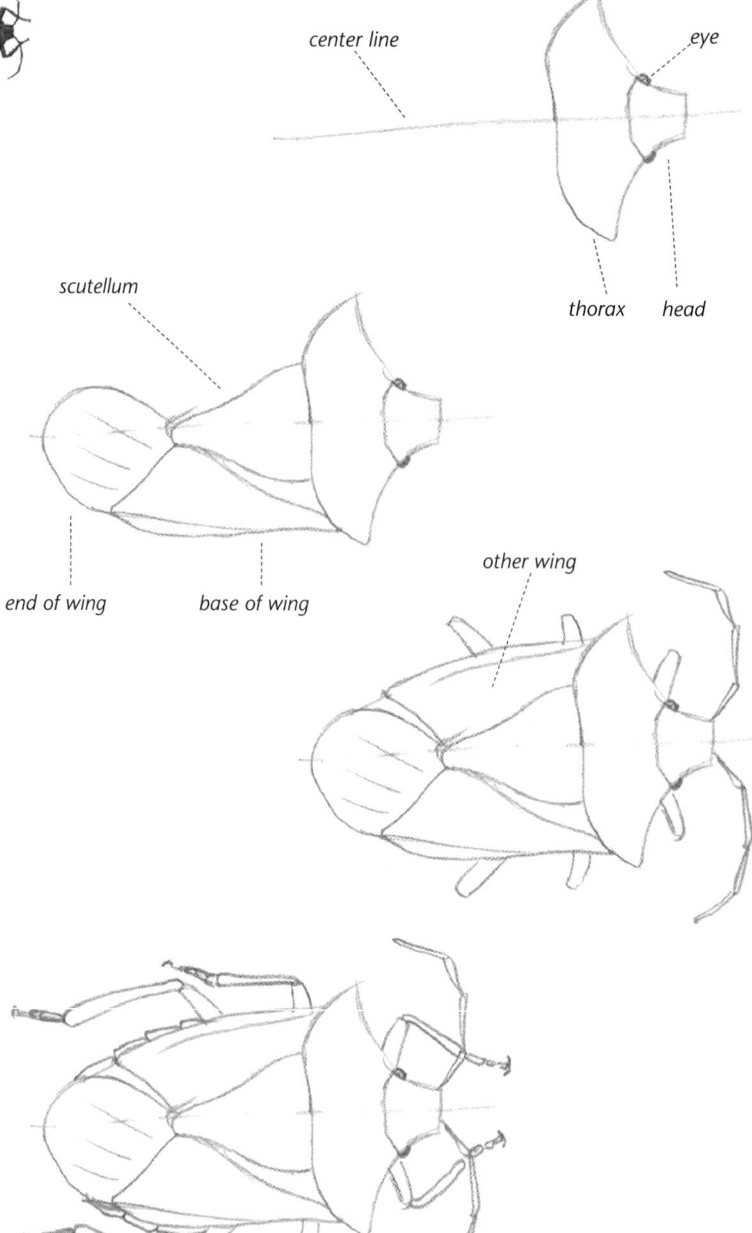

STUDY the final drawing *before you start!*

Do you see
- *three body parts?*
- *six legs?*
- *two antennae?*
- *wings (how many)?*
- *eyes?*

Does the insect look
- *shiny? smooth? fuzzy?*
- *hard? soft?*

1. Lightly draw a *center line,* then the stinky *head* with its stinky little *eyes,* and the stinky *thorax.*
2. Add the triangular *scutellum,* and one wing (the *base of the wing* is solid; the *end* is translucent).
3. Draw the *other wing,* antennae, and the first section of each leg.
4. Complete the legs.
5. Finish your drawing by adding shading, details, and texture. With a dull pencil, make a *cast shadow.*

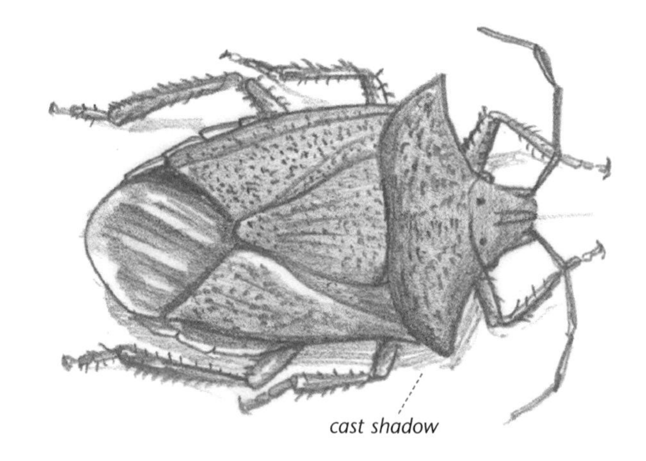

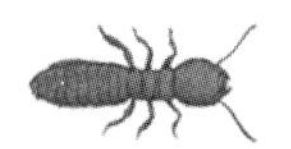

Termite (worker)

Order Isoptera

Most termite species feed on wood, which they can digest because of special microorganisms in their intestines. Termites can be very destructive to buildings. Like ants, they have a highly evolved society, with workers, soldiers, and a reproductive caste which has wings. Some species even have a special caste with nozzles in their heads for secreting a fluid to build and repair nests. With this nozzle, they can spray repellent at invaders. Beware, ants!

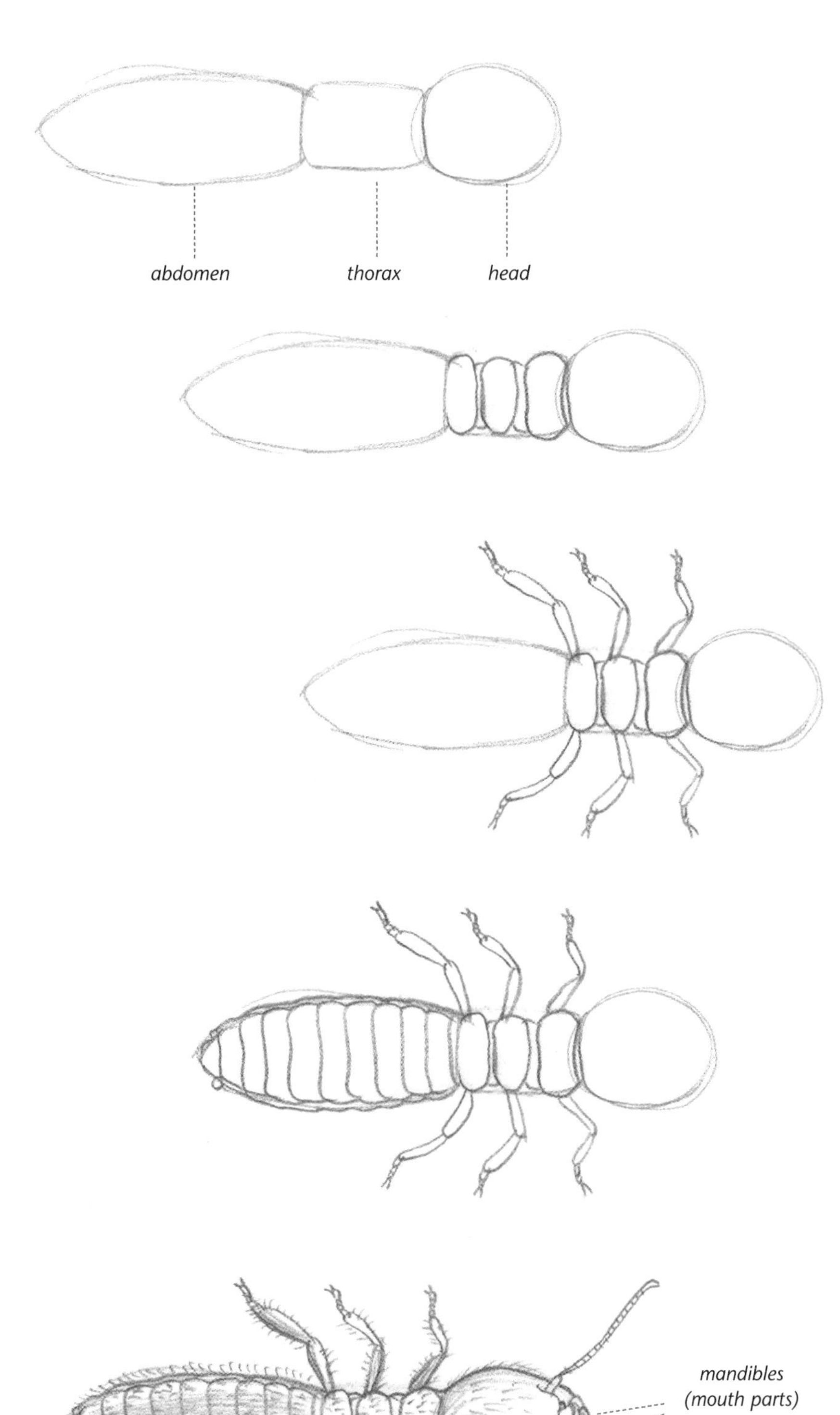

STUDY the final drawing *before you start!*

Do you see
- *three body parts?*
- *six legs?*
- *two antennae?*
- *wings?*
- *eyes?*

Does the insect look
- *shiny? smooth? fuzzy?*
- *hard? soft?*

1. Draw the *abdomen, thorax,* and *head.*
2. Divide the thorax into three sections.
3. Carefully draw a pair of legs attached to each section.
4. Divide the abdomen into ten sections.
5. Draw antennae, *mandibles* and other details of the head. Add light shading and little hairs.

Walkingstick

Order Phasmatodea
Family Phasmidae

Walkingsticks stay still during the day, doing what they do best: looking like a twig so they won't get eaten. They're so good at imitating twigs that they won't defend themselves or try to flee if handled. They can regenerate lost legs. They feed on foliage. Females drop single eggs to the ground, where they hatch in the spring.

STUDY the final drawing *before you start!*

Do you see
- *three body parts?*
- *six legs?*
- *two antennae?*
- *wings (how many)?*
- *eyes?*

Does the insect look
- *shiny? smooth? fuzzy?*
- *hard? soft?*

1. Draw a little tilted pencil.
2. Add a long, slender leg...
3. ...and another...
4. ...and a couple more...
5. ...and a couple more. Draw a twig underneath.
6. Draw antennae and abdominal segments.
7. Add a little shading, and *voila!*

Draw more twigs. See if you can make your walkingstick completely camouflaged!

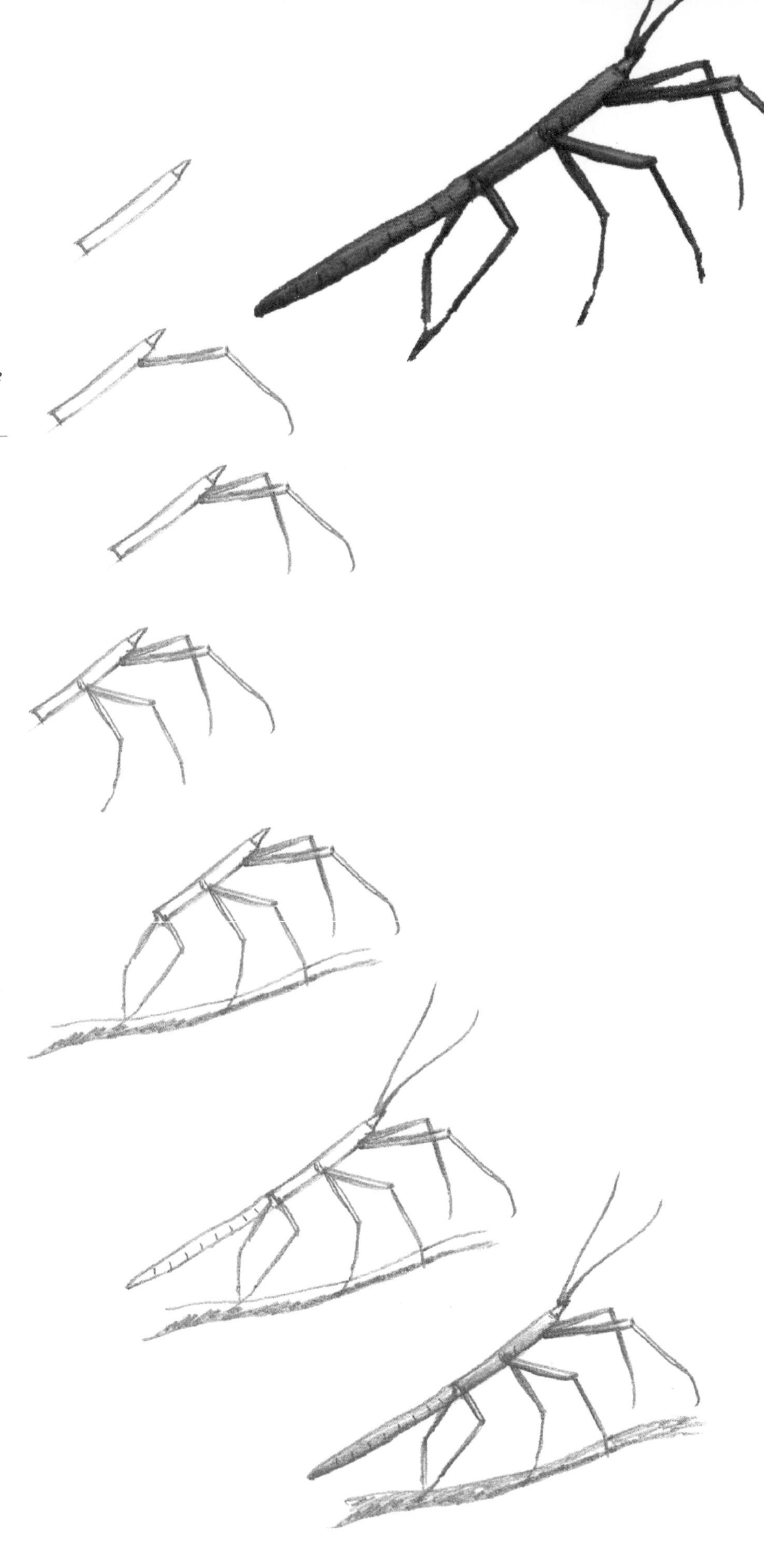

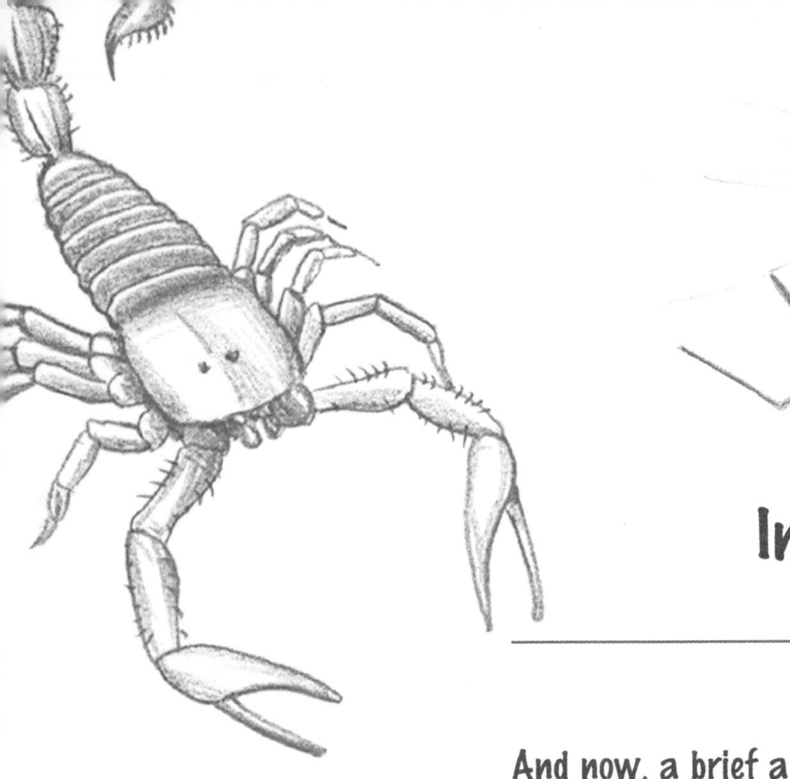

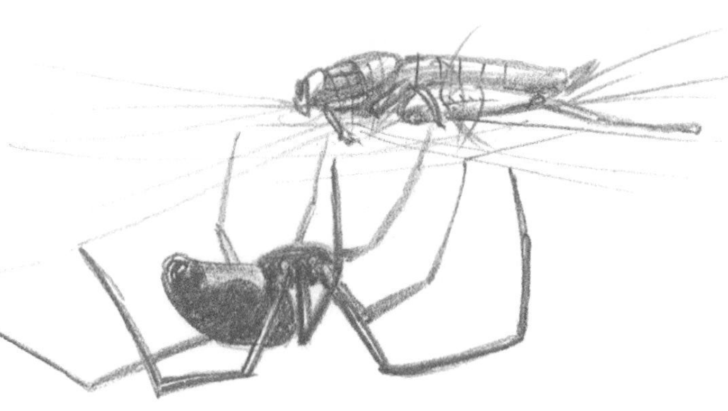

Insect Relatives

And now, a brief and learned discourse on creepy-crawlies:

As you'll recall from an earlier Brief and Learned Discourse, the primary distinguishing characteristic of members of the class *Insecta* in the phylum *Arthropoda* is the presence of six legs.

In other words, insects have 6 legs!! 6 legs!! 6 legs!!

So, if a creepy-crawly does not have 6 legs, what is it?

In the phylum *Arthropoda,* along with the class *Insecta,* you'll find a class *Arachnida* (arachnid: think spider), which includes eight-legged spiders, scorpions, mites, ticks, and daddy-long-legs (to name just a few).

Think of a school as a *phylum.* Inside the school there are classrooms, or *classes.* All the children with eight legs go to this *class,* all the children with six legs go to this (very big) *class,* and so on. And the difficult children with too many legs to count (especially because they *never sit still!!!)* go to another *class* called Myriapoda.

Obviously, I can't tell you everything there is to know about scientific classification.

Just remember this: they're all relatives.

Any one of them might show up at your birthday party.

OK, class dismissed!

You may now draw....

Wolf Spider

Order Araneae
Family Lycosidae (wolf spiders)

Wolf spiders usually live on the ground, either in a burrow, under a rock, or sometimes with no home at all. Females make a round egg sack which she drags around with her until the spiderlings hatch. Wolf spiders hunt at night. Their mottled colors make them hard to see among dead leaves and stones.

STUDY the final drawing *before you start!*

Checklist:

Do you see:
- *two body parts?*
- *eight legs?*
- *two pedipalps?*
- *eyes?*

Does it look
- *shiny? smooth? fuzzy?*
- *hard? soft?*

1. Draw a curve for the top of the head. Draw two big eyes, and six smaller eyes.
2. Add the *jaws (chelicerae)* and *pedipalps.*
3. To the sides of the body, draw three segments of the front legs.
4. Complete these legs.
5. Add the second set of legs, partly invisible where the front legs *overlap* them.
6. Draw two more pairs of legs, and the rounded *abdomen.*
7. Finish your drawing by carefully adding shading, texture, and a *cast shadow.*

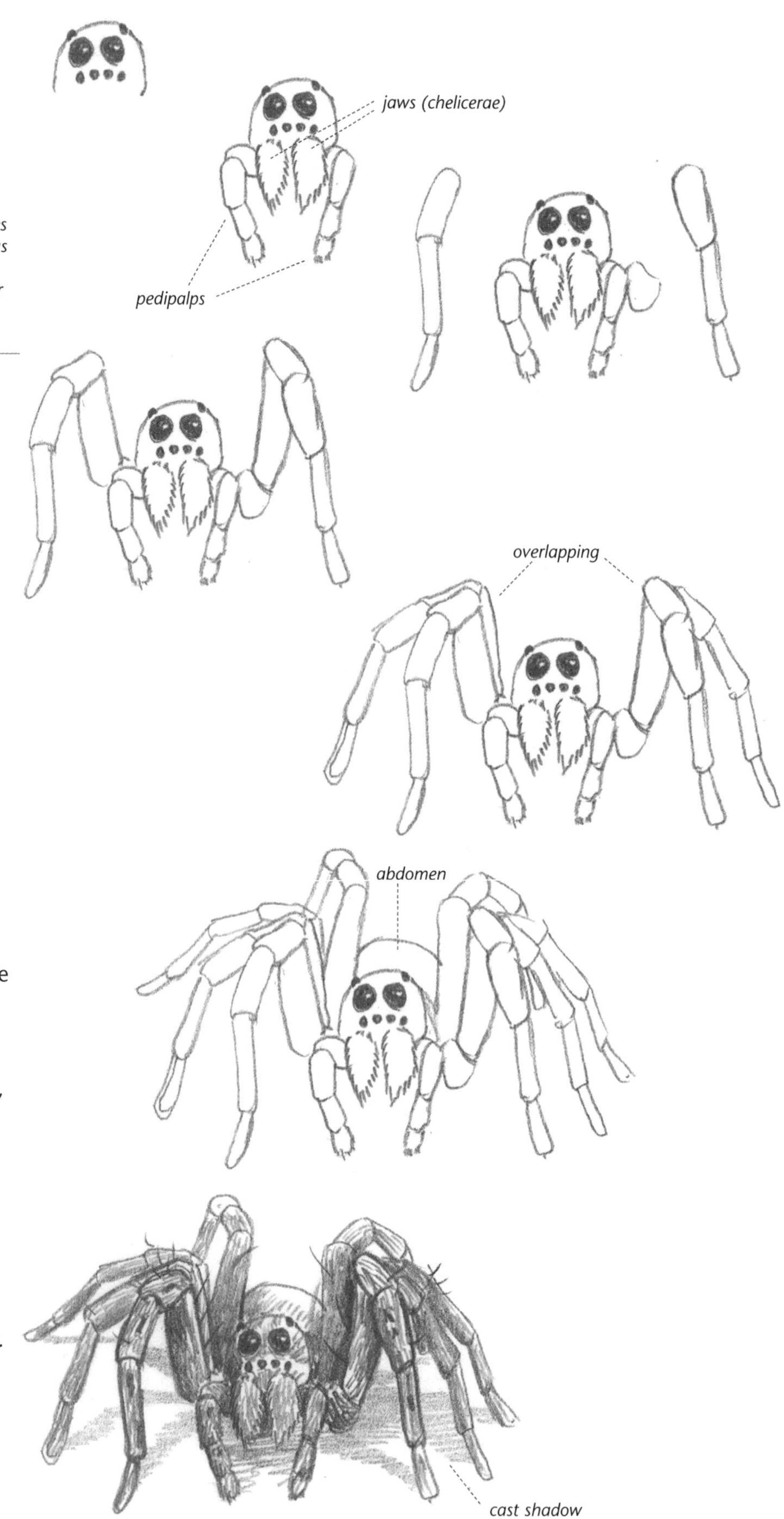

Black Widow Spider

Order Araneae
Family Theridiidae (comb-footed spiders)

This feared spider with the red hourglass shape on its abdomen usually tries to flee rather than attack. Males don't bite. Females often eat males after mating, which is why they're called "widows."

STUDY the final drawing *before you start!*

Checklist:

Do you see:
- *two body parts?*
- *eight legs?*

Does it look
- *shiny? smooth? fuzzy?*
- *hard? soft?*

1. Draw the pointed oval of the *abdomen* with its distinctive *hourglass design,* then add the small, flat oval of the *cephalothorax.*
2. Draw one leg...
3. ...and another...
4. ...and another...
5. ...and another.
6. Now add the visible portions of the other four legs.
7. Finish your drawing by shading the spider black. Add a few lines to suggest a web, and a dead grasshopper (or other insect of your choice) for the black widow's meal.

Scorpion

Order Scorpionida

Scorpions subdue or kill large insects, spiders, and sometimes lizards with a poisonous stinger. Most don't attack people, but their sting can produce painful swelling. Long ago, scorpion stings were feared as much as a lion's bite. Scorpions hunt at night, under a sky that has a constellation named for them.

STUDY the final drawing *before you start!*

Checklist:

Do you see:

- *two body parts?*
- *eight legs?*
- *two pedipalps?*
- *eyes?*

Does it look

- *shiny? smooth? fuzzy?*
- *hard? soft?*

1. Start by making the main body shapes.
2. Add lines on the *abdomen,* and carefully draw the sections of the tail, with the stinger at the end.
3. Draw a clawed *pedipalp...*
4. ...and another.
5. Now add four walking legs, first on one side...
6. ...then on the other.
7. Add shading and bristly hairs to complete your drawing.

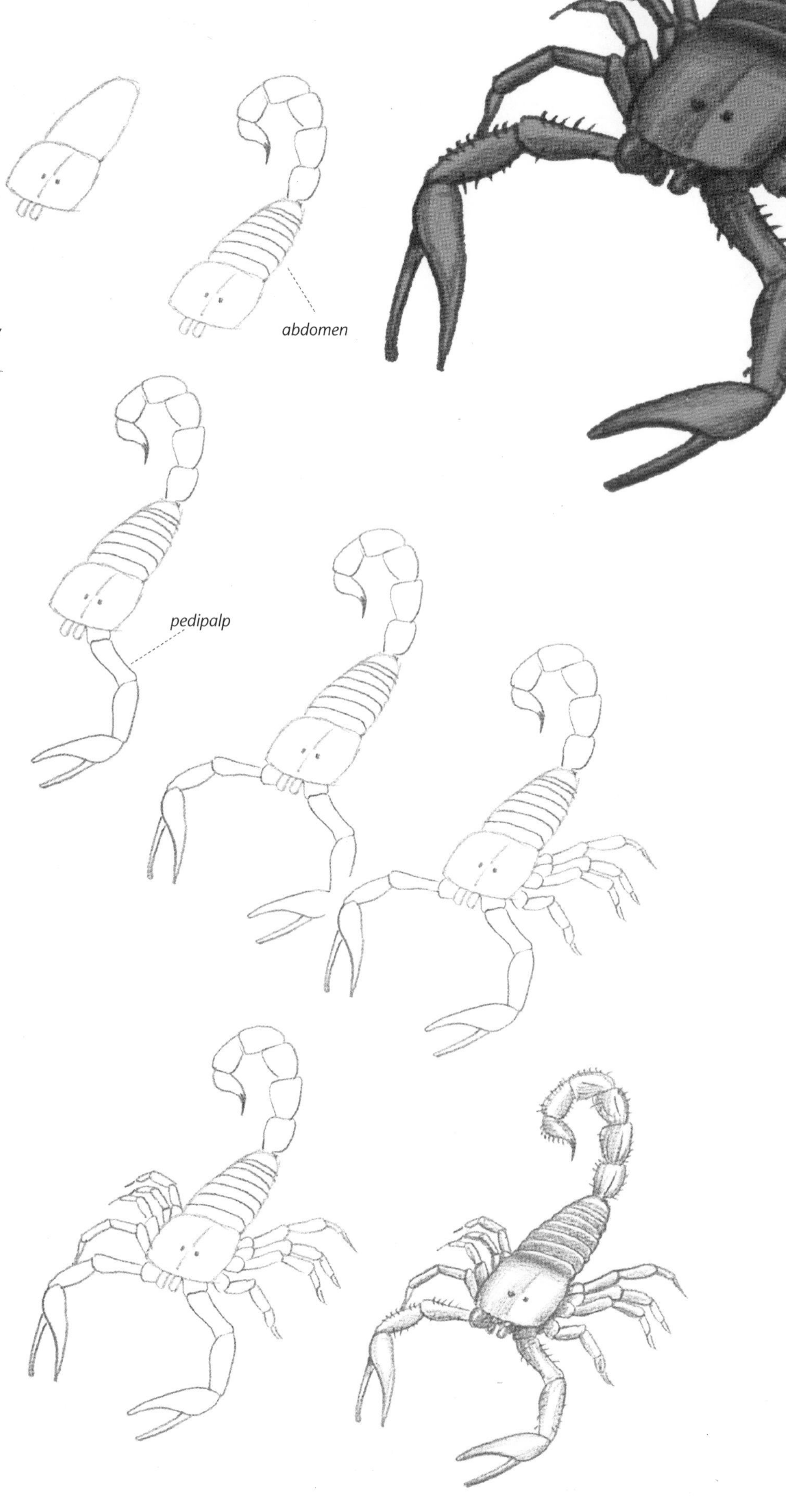